The
25 Most
Common
Problems
in
Business

(and How Jesus Solved Them)

The
25 Most
Common
Problems
in
Business

(and How Jesus Solved Them)

Jim Zabloski

BROADMAN
&HOLMAN
PUBLISHERS

Nashville, Tennessee

Published by Broadman & Holman Publishers,
Nashville, Tennessee
Acquisitions & Development Editor: Vicki Crumpton
Interior Design: Leslie Joslin
Printed in the United States of America

4260-79
0-8054-6079-9

Dewey Decimal Classification: 174
Subject Heading: BUSINESS ETHICS / JESUS
CHRIST—PUBLIC MINISTRY
Library of Congress Card Catalog Number: 96-22552

Unless otherwise noted, Scripture quotations are from the
Holy Bible, New International Version, copyright © 1973,
1978, 1984 by International Bible Society.

Library of Congress Cataloging-in-Publication Data
Zabloski, Jim, 1958–
    The 25 most common problems in business
(and how Jesus solved them) / Jim Zabloski
        p.   cm.
    ISBN 0-8054-6079-9 (pbk.)
     1. Management—Religious aspects—Christianity.
2. Jesus—Leadership. 3. Success in business. 4. Executive ability—Biblical teaching. I. Title.
HD38.Z27 1996
658—dc20

96-22552
CIP

00 5 4 3

*To the late Dick Marant who taught me
that in this day and age it is possible to run
a thriving business ethically*

and

To Linda, Ross, and Taylor.

CONTENTS

INTRODUCTION

After studying business strategies for twenty-five years, after observing best-sellers in the field come and go, after watching managers and businesspeople use everything from "Theory Y" to managing in a minute, I concluded that someone ought to have written a book based upon well-established principles of management rather than upon current trends. After speaking with businesspeople who expressed a need for a book explaining how Jesus would handle certain situations, I followed their urging and wrote the book you now have in your hands.

People don't run a business on theory. They run it on day-to-day practices. When you face a crisis situation and need help, the last thing in the world you want is a book on "the simplified theories of cost reduction and analysis thereof." You don't want theories. You want to know how to get cash flowing, how to hire a new employee, how to delegate responsibility, or how to market your product better. You want it logical, practical, and useful, and you want the information now. What businesspeople ask is this: How do I handle the problems I have *now?* How do I know it will work for me? Is this stuff provable?

Business as we know it must change. Like an orange tree, the best way to make it bear fruit is to hack at the roots, severely prune the branches, and replant it in good soil. At first the tree goes into shock, but once it has recovered, it bears double the yield of fruit. So it is with business. Get it planted on the right foundation and it will succeed. Build your business on the latest hot-selling title, and it will fade as soon as the book goes out of print or as soon as it's replaced by a newer book.

We will examine the business philosophies and strategies of a man whose ideas and products have remained on the market for several thousand years. The ideas are timeless, and they work. Jesus Christ built what some only dream of—an organization lasting thousands of years, comprised of highly self-motivated and self-fulfilled employees with little or no aspiration than that of the good of the organization. How did He do it? Furthermore, how can we? Can a businesswoman or businessman today take the same principles and teachings of Jesus Christ and apply them to the work they have undertaken? This book is designed to take Christian principles out of the church and into the business world, and to take a unique look at today's business practices and management styles by comparing them to Jesus Christ's style. I would never say that Jesus did all the things I mention herein, but after studying His methods and philosophies, I believe He would have considered them. Jesus did not run a business. That was never His intent. But He left behind a way of life for us to follow, and that way must extend beyond the boundaries of the church and into our personal and business lives. I believe we should and can run our businesses as He would run them.

For quick reference, I've indicated where each teaching or practice can be found in the Bible, and then while staying true to the stories, took some artistic liberties to present those passages in a colorful way. I have incorporated some historical background to help clarify the passage or to fill in some plausible gaps.

If the first question asked by businesspeople would be, "How would Jesus handle this?" then the world would be a different place indeed. This book will help you start operating along that path. Many of Jesus' practices and teachings go against the grain of popular theories. Some of Jesus' ideas are as controversial now as they were two millennia ago. So what else is new?

CHAPTER 1

AGENDAS: MEETINGS

"Committee" is a noun of multitude, signifying many, but not signifying much.

—ANONYMOUS

A committee is a gathering of important people who singly can do nothing, but together can decide that nothing can be done.

—FRED ALLEN, COMEDIAN

A group of religious leaders banded together with a group of political leaders for a showdown with Jesus. The Pharisees loathed the Herodians. They merely tolerated each other's presence on the planet to avoid conflict. Herodians were followers of Herod, the monstrous king who thirty years earlier had all the Jewish male babies slaughtered for fear that from them a king would arise. Pharisees were strict followers of the law and all of its thousand points of darkness. Yet for all their animosity toward each other, this day they formed a partnership in an attempt to trap, and hopefully arrest, Jesus.

Jesus watched as the two groups approached Him. A crowd of listeners had already gathered around Him, so He had the audience He needed. He knew the leaders' intent. He read their faces—stony, ashen, angry, pious. He had prepared for a showdown but none so dramatic as this. To bring the law of Moses into question was one thing; to question civil law was another matter altogether.

"Wonderful Master and Teacher," oozed one of the leading Pharisees, "we know You are an honest man and that You care not what others think of You."

Jesus glanced at the crowd around Him. They muffled their chuckles. Could they see where this meeting was heading?

"We've been pondering something all day, and wondered if You could tell us what You think. Is it lawful to pay taxes to Caesar or not?"

The Herodians nodded to each other in gleeful approval. One nodded to a Roman guard who took several steps toward Jesus to prepare for His arrest. If Jesus answered yes, the Pharisees would have Him arrested for breaking one of their laws. If no, the Herodians would arrest Him for insurrection. The perfect plan laid by the perfect group. The pause for thought took but a moment.

"Show Me a coin," Jesus said. He examined both sides. "Whose name is on this? Whose picture is this?"

The leading Pharisee answered, "Caesar's."

"Then," Jesus said in a matter-of-fact tone, "give to Caesar what is his." He turned back to the crowd. The Pharisee signaled the guard to move toward Jesus who turned back to finish His statement. "And," He said to the Pharisee, "give to God what is God's."

The two factions joined again as one and left in a fury. The meeting of the minds had ended.

—MATTHEW 22:15–22

During the days of the Revolutionary War, Oliver Cromwell became so angered when he heard that his troops were raping women and stealing goods that he formulated what could be termed a gallows meeting. He set a mandate that anyone in a troop accused of doing such atrocities had to meet with his troop under the gallows from which hung a rope. The story goes that the men would roll the dice, all of them, and whoever lost the toss would be hanged for the crime. In no time, the decision to behave ran through the troops, and the meetings by the gallows dwindled to nothing.

I suppose some managers would like to consider such a policy if it meant doing away with meetings. We attend a lot of them. The average executive spends three and a half hours per week in formal meetings and another eight hours in informal meetings. "It has been estimated that every day of the year eleven million meetings are held in the United States alone. That figure extrapolates into a conservative guesstimate of fifty million daily meetings in the world."[1] From those meetings, you have to ask yourself, "What on earth are we really accomplishing?" Imagine what a different world we would live in if all those people were actually working! No wonder meetings bring such a negative connotation.

I MEET, THEREFORE I AM

Think of meetings as a tennis match. For there to be success, both tennis and meetings require preparation, practice, a great deal of going back and forth, and an understanding that someone may win and someone may lose.

Why do we so dislike meetings? Perhaps it is because they breed like an amoeba. Nearly every meeting subdivides itself and creates another meeting. There is no end. One meeting creates another from which come two more and two more and on and on it goes. Can meetings be handled properly? More importantly, can we learn from Jesus how to handle agendas and meetings? I believe so.

The Gospels do not record in detail Jesus' daily affairs of three years. As you study the books recording Jesus' life, one thing stands out. The writers, for whatever reason, recorded only meetings between Jesus and someone else. Whether with a large group, His small staff, an individual, or with His God, Jesus' story is a tale of meeting after meeting. Notice that Jesus never came unprepared. He was never caught off guard by His encounters with people. That is the first lesson to learn from Jesus. Before you even have a meeting, ask yourself why you are having this meeting and what you hope to achieve from it. Obviously, if you can't answer the questions, don't hold the meeting.

Meetings need to be as well prepared and organized as a book. No author I know just sits down and writes. We formulate plans, make outlines, do research, and then prepare some more. So it is with meetings. Those that are a waste of time are the ones that demonstrate the least preparation time. Those are also the longest. The length of a meeting will be in inverse proportion to the amount of time one prepares multiplied by the number of people attending.

The second thing to notice about Jesus' encounters is that He kept His focus. There are various kinds of meetings: brainstorming, problem solving, pep rally, and decision making among others. Regardless of the kind of meeting being held, each must have at its foundation the direction of furthering the company's goals and objectives. If the meeting is not in keeping with company objectives, cancel it.

Most companies schedule routine meetings. Routine meetings, as a rule, are a waste of time because the meeting rests upon the bedrock of "every Thursday at 9:00" instead of "customer satisfaction is dropping" or "staff morale is low." I prefer meetings that are preplanned but are odd in terms of days and times. It keeps people on their toes and breaks up the monotony. I often hold pop meetings with my staff. "Meeting in five minutes in the conference room, everyone! Bring something to write with. Let's go!" This adds an air of excitement, and meetings need all the excitement they can get.

SUCCESSFUL MEETINGS

Let me give you several clues to making a meeting a success.

Plan extra time for the meeting. If it ends early, people are pleasantly surprised. If it runs over by twenty-five seconds, you start to lose them to their watches.

Start meetings on the dot, regardless of who's there. End them on the dot, regardless of who's awake.

Consider penalizing people for being tardy. Here are two ways to do this: $1 per minute late or $1 per minute late per persons already seated (that's the number of people you held up). I explained that to a staff member who was habitually late to my meetings. "There are eight people sitting here. You are five minutes late. That means you have wasted this company forty minutes, not five. Time equals money. I know exactly what these people are making per minute. The next time you come in late I will prepare an invoice for you for the amount of money you cost this company." The company managers even discussed implementing this idea for management meetings.

Eriez Magnetics in Erie, Pennsylvania, thinks they solved the problem of meetings starting late and running over by allowing meetings only before 9:00 A.M. and after 4:30 P.M. The idea works for them, but it is not without its problems. It is a bit time constrictive, especially for people with families and those who have long commutes.

Schedule meetings at odd minutes such as 9:10 or 12:20. It is easier to remember than meetings held on the half or quarter hour because of its uniqueness.

To keep things lively, provide food only at breakfast meetings. The food is generally lighter and people are fresher. Lunch meetings are great as long as lunch is served at the conclusion. Otherwise people turn sluggish and lose creative juices. Save lunch meetings for special occasions.

Send out an agenda beforehand for planned meetings. People ought to walk in knowing what's going on. Tell the attendees what it's about. Tell them also what you want solved, how much time will be spent on each point, how long the entire meeting will last, how they should prepare, and what they should bring.

If you must hold brainstorming meetings, do it once a year. Experience shows that most brainstorming meetings end up being only a slight drizzle. Brainstorming requires a fair number of people to give it energy, but by default only 20 percent of the group will really contribute while the other 80 percent sit idly by. Better to consider holding regular two-person meetings where people are more inclined to share creative ideas.

An undirected meeting is a danger, even under the team concept. Someone has to lead. Good meeting leaders don't monopolize the meeting; rather, they see that everything goes smoothly. I often begin my meetings by laying down some ground rules. "All right, gang. This is a brainstorming meeting. Rule number one: There will be complete freedom of opinions. Rule number two: No fighting or diminishing another's idea." You get the point.

Every meeting lends itself to conflict. Conflict in meetings is healthy. Jesus' meetings with the religious and political leaders of His day were pregnant with conflict. His meetings didn't lapse into snide remarks or sarcasm, name calling, shouting, withdrawing, quick concessions, or overpoliteness. Don't allow them in your meetings either. As a leader, you must keep the momentum going, even at the risk of knocking over a hornet's nest. At least things get running again.

All of this is possible so long as you don't have one person in the meeting with an argumentative spirit. The nineteenth-century preacher D. L. Moody said, "The best way to show that a stick is crooked is not to argue about it, or to spend time denouncing it, but to lay a straight stick alongside it." Argumentative people don't want to see it straight; they just want to argue. It's like baseball coaches who go out and yell at the umpire, delaying the game for everyone else It never changes anyone's mind, and it seldom serves a purpose. Dismiss the argumentative person from the room as the ump might from the game and get on with it. You and the fans will be glad you did.

Along the same lines, one seldom hears anything about meeting etiquette. Besides the rule about arguing, there are several other guidelines attendees should remember. You might want to print these out somewhere and hang them in your meeting room as motivation.

Rules for This Meeting

I will not argue.
I will not bore.
I will admit when I'm wrong.
I will let others do the talking.
I will respect every other opinion besides my own.
I will find creative ways to dramatize my point so everyone understands.
I will not pretend that I know what I'm talking about when I really don't.

Let me add one point here about the rule of dramatization. Some of this comes from being an elementary school teacher for years, and some of it comes from studying Jesus' techniques when trying to prove a point by use of parables. Find creative ways to use dramatic, nonreadable visuals to drive home your point. Except for financial people and the legally blind, most human beings are visually oriented. Yet we make people sit through hour after hour of endless talk with no visual imagery besides the agenda sheet in front of them. Ever wonder why people doodle during meetings? Because they're bored, yes, but also because they are visualizing their boredom.

I'm not asking you to walk in wearing a clown outfit. (One need not emphasize what they may already think of you.) Let me give you a couple of illustrations to get your creative juices flowing. I have working for me a group of this country's most talented and brilliant editors. Because of their talent, they are also perfectionistic. Because of their perfectionism, I must wrestle with them to let a book go to the printer lest they proofread it "just one more time." They have very strong opinions about what is proper and improper, which makes our product the highest quality product on the market, but they also can tend to disagree vehemently among themselves over the use of one word versus a similar, acceptable word. To prove my point, I walked into a meeting holding a large bell. I emphasized the point that we all recognize it as a bell. I rang the sucker as loud and as long as I could. Then we all agreed that the bell rang. I asked them exactly how many dingdongs did they hear. Blank faces. My point? This bell is like quality. We all recognize it when we see it, but not everyone sees it exactly the same. They never forgot the example.

Another illustration comes from an international sales conference I attended several years ago. The speaker, author Patsy Clairmont, told of her struggles, frustrations, and over-commitments. She then pulled from a bag a wad of tied up, intermingled, hopelessly tangled rubber bands and said that this illustration pretty well demonstrated her life at one time. I never forgot the illustration. Jesus often used illustrations to get His point across.

Learn to read your audience and do something about it. I'll never understand how professional speakers get to be professional speakers without the skill of audience reading. Jesus was an absolute master of reading His audience. He knew when they were hurting, angry, or frustrated. Reading your audience takes a great deal of training, even if there are only five or six people in it. I've watched people stare at the conference table while some member droned on and on without a clue as to the reaction of those around him. Ditto for public speakers.

As I graduated from college, putting on my robe and cap, a well-known national speaker entered the great hall of graduates. He saw the tears and the smiles, and he no doubt sensed the excitement in the room. He had prepared a big speech for which we were not ready. Wisely, he chose to approach the microphone, called us all to attention, and uttered some of the shortest but most memorable words I had ever heard. He said,

"Students, I just want you to remember one thing. God does not bless your success; God blesses your faithfulness." He stepped from the platform and exited. He read that room perfectly. He stood up, spoke up, and shut up. The official graduation speaker spoke later that evening for an hour and twenty minutes, and I do not remember one word he said.

Meetings are what they are because we are what we are: imperfect. But we must strive for improvement both in ourselves and in our meetings with other people. Jesus gives us some great examples in the Bible. The rest is up to you.

PRACTICAL TIPS

1. Hold the majority of required meetings in the morning when people are fresh.
2. Keep brainstorming meetings to once or twice a year.
3. Start meetings on time. Period.
4. Don't come to any meeting unprepared, and don't let others come unprepared either.
5. Always try to illustrate your main points visually and dramatically.

CHAPTER 2

APPEARANCES: DRESS AND DIET

Blessed are those who hunger and thirst . . . for they are sticking to their diets.

—TROY GORDON

I base most of my fashion taste on what doesn't itch.

—GILDA RADNER, COMEDIENNE

It was a hard life. Among the crowd sat the poorest of the poor. The Romans had taxed, double-taxed, and triple-taxed the people. Duties were placed on purchases, on travel, on entertainment, and even on worship. A man's wages were eaten up paying for the luxuries of the Roman empire to which the Jews did not belong.

Filled with compassion, Jesus looked at the multitudes in their worn, weathered clothing. Their faces showed a people who were tired and discouraged from trying to survive, let alone get ahead. Their diets were partially based on the Hebraic laws and partially based on what poor selection was available after the Romans took their share. Beautiful, young women who but a few years before attracted their spouses now gazed on Jesus through exhausted eyes. Men who yearned to play the lyre forsook their musical talents for the few shekels that woodworking brought.

Jesus sensed their frustration. He told them not to ask themselves questions such as "What should we eat?" and

"What should we drink?" and "What should we wear?" He told the crowd not to worry about tomorrow. He admonished them not to fret over the food they ate or the things they drank. He asked them to stop worrying about life and suggested they start living it. Life, He said, was more important than food and clothing. He told them to handle each day as it came, one at a time, no more and no less. Having gone hungry Himself, He understood. Having but one set of clothes and no place to rest His head, He empathized with them. Having been there, He could console them, and console them He did.

—MATTHEW 6:25–34

In many ways, the world in which you live is not so very different from the world Jesus and His contemporaries lived in. They too had to deal with pretenses, image, dress, attitudes, diet, and stress. In fact, in some ways, their lives may have been harder. It's not often you hear about a man being crucified these days for insurrection against our government or for belonging to a particular religious group. In Jesus' day, these things happened daily. Looking like a criminal could land one in the dungeon. They worried a great deal about appearances, I'm sure. Today, your appearance still "talks" to others without you saying a word. People judge you by it, much as they did two millennia ago.

YOU ARE A PACKAGE

We all project different images to different people. The image you project to your superiors will be different than the one you reveal to your spouse. Your subordinates will see you in a very different light from the way your siblings see you. So there's no getting around it. Whether you like it or not, you project an image. Jesus understood that. Like an old slide projector, the image you portray—whether fuzzy, clear, pleasing, or repulsive—is entirely up to you and how you control the mechanism. It also has to do with what's on the inside. Try as you may, you won't project an image of beauty if the only slides you have are of horror scenes. But that's another chapter altogether.

In today's business world, as in food packaging and marketing, the package is everything—or so we are told. We are encouraged to dress for success. Yet as you study the business principles of Jesus, something seems out of line with what we're being told today. Success? In a strange way, Jesus certainly had it. Few of us will be remembered for our works two thousand years from now. Did He dress for it? Not exactly. He knew what we fail to recognize today; specifically, Jesus knew that our appearance has less to do with the trappings and more to do with the inner being. Clothes alone do not make the man or woman. They merely accentuate what lies beneath.

If everyone were suddenly garbed only in a white seamless gown, what image would you portray? In that context, how you appear to people takes on new meaning. It is just this meaning that Jesus was trying to emphasize. Ask yourself, what image do you portray by your:

- Speech? Do you have a regional accent? Is your volume loud or too low? Is your tone nasal or gruff? Is it peppered with sarcasm or negativism? Is it friendly and engaging?

- Dress? Do you dress to impress? How can you hope to please everyone? Would your styles look good on every one of your gender in the office? Are you old fashioned? Too conservative?

- Physical characteristics? Are you bald? Short? Tall? Do you have a spare tire or mail-pouch thighs? Are your teeth straight and white? Are they all there?

- Possessions? Is your car pretentious? Do you really need all the house you have? Do your jewels jingle when you walk? Are you trying to prove a point by your possessions or nonpossessions?

- Etiquette? Do you come across as being well-bred or ill-bred? Can your good manners carry you through bad situations? Could you advise others in the laws of etiquette?

- Composure? Are you in control at all times? Do you want to be? Can others count on you when they're losing it? Are you temperamental or moody?

- Entertainment? Do you prefer to go bowling or golfing? Would you rather watch a tennis match or a football game? Do you go camping or touring? What kind of movies do you prefer?

DRESS AND YOUR IMAGE

Billionaire Aristotle Onassis once said, "Appearances count: Get a sun lamp to keep you looking as though you have just come back from somewhere expensive; maintain an elegant address even if you have to live in the attic."[1] Another billionaire, Sam Walton, said, "We're not ashamed of having money, but I just don't believe a big showy lifestyle is appropriate for anywhere. . . . I still can't believe it was news that I get my hair cut at the barbershop. Where else would I get it cut? Why do I drive a pickup truck? What am I supposed to haul my dogs around in, a Rolls-Royce?"[2]

Dress and image are not everything to everybody. Before you frustrate yourself to death and stress yourself out, remember several points. First, you do not need the income of Onassis or Walton to dress nicely. It costs practically nothing to be neat. My mother often said of her home that she might have dirt floors, but they would be clean dirt floors. The same goes for apparel. You may not be able to afford a thousand-dollar suit (I know I can't), but you can avoid wearing wrinkled, frumpy clothing. Second, let them not see the clothes; let them see you. If your value rests on what hangs in your closet, what will you do when moths eat through your clothes or fire destroys them? That is what Jesus tried to drive home. What is on the inside is most important.

One way to focus more on the inner person is to avoid extremes. Styles are for those with a poor self-image who care about what people think. Ever look at political leaders during a State of the Union address? Talk about uniforms! If your tendency is to dress more conservatively, break out of the mold occasionally with something slightly fashionable or even flashy. If you tend to overdo the purples, reds, and hot pinks, tone it down to at least the three primary colors. Hot colors are great if you're going hunting and don't want to get shot; they are not appropriate for business settings.

Dress in clothes you feel natural in. Never sacrifice comfort for style. I don't care how great the male models look in European-cut suits; I won't wear them. I feel awkward, which makes me look awkward. Then I become awkward. You become the clothes you wear, it is said. I believe it. When my two sons don their Batman and Robin costumes, they become the superheroes. They leap buildings (couches), they battle evil menaces (Mom), and they destroy the tickle monster (me). Ask any soldier, officer, or actor: once you put on the clothes, your tendency is to act out the part. If you want to feel like a professional, dress like one, but do it with class.

A standard gag among clothiers says that "a bad fitting suit never seems to wear out." Leisure suits will be hanging in some men's closets until the next nuclear meltdown, and they only cost a few dollars! What a bargain. Clothing follows the same rule as furniture. Buy half as much as you think you need, but pay twice as much as you think you ought. You don't need seventeen $120 suits; you need five $450 suits. They will, because of their craftsmanship and quality, look better and last longer. In the long run, they are the better bargain.

DIET AND YOUR HEALTH

Another area to consider when working over your image is your diet and your overall health. My wife came up with a little saying that helps me keep things in perspective. She said, "FAT—You are what you eat. STRESS—You are what eats you." Now let's discuss how both of these factors influence your appearance and image.

Fat affects the circulatory system and the heart. If you are a man, this fact will interest you: fat in the diet decreases testosterone production by 30 percent, says a University of Utah study, thus reducing a man's sex drive proportionately.

Fat in your diet can be cut by eliminating candy bars, potato chips (150 calories and 9 grams of fat in 10 chips—and who can eat just ten?), and granola bars. The best snack foods are raw fruits and veggies, cereal with skim milk, bagels or soft pretzels, diet fudgesicles, popcorn, pretzels, and vanilla wafers. Replace ground beef with ground turkey. Do what you can to drop the fat and the appearance of fat from your diet.

The second most critical area that affects our outward appearance is inward stress. Mistakes are most often made when leaders are tired and stressed. Great computer systems are worth looking into, but no system can ever replace refreshed personnel. Are your people stressed? Are they looking wiped out day after day? Stress causes you to lose sleep. Most Americans have no idea what it feels like to be sharp witted because they are operating on less than six hours of sleep a night.

Stress in the 1960s was more manageable. You had a crisis. You got through it. You rested and prepared for the next one. Today there are no breaks between crises, and most of the time they overlap. Why do you think Jesus took the time to talk to people about stress and worry? He knew even then how much it affected peoples' lives and performance.

Handle stress through planning. Stress comes most often from poor planning. Examine your next major stressful situation and see if you don't agree. At the root of every crisis, someone somewhere blew it in the planning stage. But that's OK. Don't get stressed out about getting stressed out. It is normal to be stressed. In fact, I think a little bit is healthy. Handling it is the basis for getting through it. Here are some ideas to follow.

When stressed, distract your mind by playing or exercising.

Relieve stress by taking your mind off yourself and doing something for someone else.

Watch your work schedule. Last year I found I had taken only three vacation days from January through November. I should know better, and so should you. The body needs refreshing more than that. Sometimes I feel like the father who kept bringing work home night after night. His six-year-old asked him why, and he replied that he didn't get all his work done at the office. His son helpfully answered, "Then why don't they put you in a slower group?"

One of the major forces against stress is humor and laughter. Laugh more often at the things that bring you stress. That is the bottom line of what Jesus was teaching the people. Why worry about tomorrow, what you will wear, or what you will eat? Let tomorrow worry about itself. Stake your chips more in yourself than in your closet or cupboard. Take one day at a time, and your appearance will take care of itself.

PRACTICAL TIPS

1. Locate three areas of your appearance that could use improving.

2. The next time you buy clothes spend a little extra on quality.

3. Cut the fat in your diet by 50 percent—NOW!

4. Locate a respected massage therapist to hire during overly stressful times.

5. Begin an exercise program to increase stamina and reduce stress.

CHAPTER 3

ATTITUDES: OPTIMISM AND A POSITIVE WORK CLIMATE

The Concorde is great. It gives you three extra hours to find your luggage.

—BOB HOPE, COMEDIAN AND ACTOR

If there is no wind, row.

—LATIN PROVERB

Jesus and His twelve retreated to the remote village of Bethsaida. His renown followed Him from town to town, and though He sought rest here, He found none. Every town through which He passed called out for help. Every villager He saw had a need. Every voice cried His name.

A band of thirteen men passing through town could only mean one thing—help had arrived. Word spread quickly to the surrounding villages and towns. Jesus and His men retreated to a hillside outside the city. He could see the crowd swell below. Fifty, several hundred, several thousand. The human glacier carved its way toward Jesus. By late afternoon, more than five thousand men and their wives and children surrounded the Provider.

Jesus asked Philip, the mathematician of His staff, to estimate the head count. He asked Philip how much money it would take to feed so many.

"Feed them? Jesus, we don't have that kind of money. Eight month's wages would barely be enough to feed them one bite per person. Send them away to buy food."

Andrew, the young disciple with little math skill but with simple faith, wanted to join in on the conversation. Andrew said, "There's a little boy down front with five barley loaves and a couple fish. Will that do?"

Taking a quick breath, Jesus stood, turned to Philip and Andrew, and said, "Yes, that will do. It is enough. Divide the crowd into groups of fifty and have them sit in the grass. Bring me the loaves and fish." Jesus took the loaves and broke them into a large, waist-high basket someone had been carrying. Ten halves. He took the fish and broke each. Four halves. Even the mathematician failed to realize what Jesus had done as He raised the basket up to the sky, blessed it, and then strained to keep it up. With a crash He dropped the basket which overflowed with broken fish and broken loaves. Each disciple followed His example. Lifting baskets with a few broken pieces and dropping baskets running over with food. Word of what was happening reached the crowd long before the food did. Excitement electrified the air.

—JOHN 6:1–13; 3:17

Nothing discouraged Jesus. Nothing held Him back. He saw opportunities in every situation. He found the positive in every negative. Good turned from evil. Plenty came from little.

It is said that attitude is demonstrated by action. No man in history ever demonstrated a more positive attitude through his actions than Jesus. Everywhere He went He attracted crowds. His outlook, His words, and His actions brightened people's lives. Someone once said to me that if Jesus had never performed miracles, the crowds would not have followed Him. To which I say, "Nonsense!" This land is filled with motivational speakers who spread a positive, optimistic message, and they fill stadiums with merely a message. No miracles are performed. I contend that Jesus had a message worth hearing; He spread good news. This is what drew the crowds, not the miracles. Where Philip saw hungry masses, Jesus saw hope. Where Andrew saw two fish and five loaves, Jesus saw a banquet. It all depends on your attitude.

YOUR OUTLOOK NEEDS AN IN-LOOK

It's like the story of the two bricklayers. A pedestrian stopped to admire the skill of two men laying brick upon brick. To the first he asked, "What are you making?" The gruff laborer replied, "About $9.50 an hour." Nonplused, the passerby stepped over to the next bricklayer and asked, "Say, what are you making there?" The happy reply came back, "I'm making the greatest cathedral in the world!" One man is a pessimist; one is an optimist. How we see things depends on how we approach them, and it also has a great bearing on the outcome.

Optimism is less difficult to describe than it is to define. Optimism keeps the sailor's eyes pealed for the shore as he makes his way home. Optimism makes the cancer patient live one more day. Optimism tells the business owner to open the shop doors in the morning. Optimism moves the heart from "I can" to "I will," and often to the great "I did it." Optimism dug the Panama Canal. Optimism placed man's footprint on the moon. Optimism time and time again changed the course of history.

Optimism is often associated with enthusiasm. Optimism comes from the French word meaning "best or greatest" and from the Latin word meaning "power." Enthusiasm comes from the Greek *en + theos*, meaning "in God" or "inspired by God." Put them together and what does it mean? The best power inspired by God is optimism! Jesus often spoke of faith. Isn't that optimism? Moving mountains takes faith, but it also takes a lot of optimism. It takes faith in God, and a positive attitude that it can be done. However, it can run amuck without one essential ingredient: organization (from the Latin meaning "tool" and the Greek meaning "work").

The second bricklayer in our illustration may have believed he was building the greatest cathedral in the world; but unless he laid the bricks upon each other in a systematic form, he would undoubtedly end up with something more akin to a brick oven than a cathedral. Optimism and enthusiasm must be balanced with organization to accomplish anything. It must be channeled.

This reminds me of the frustrated mother whose twin boys were identical opposites. Jason was the eternal optimist, and Michael the eternal pessimist. For Jason, every cloud had a silver lining; for Michael, every cloud held a storm. The mother grew tired of wanting to please her boys by treating them alike. No matter what she tried, one loved it and the other found something to complain about. Finally at wit's end, the mother dragged the four-year-olds to a psychologist and begged him to do something.

"Well," said the doctor, "the answer is balance. If we submit pessimistic Michael to good things, he'll become an optimist. If we put Jason in a bad situation, he'll see the bad side."

So at the doctor's recommendation, both mother and doctor watched as the children were placed in separate rooms. Gloomy Michael sat in a room surrounded by new toys, computers, games, and puzzles. Mother listened in to hear him exclaim, "I know Tommy has a bigger truck than this. You call this a computer? I'll probably cut my finger on this box."

The mother walked into the next room watching Jason gleefully sitting in a three-foot pile of manure. Manure! She gasped as she watched her optimist toss shovels full of manure into the air. Then she overheard him saying to himself, "Come on. Come on. With a pile of manure this big, I know there's got to be a pony in here somewhere."

One interesting note about optimism and its effect on attitudes: enthusiastic optimism is contagious. Like a happy virus, it spreads quickly, infecting everyone around with its potent, positive medicine. That's why I love to attend motivational seminars. One national speaker I admire walks through the audience before his speech hugging and laughing with people. He makes them feel good even before he tells them how to feel good. Like any virus, though, optimism has its antitoxins.

OPTIMISM AND ATTITUDE KILLERS

Fear. The smell of fear is the smell of death for a positive attitude. Fear starts rumors. Fear breeds an "I can't" attitude. Fear keeps us from forging ahead into unseen waters. Fear avoids risks.

Distrust. Trust is a vital culture for optimism. Distrust is a breeding ground for negativism. Distrust says, "You lied to me so I cannot believe."

Resentment. Optimism cannot survive under a snarled lip. Even the optimist knows a dog who bares his teeth is not smiling, even if he's wagging his tail. Optimism runs from resentment.

Indifference. Who cares?

Insecurity. This is a weaker toxin than fear. Insecurity says to optimism, "I don't think I can." It precedes fear's "I can't."

Anxiety. Nervousness shakes the foundation of optimism. Worry rattles its bones. Anxiety questions the possible and changes it to impossible. It says, "Yeah, but what if?"

EIGHT LESSONS ABOUT ATTITUDES

A positive attitude in your workplace can change the undoable to the doable. Leadership is essential. A raft full of positive, optimistic survivors won't last long if the captain knifes a hole in the boat. Remember that optimistic and enthusiastic attitudes spread. You must be the carrier. Over the years I've learned a number of lessons on this subject. I believe you'll find them as helpful as I have.

LESSON 1: PEOPLE WILL BECOME WHAT YOU EXPECT THEM TO BECOME

Do you remember the education experiment from a few years ago called the Pygmalion Effect? In essence, a number of school teachers were told at the beginning of the year that certain students were failures and that others were brilliant. In truth, all students in the group graded in at the same ability level and academic standing. The results of the experiment were predictable. At the end of the school year, the students with the lowest class scores were the ones the teachers had been told would fail, and those who excelled were those who had been primed by the teacher to do so. So it is with your staff. If you place limitations on them, they won't disappoint you. You must believe they are all successes in the making, that they are possibilities, that they are all the grade-A students.

LESSON 2: YOU ARE A MIND WITH A BODY, NOT THE OTHER WAY AROUND

In our sex-crazed society, this ditty hits home more than ever. While I am saddened at the tragic story of *Superman*'s leading actor Christopher Reeve being crippled by a fall from a horse, I am also encouraged by his wife's indomitable spirit. She has her attitude together. She said in a *20/20* interview with Barbara Walters that the body she sat next to, the body which required a breathing apparatus strapped to his chest was not Christopher Reeve. Chris was inside. What she saw was but the shell holding Chris in. So it is with us. She understood that, kept in perspective, we are limited only by what we think limits us. There is more to the human spirit than meets the eye.

During my college days I had become discouraged to the point of quitting. I recall sitting outside the dean's office, waiting for my appointment. Inside his office I overheard a young lady tell him what a pleasure life is, and how wonderful it is to be alive and to be able to go to school. For more than thirty minutes I listened to her positive outlook on life. When the time came for my appointment, the dean saw her to the door. There, passing before me, I viewed an eighteen-year-old girl no more than three feet tall riding a wooden tricycle specially built for her horribly contorted limbs. He opened the door for her as she rode away, and I exited with her, determined never again to complain about my lot in life. She had learned Attitude Lesson 2, and without knowing it, she taught it to me.

LESSON 3: IT'S NOT WHAT YOU HAVE, BUT WHAT YOU USE THAT COUNTS

You've heard stories of bright young students with incredible IQs who end up spending their lives delivering pizzas. The world will never know how many people dropped their potential at life's door and walked away. You may not be the most brilliant manager in the building, yet alone in town; but remember that men and women more brilliant than you have tried and failed, and more often than not have never even tried. Use whatever God-given skills you have, and forget about the competition.

LESSON 4: ATTITUDES ARE OUTWARD DISPLAYS OF THE HEART

Jesus said that as a man thinks in his heart, so he will demonstrate. A Chinese proverb states it this way: Assume a cheerfulness you do not feel, and shortly you will feel the cheerfulness you assumed. Attitudes are a paradox. If you fake a positive attitude and an optimistic outlook on life, you will become positive and optimistic on the inside. Then, from what is inside, you will show outwardly. Talk about a win-win situation!

LESSON 5: BAD ATTITUDES ARE CONTAGIOUS

Just as good attitudes are contagious, so are the bad ones. I have seen them destroy relationships. I have seen careers ended because of them. The reason I have been unfortunate enough to have seen the result is because someone in authority failed to nip it in the bud when it surfaced its ugly head. Bad attitudes spread faster than fire and in a work situation can be more damaging. Computers and desks can be replaced—ruined lives and careers not so easily. It is less painful to do minor surgery than to bury the remains.

LESSON 6: PHYSICAL, EMOTIONAL, AND MENTAL STRAINS AFFECT OUR ATTITUDE

I don't care which motivational speaker or writer you talk to, they all will tell you the same thing. You must stay fit emotionally, mentally, and physically, or all the positive attitude in the world will do you no good. Fatigue is a tormentor that spares no mercy. You cannot be at your optimum optimism if you are frazzled with fatigue. Get your rest. Stay in shape. Relax occasionally. You are in a fight for your mind and your life. Take care of yourself. Doctor's orders.

LESSON 7: YOU HAVE ABSOLUTE CONTROL OVER YOUR ATTITUDE

Try as you may, you can't control taxes. You can't make a red light green when you're in a hurry. You can't make ice cream that doesn't melt. You cannot make the sun rise faster. There are many things in this world we cannot control and shouldn't waste our time trying to. However, there is one thing you can control, and only you can control it. It is your attitude. I can't change your attitude, nor can you change mine. On this flight you are the captain, flight attendant, and passenger.

LESSON 8: LOVE YOUR WORK

No one gets paid to do what he really wants to do. When you get right down to it, sports figures and world-class musicians, rock singers and politicians, businesspeople and ministers would all rather be doing something else. We all would rather be with family and friends. We all would like to spend our days on earth full time with the people who matter most. But no one pays us to do that, so we work. If you must go to work, even when you don't want to, why not practice Lesson 8 and learn to love it. If you can love it when you hate it, imagine how much better you'll feel when you start to like it.

Instead of getting out of bed complaining about going to work, remember and say to yourself, "I could be going to the

unemployment office this morning. Thank God I have a job."
When you are preparing your morning ritual, say to yourself,
"I can't wait to see . . . " and name someone at work you'd like
to see upon entering. On your way to work, list some things
this job has provided for you: the clothes you put on, the place
you live in, the vehicle you travel in, and the food you eat.
Once you begin to see how much better off you are than the
majority of the world, you will begin to appreciate your work.
The more you learn to appreciate it, the more you'll learn to
love it.

HOW TO IMPROVE ATTITUDES

Are you convinced now that you need to develop a positive
attitude? Would you like to see it spread to your staff? What
about your family? Let me give you twelve pointers to get you
started. These are as practical as I can make them.

Treat your followers with respect. You will not find in the
words of Jesus even the hint of disrespect toward His staff. He
honored them by treating them as He wished to be treated.
There were times when He held His ground or had to disci-
pline a worker, but He always did so with dignity and respect.

Boost self-esteem by treating each one as important. Everyone in
your organization is here for a purpose. It is your job to find
that purpose and to be sure that everyone is plugged in to the
right job. Let each person know that the job will not get done
unless they do it, and that they are vital to the health of the
body.

Do not compare one to another. No father should compare his
athletic son to his musical son. No mother would compare
her twins. Neither should you compare the skills of one staff
member to another. When you compare people, it only
inflates the ego of the one you raise as superior and, obviously,
deflates the other person. The flip side is that even the winner
comes out the loser, because ultimately his ego is built on
comparisons. He will soon realize that his worth is relative.

Emphasize the successes not the failures. While I am not a fan of B. F. Skinner, the behaviorist, I recognize that his work does have some merit. His theory is that if you repeat an activity often enough, it will become engrained and will become a habit. We teach our children early on to brush their teeth every night so the habit will continue. I'm told that any exercise program continued for four weeks will become a permanent pattern. So it is with successes and failures. Fail often enough, and defeat takes its toll. You must emphasize your people's successes and deemphasize their failures. They already feel badly about the mess-ups; they don't need you harping about them. Rather, find what they do well and recognize it.

Avoid competition and contests, but set individual targets. Team effort is the best way to build a positive attitude among your staff. Jesus built a team. Military leaders build teams. Sports is often comprised of teams. I am not saying that team competition is bad, but winner-take-all attitudes among your staff will ruin the positive attitude you are trying to build.

Don't hog the credit. If you want to breed a bad attitude among your employees, just take credit for something they did. No one wants to rally behind an egomaniac. It's hard to be optimistic about your ideas if they all belong ultimately to someone else.

Trust your followers' motives. I live under the premise that deep down people are good and want to do the right thing. People don't want to fail. They really do not want to disappoint you, and unless you deserve it, they truly are not out to destroy you. Things happen. Bad ideas come along and mess things up. All in all, chances are the people you have working for you are a wonderful lot, and you need to give them credit for being honest. They usually have pure motives and good intentions.

Believe your work has importance and urgency. You have two options with regard to your work. You either need to get behind it, dig into it, enjoy it, and see it as some vital contribution to society as a whole. Or you need to quit. Get in or get out of line. If you stay in line, then do it with all the fervor your heart can muster. Do it as if it were your last day on earth.

Shake hands, and smile enthusiastically. Every person you meet is the greatest person on earth. Treat them as if they are and they will respond in kind. Whether you are a man or a woman, shake hands with vigor. Grab someone's hand like you grip the stuck lid on a jar of pickles. Look people in the eye and smile. Pretend they are about to give you a huge check that will forever end all your debts.

Praise your people. Find something good to say to every staff member within reach every day. You may have to look for things. Even if they are working on the same project day after day, praise them for it. Praise them for their work area looking nice. Praise them for holding down personal phone calls. Praise them for their attitudes. The more you sincerely praise, the better they will become.

Occasionally hold a pep rally for your staff. My staff knows I loathe meetings, even good ones. I consider good meetings an oxymoron. On occasion, however, I use the meeting format just to rah-rah my people. Try it. Watch their reactions. Call your staff together, come in last, and let them have it. Tell them how much you appreciate them. Tell them how wonderful they are to work with. Tell them you couldn't get along without them and you just wanted them to know. Then dismiss them. Boy, you'll make their day and increase their positive attitude quotient fourfold.

Read the Bible. I realize that the readers of this book come from all walks of life. I know some readers will have great faith in God, some will have little, and some none. Regardless of your denominational or religious background, I cannot emphasize enough the need to read this great Book—the Bible. The thread of hope runs throughout its pages. Its words of inspiration have changed hearts for more than six thousand years. Nations started because of it. Kings clutched it in death. So what is your excuse not to read it? It is required reading if you hope to make the grade in Optimism and Attitude 101.

PRACTICAL TIPS

1. Determine immediately to infect your staff with the virus of optimism.
2. Remember that people will rise to your expectations.
3. Ask a friend to recommend a version of the Bible to you and begin reading it.
4. Nip bad attitudes in the bud.
5. Find something positive to say to someone every day.

CHAPTER 4

COMMUNICATION: HINDRANCES TO GOOD COMMUNICATION

Thoughts unexpressed may sometimes fall back dead; but God himself can't kill them when they're said.
— WILLIAM MCKENDREE CARLETON, AMERICAN POET

It's not what you say, it's how you say it.
— ANONYMOUS

As the dust encircled the thirteen men who covered their faces with their sleeves, Jesus coughed a command to continue on and buy some food at the nearest village. He watched as they became smaller in the distance. Exhausted from His travels, Jesus leaned His back against a round stone well. The dust settled, and the sun beat its full power down to midday temperature. His eyes closed.

A woman came to draw water. Jesus said to her, "Will you give me a drink?" He ran His tongue over His cracked lips.

"Excuse me? Were You talking to me?"

Jesus shielded His eyes to look up at a purple-clad woman with dangling earrings and jangling bracelets. Delicately she removed an empty water pot balanced on her head and placed it next to Jesus. She was a Samaritan. His culture had taught Him to treat her as lower than a dog, but He saw beyond culture. His teachers told Him as a youth never to speak to such a woman. She did not expect His kind to speak to her kind. But He did.

"Please, if you would, draw Me some water."

She responded, "I am but a Samaritan woman, and You speak to me?"

His thirst for water and conversation transcended years of cultural prejudice. He spoke; she listened. She spoke; He listened. Two strangers in need of conversation shared more in common than water. Their desire for water brought them together, but her desire to learn more about the living water Jesus spoke of kept them together until the disciples carrying food arrived.

—JOHN 4:5–30; MATTHEW 11:15

Communication is best defined as getting an accurate message to an appropriate source in an effective manner. Anything less than that is simply disseminating information.

For every person on the planet there is at least one good excuse not to speak to any other person on the planet. Perhaps you fancy yourself a great conversationalist. Ask yourself the following questions and rate yourself 1 through 10, with 10 as the strongest response.

I find it difficult to select a topic for conversation.	1 2 3 4 5 6 7 8 9 10
I embarrass myself by talking about taboo subjects.	1 2 3 4 5 6 7 8 9 10
I mispronounce names and words.	1 2 3 4 5 6 7 8 9 10
I forget people's names quickly.	1 2 3 4 5 6 7 8 9 10
I overuse slang terms.	1 2 3 4 5 6 7 8 9 10
I find fault with what others are saying.	1 2 3 4 5 6 7 8 9 10
I cannot keep a conversation going.	1 2 3 4 5 6 7 8 9 10
I am as clumsy at ending a conversation as beginning one.	1 2 3 4 5 6 7 8 9 10

How did you rate? Anything above a 16 total, and this chapter (and the next) is for you. We all need to recognize the things that make us poor conversationalists before we try to improve. Improve what? First, find the weak link in the chain, and then begin to repair it.

WE DON'T TALK ANYMORE

Some obstacles to communication are obvious. People hear only what they want to hear. Jesus said several times throughout His brief teaching ministry, "He that has ears, let him hear." The problem of hearing is as old as recorded history, and the first problem is our selective screening of information. The dilemma increased exponentially with the onset of billboards, television, and computers. We *must* screen out information to keep our sanity. Our culture has become adept at it. Because people spend so much time learning to tune us out, we must work even harder to capture their attention. We must learn to get people to tune us in.

Another obstacle, at least in the business world, is staff turnover. In an organization of less than a hundred, it is not at all unusual to have a completely new staff in ten years. In fact, that is the norm. After ten years with the same company, I find myself one of the three senior staffers. In this scenario, we find it nearly impossible to generate communication with any measure of continuity. The memo or policy sent disappears with each terminating employee. Information does not get passed when a new staff member is trained. We spend our time teaching systems. Repetition seems the obvious answer; however, your remaining employees do not want to hear the same messages again and again.

The third blockage to good communication is also the easiest to eradicate: corporate red tape. You know what I mean— memos with "cc's" stamped all over them, "return response by" and "urgent" meaninglessly attached to them. Nicely packaged but ineffective paper shuffling breaks down a relatively simple process into a pyramid of problems.

Even beyond the corporate level and down to the one-to-one conversation, we face difficulties. This is critical, because corporations don't communicate; people in corporations do. I despise it when someone says, "I got a memo from headquarters." My response is generally, "What, all five thousand people signed it?" The greatest communicator in history dealt with individuals (like the woman at the well), and though the Sermon on the Mount is beautiful, there is no record of lives that may have been changed because of it. The woman at the well, on the other hand, ran and told the entire town of her one-to-one conversation with Jesus. As a result, many Samaritans believed because of her testimony.

One hindrance to great conversation is what author and lecturer Charles Ford called "conversational fat." Essentially he said that even in our efficient society we waste two hours a day (520 hours per year) in irrelevant conversations. Chitchat before meetings, rabbit trails during meetings, and supporting information after meetings takes up time that could be better used to tell your hardworking staff member what a great asset he or she is to the company.

At times we use poor word choices that mix up our intent or our message. It is like the nurse working in the psychiatrist's office who received a stern reprimand. "Nurse Bilge," the irate doctor insisted, "when you answer the phone, please say, 'We're awfully busy at the moment' instead of saying 'This place is a madhouse!'" The right choice of words often can make or break a conversation.

You may remember the poster that declared that the fifteen most important words in the English language could be broken down thusly: "I am proud of you," "What is your opinion?" "If you please," "Thank you," and "You." Knowing the right words makes choosing the wrong words more difficult. The more words you know, the more likely you are to select the appropriate one at the proper moment. One little boy placed an ad in the local newspaper that read, "Lost—one dog. Brown hair with several bald spots. Right leg broken due to auto accident. Left hip hurt. Right eye missing. Left ear bitten off in a dog fight. Answers to the name 'Lucky.'"

Some words, like *lucky*, convey a very different meaning than the little boy's view. To him, *lucky* meant full of great fortune. The dog is still alive despite his accidents. We chuckle at the name because our experience with the word tells us that if the dog were lucky he would have avoided all his calamities.

When you place the word *prompt* on the notice for an upcoming meeting, does your staff respond with a chuckle? When you say that a policy applies to all employees, is there a rolling of the eyes? Words convey a meaning because words convey a history. It is unlikely that the words *Choochie Anna* mean anything to you. You do not have their history to draw upon, but for me they evoke memories of an elderly Polish aunt with loose fitting dentures frying French toast for me at breakfast. Some of your employees have a history behind the words *deadline, review, probation, lunch*, and *flextime*. That history may not be the same as yours; therefore, the meaning will differ, and you must discover what others mean by the words you choose.

BODY LANGUAGE

For some a disconcerting hindrance to communicating is eye contact. The Gospel of Luke records an incident in which Jesus forewarned Peter that he would deny Him. When Peter did, Jesus looked at him, and Peter wept bitterly. Incredible amounts of communication took place with no words spoken.

Various cultures respond differently to eye contact. Americans, for example, will make eye contact for only about a second before one or both people look away. Any longer than that and emotions are heightened and the relationship grows in intimacy. Americans look at approaching people on the sidewalk just long enough to show an awareness of presence. What about the rest of the world? In some parts of the Far East, looking away during conversation is an insult. I have been to England a number of times where the ever-polite listener stares with occasional blinks that indicate a hint of interest. Shifting eyes are equated with shiftiness and dishonesty. Staring eyes indicate a power play and a challenge. Blinking eyes evoke thoughtful images, as do squinting eyes. Saying, "I really respect him," while rolling your eyes to look at the ceiling conveys a different message than saying it with a slow, methodical blink.

The entire body as well as the eyes convey meaning in conversation. What you see is not what you say at times. In every culture people speak differently with their bodies. Arabs may stand so close together during conversation that they feel each other's breath; Americans maintain an arms-length invisible bubble or personal space when conversing. Kinesics, the study of body language, tells us that visual images often speak louder than words. An otherwise calm interviewee may nervously but unknowingly tap his foot. Crossing arms is a dare-me position. Hands clasped above and behind the head reveal an open invitation to share information. Arms outstretched, hands tucked in pockets, legs crossed ankle to knee, head tilted to one side—all these reveal a message, and not understanding the message can become a hindrance to good communication.

HOW YOU SAY IT

Another barrier to getting the message across is a difficult one to nail down, but we call it tactlessness. It is easier to describe *tact*, than *tactlessness*. Tact is like a girdle. It enables you to organize the awful truth more attractively. It may be difficult to be the bearer of unpleasant news, but delivering it with tact helps ease the blow. A friend of mine, Jerry Jenkins, tells the story of having to fire a large number of staff members upon his promotion to management. He jokes about having bluntly put in a memo to all that "firing will continue until morale improves around here." To say something tactfully, follow this rule: Soften the blow, but be sure the message still comes through.

I almost avoided putting this next communication barrier in because it may sound preachy, but bear with me. *Gossiping* is a hammer that breaks down trust. Once you have gossiped to an employee or another staff member, or allowed them to gossip to you, trust is forsaken. Later when the need arrives for you to take the worker of whom you gossiped into a confidence, it is unlikely that the employee will want to. Trust is one of those nebulous things that good communication requires, but which writers have a difficult time capturing. All humans have a fragile trust barrier. Once it is shattered, it seldom can be repaired. Some people trust politicians; others do not. One group trusts used car salespeople; one group does not. One person believes his family doctor; another person gets a second opinion. Trust is an important part in conversation, and gossiping is the radioactive cloud that melts the wall of trust.

I had (past tense) a good friend who fed me a steady diet of gossip for years. Many of his conversations began with "Well, apparently . . ." Finally, I wised up and realized that I stood a good chance of being on the sending end of his "Well, apparently's" to someone else. He who gossips *to* you will gossip *of* you. Shut off any conversation that begins with "Don't tell anybody, but . . ." Acting legend Errol Flynn once said, "It's not what they say about you; it's what they whisper."

BEHIND DOOR NUMBER ONE

The two final big hindrances to communicating effectively are closed doors and one-way communication. Let's look at each.

In the ideal situation, management and staff have open communication. Any employee can have access to any manager for any reason at any time. Companies like McDonalds have made strides to achieve that goal by tearing off the doors to all their offices. While that may seem drastic, if not financially unsound, the concept is valid. Closed doors tell your staff that (1) either you are too busy for them, (2) you are holding something back from them, or (3) you are busier than they are and inaccessible. Seldom does a closed door connote a good meaning. While it allows you privacy, it also blocks opportunities to develop friendships, increases frustration levels, slows resolution of crises, and causes hurt feelings.

It is possible to have a closed-door policy without having a door in the office. Our office layout is a series of mazes and cubicles; yet without doors one man manages to tell people that his six-by-six office is off limits to drop-ins and social butterflies. He puts his briefcase on the visitor's chair and has his back toward those who enter.

The last problem will be dealt with in greater detail in the chapter on improving your communication skills, but briefly consider one-way conversation. One-way conversation implies that it is the receiver's responsibility to "get it" once you have delivered it. But with all the possible barriers listed above, the chances of them getting it simply because you delivered it are slim. Communication generally requires feedback or dialogue of some sort. It is a two-party affair. Few people are good at it. Jesus and the woman at the well had comfortable dialogue. What seems natural to us, for them took great courage, an understanding of their limitations, and a determination to overcome communication barriers. It is said that before an addict can be healed, he must first know and recognize that he has a problem. Not knowing or acknowledging that one has communication barriers is the greatest of all hindrances to communication.

PRACTICAL TIPS

1. Write down your greatest areas of weakness regarding communication.

2. When asked to participate in gossip, remember the consequences.

3. Vow to do more thinking and less speaking.

4. Remember that your words may mean something else to the listener.

5. Observe body language and watch others' eyes as you converse.

CHAPTER 5

COMMUNICATION: IMPROVING YOUR COMMUNICATION SKILLS

Think like a wise man but communicate in the language of the people.
— WILLIAM BUTLER YEATS, AUTHOR

Everything that can be said can be said clearly.
— LUDWIG WITTGENSTEIN, AUSTRIAN PHILOSOPHER

While passing from village to village, Jesus stretched forth His hand touching and healing all who wished it. The small band of followers swelled to a crowd of thousands as He reached an amphitheater-shaped hillside. Jesus seized the opportunity of addressing so many people at once. It was no accident that He led them here, for the acoustics allowed Him to speak at nearly normal volume while the rocks reverberated His words. The place was perfect.

The time was perfect. Jesus observed the pain and frustration on many faces. He looked at old men scowling from anger brought on by inconsistent leaders who used the law to their own ends. His eyes passed over the crowd as He looked directly into the eyes of a known prostitute sitting alone. He knew some of these men from boyhood. Priests were peppered throughout the crowd. Divorced men sat with their new younger wives while divorced women sat alone. A wealthy merchant wrapped his silk robe around him as he sat next to a beggar wrapped in twelve-year-old rags.

The crowd hushed. Jesus took in all He surveyed. Of the two thousand on the hillside, He sat last. He told the crowd His interpretation of the sacred laws. He spoke of salt and light, of divorce and remarriage, of oaths and vows, of murder and adultery, of riches and poverty, of praying and giving. He warned of judging each other. He admonished the rich and encouraged the poor. In several hours He communicated one of the most significant messages ever recorded. He spoke with authority, and when the crowd dispersed, everyone—the priests, the rich man, the prostitute, the beggar—walked away with a message meant just for them.
        —MATTHEW 5:37–48

Like the Walrus in *Alice in Wonderland*, we talk of so many things: of shoes, and ships, and sealing wax, of cabbages, and kings. How we talk is as important as what we talk about. People will judge us by what we say as well as how we say it. Henry Higgins bellowed the plea, "Why can't the English learn to speak?" in *My Fair Lady* after enduring Eliza Doolittle's butchering of the English tongue and proposed that he could transform the poorest commoner into a ravishing socialite if only she would learn to speak correctly.

At the close of the Sermon on the Mount, we are left with the words, "The crowds were amazed at his teaching, because he taught as one who had authority, and not as their teachers of the law" (Matt. 7:28–29). Jesus spoke with authority. We all have a way to go in our ability to communicate as effectively as He did. Once we know that we have communication problems, we must identify and resolve them. Don't be bashful. We can all improve in one or more areas: listening, speaking, or writing. Let's take each section and break it down into palatable chunks to sharpen our communication skills.

YOU'RE STILL NOT LISTENING

The first hurdle to overcome is shyness. It is simple for us boisterous folk but may take some doing for the truly shy person. Try this. When introduced to someone, grab their hand firmly but warmly. Then look directly at the person's eyes, smile, and say with enthusiasm, "Glad to meet you."

Shyness is not an inherited trait. There are no shyness genes. It is a learned behavior that can (and must) be unlearned if you aspire to be a leader. Shyness is often viewed as a sign of weakness . . . a burden leaders cannot afford to bear.

Practically, there are ways to overcome shyness, or at least give the appearance of overcoming it. (1) Practice making eye contact. If this is too difficult, then look at the bridge between the eyes of the other person. They will not be able to tell that you are not actually looking at their eyes, and this exercise will help build your confidence. You may even find your eyes sliding a bit and making contact with theirs. (2) Force yourself into a good conversational position. Sit in the front of the classroom instead of choosing the back seat. In a circular seating arrangement, choose the chair that places your back toward the door. That way when new people enter or exit, the crowd will inadvertently look at you and allow you to make contact. (3) Up your pace. Ever see managers whip around the office like greyhounds out of the starting gate? Don't they look important just by the determination in their walk? I have a long-held secret to share with you. Managers have learned the art of what I call "constructive nothingness." We really aren't headed anywhere when you see us rushing about. It is a ruse. Make people believe you are on a mission. (4) Respond. Speak when spoken to, and do so at a volume to be heard. If opening a conversation is difficult, at least take the initiative to answer when addressed. Gage yourself by the number of times someone says to you "excuse me" or "what" or "I didn't catch that." Turn up the volume. People really do want to hear what you have to say, or they wouldn't ask in the first place. They will listen.

Most people, unfortunately, are poor listeners. In my business travels I can recall one or two people who genuinely showed interest in our conversation by the way he or she listened. Listening is more than one-half of communication as many counselors will tell you. A lady walked into the marriage counselor's office and said flat out, "I want to divorce my husband." The counselor asked her, "Well, do you have any grounds?" to which she replied, "Oh yes, we have almost two acres." The puzzled counselor responded with, "No, you don't understand. What I want to know is, do you and your husband have a grudge?" The lady answered, "Actually, we don't. But we do have a lovely carport." The counselor shook his head and said, "Ma'am, I'm sorry. I just don't see any reason why you should divorce your husband." The lady looked at the counselor and said to him, "It's just that the man can't carry on an intelligent conversation. He never listens!"

Listening appears to be a weaker position in terms of communication. Jesus, the classic servant-leader, spoke for hours on the mount while perhaps thousands listened. Based on the subjects He addressed, however, He must have done a great deal of listening first. He could not have known what to cover without first hearing the need. He could have talked about war. He could have brought up the Roman empire. Apparently, those things were not on people's minds or lips as much as the issues of adultery, riches, and prejudice. Influential and important people generally talk less and listen more.

How do you develop a listening mentality in your organization? Begin by establishing a nonthreatening forum for expressing ideas. The first employee who rolls their eyes back, humphs, or comments negatively at another's suggestion must be dealt with immediately and sternly. Those involved must have the assurance no idea is stupid, irrelevant, or inferior. Slam the door shut on that attitude, and others will feel freer to contribute. Establish the ground rules for contributions at every meeting until employees feel free to disagree, but they can do so with the right attitude. Not every idea is appropriate, and you don't want to give the impression that you will act on all of them. However, if there is to be a naysayer in the crowd, it ought to be the leader of the pack and not one of the pack. If Bob Job disagrees with Sally Sweet, that breeds discontent. If one with authority disagrees, then the group is likely to continue finding other solutions.

WHAT ARE YOU TALKING ABOUT?

So you think you are a great communicator? Everyone always understands everything you say? Honestly answer the following questions with a yes or no.

1. Do you actively listen to others' ideas?
2. Do you use descriptives to bring your message home?
3. Do you use others' ideas more often than your own?
4. Do you purposely ask more "why" questions than "who, what, when, where" questions?
5. Do you offer encouraging words to everyone you meet with?
6. Do you let the others do more talking than listening?
7. Do you jump in with solutions to problems?
8. Do you always let the employees solve their own problems?

If you answered no to any question besides 7, keep reading. Did you get all the answers right? Then keep reading because anyone who has all the answers has much more to learn than the one who knows he doesn't know.

I love conversing with great talkers. I enjoy listening to spellbinding motivational speakers who can command the English language like a general commands his troops. Nothing makes me cringe more than a speaker who repeatedly uses pet words like *moot, paradigm shift,* or *irregardless* without a clue as to their proper usage. Poor talkers often overuse the phrases *frankly, so to speak, in other words, you know, by the way, you see,* or *for what it's worth.* Eliminating them from your conversation will be as easy as asking others to point them out to you when you use them. Believe me, for what it's worth, they will be more than happy to see you eliminate them, so to speak, from your vocabulary, you see.

Another way to improve your speech is to eliminate fad words or slang often associated with youth. Professionals should be aware of slang expressions and can use them at will when speaking to a group of teenagers, but they are out of place in a formal meeting among adults. Teens also will express a conversation with dozens of "so I said, then she said, so I said, then he goes, then I go." It is bad enough to find it in published modern-day novels; it becomes unbearable in face-to-face conversations.

In addition to those guidelines, follow these "ten commandments" of conversation to improve even further.

I. Thou shalt not be right all the time.
II. Thou shalt not be ridiculously dogmatic about everything.
III. Thou shalt not use the words *always* or *never* in thy vocabulary.
IV. Thou shalt not believe the universe revolves around thee.
V. Thou shalt not be insincere in thy compliments.
VI. Thou shalt not interrupt.
VII. Thou shalt not be argumentative.
VIII. Thou shalt not be discourteous.
IX. Thou shalt not speak of that which thou knowest not of.
X. Thou shalt not lie. (This one's not original with me, but I have permission to quote it.)

After reading that list, you may be wondering what on earth you can still talk about. Avoid talking too much about your private life, the faults of friends and family members, the climax of a suspense thriller, or shady stories. Other than that, the world's a banquet of conversation pieces. Talk about football, swimming, skiing, diving, synchronized swimming, the

Olympics, soccer, or chess. Talk about door-to-door salespeople, telephone solicitors, chain letters, IRS audits, bank fraud, or tax cheats. Talk about magazine or newspaper articles, documentaries, movies, or books. Talk about budgets, improvements, capital expenditures, training, problems, and solutions.

SOME RADICAL IDEAS TO INCREASE COMMUNICATION

There are a number of ways to increase the opportunities for communication among employees. Some companies have come up with radical ideas. For instance, Walt Disney Productions insists that all employees wear a name tag. The uniqueness is that all tags only bear the wearer's first name, and even the president wears one. Everyone is encouraged to speak on a first name basis. When designing the new engineering complex for Corning Glass, managers suggested that escalators be installed instead of elevators to increase the chance of other employee contact. Some companies hold rap sessions in a park setting to remove the formalization, while others intermingle departments rather than compartmentalizing them. If you look around, you will find many ways to increase communication in the company setting in addition to those just mentioned.

You will know communication is developing if your organization has one or more of the following attributes.

Informality is the norm. No one calls anyone mister, miss, or missus. Stock people address the president as Tony and not as "sir." I am not sure why, but financial institutions seem to have the most difficult time adjusting to this idea. There is something inviting when a patron can call the bank president Shirley instead of Mrs. Jamison. Ditto for employees.

Informality is balanced with professionalism. Employees do not take two-hour lunches, nor do employees wear sloppy clothes. Remain informal in conversation but professional in demeanor.

Systems and decor lend themselves to increased informal conversation. I prefer round tables to long cafeteria tables for face-to-face contact. No one sits at the head of the table that way. Some companies have far too many tables set up in the cafeteria to entice informal discussions. Fewer tables forces employees to sit with each other. A little bit of "squeeze over please" is good for breaking the ice. Conference rooms ought to be equipped with devices needed to aid interplay of ideas such as blackboards, note pads, pens and pencils, and video equipment.

Openness of ideas is expressed freely, even if it brings intense conflict. I despise company politics. Nothing destroys open communication faster than fear that the president's son or friend is sitting in to report everything that is said. I once recommended using another exterminator for our facility because the one we were using stained the walls, smelled up the halls, and made no house calls. At the end of the month, we were paying five times what a nationally advertised company estimated for me, and we still had ants in the cafeteria cupboard. But, alas, our exterminator happened to be a good friend of someone in management, so we opted for poor service at five times the price rather than fire the bum. No one but me dared bring up the issue. They preferred to let ants crawl all over their computer keyboards (it happened) than complain. Does that sound too harsh? There is no room for politics in the line of communication in a business. Jesus knew and understood this.

Once you have determined to incorporate those four attributes, move on to ways of opening dialogue. They can be as simple as discussing the results of customer surveys, opening suggestion boxes to public criticism, publicly praising performing employees, or asking spouses of employees to offer their suggestions. Let your staff come up with other ways. Often just asking them, "How can we better communicate here?" will result in a cornucopia of ideas.

Of course, there are some basics you learned in school with regard to communication and dialogue. Remember these?

- Encourage questions.
- Give and get feedback.
- Give clear instructions.
- Repeat the instructions.
- Summarize the conversation.

Great ideas, I believe, but who has time for all of that at every conversation or meeting? I sure don't. What about when training someone or giving instructions? Even less time! Have you ever caught yourself saying, "By the time I've finished telling him how to do it, and followed up to make sure he understood what I said, I could have finished the job myself!"? Unfortunately, the reality is that you will need to spend a little more time when giving instructions. Time spent up front is less frustrating than having to redo the project because of miscommunication.

Try this experiment out on a number of people, and you'll see what I mean. Hand someone a blank piece of paper and read these simple instructions: (1) Fold the paper in half. (2) Tear off the upper right-hand corner. (3) Fold in half. (4) Tear out the lower left-hand corner. (5) Tear out the center. This exercise will help both you and the participant see the need for clear directions and full understanding because interpretations will often vary.

A MEMO ABOUT MEMOS

A memo at a certain company went something like this.

From: Marketing

To: Sales

Subject: Marketing Forecast

Sales and income figures show an easing up of the rate at which business is easing off. This can be taken as ample proof of the government's contention that there's a slowing up of the slowdown. Now, to clarify that, it should be noted that a slowing up of the slowdown is not as good as an upturn in the downturn. On the other hand, it's a good deal better than either a speedup of the slowdown or a deepening of the downturn. Also, it suggests that the climate is about right for an adjustment of the readjustment to rate structures.[1]

Let's face it. Memos are the bane of a company's existence. They are overused and under-read. Memos stifle creativity, kill interactive communication, and flood file cabinets. They are voiceless messages with no intonation or feeling. They beg the reader to infer the hidden meaning and to interpret it as they see fit. To put it bluntly, memos are a waste of everyone's time and effort. Some days I sit at my desk and say to myself, "So help me, the next person who walks in here and puts a memo in my in-box is going to get socked in the beezer." I dream of the day when some visionary president rids the country of time clocks and memos, but not necessarily in that order. Until that day, I'm afraid memos will be with us, so we might as well learn to adjust and file them. Just remember, filing systems are designed to retrieve things, not store them.

Most word-processing software now comes with preset memo sheets. That saves the aggravation of getting a memo from someone with no identity as to the sender. I have been in business for twenty years and have never read one word on memo basics. Chances are, neither has your staff. Feel free to use this material in your next memo or when teaching a Memos 101 class. I'm afraid some of my attitude about these little things may show through a bit. You understand.

ZABLOSKI'S RULES FOR MEMO-IZING

1. For heaven's sake, put your name on the thing. How do you expect me to give you an answer by next Monday if I have to spend a week hunting you down to see if you sent it?

2. Date it. That'll give me some idea how many months it's been sitting at the bottom of my in-basket.

3. If you are going to ask the logging industry to cut down a tree just so you can send me a memo, at least have a purpose for it. Tracy's birthday party doesn't count, either.

4. Don't be so technical. I have no idea what a mega-gig or a serial port with a bus is. I interpret it to mean a great party at the bus terminal where a hip band serves cereal. Just tell me my computer won't be fixed until Thursday so I can go home or play golf.

5. Be brief. Unless you'd rather ramble on endlessly without any possible provocation or understanding as to where periods, question marks, or things should end. At all.

6. Stick to one subject. I estimated that I have spent a total of three and a half years trying to decipher memos with four unrelated items on them, and another six months trying to figure out whether to file the thing under Reed Olson, Cafeteria Duty, Postage Increase, or February.

7. Direct it to the right person only. There's little to be said for receiving a memo with a "cc:" on it indicating a copy was sent to the president and all upper management, especially when the memo is about something stupid I did or said that would make them think I am some sort of slimy invertebrate with the personality of an orange.

Learning the rules of communication takes time and effort. All the information in this chapter should make you a great communicator, but only if you apply it and take it to heart. Be patient. It took Jesus thirty years to perfect His communication skills. It may take us a lifetime.

PRACTICAL TIPS

1. Begin looking people in the eye when talking to them.

2. Listen to people's words as well as to their hearts.

3. Find three ways you can improve your speech this month.

4. Ask your staff to suggest ways your organization can better communicate.

5. Train yourself and your staff to say it rather than write it.

CHAPTER 6

CUSTOMERS: HOW TO HANDLE CUSTOMER COMPLAINTS

Revolutions are not about trifles, but spring
from trifles.
—ARISTOTLE, GREEK PHILOSOPHER AND TEACHER

Handle people with gloves, but issues barefisted.
—DAGOBERT D. RUNES, EDITOR AND PUBLISHER

Martha and Mary had lived together since the death of their parents. Martha, the elder, the wiser, the worker, had taken care of Mary. She allowed her mothering instinct to fill the void in Mary's heart. She taught her as much as a woman could teach, but Mary always wanted more.

Martha had the gift of hospitality, and she tried to lay the mantle of that gift on Mary's shoulders, but Mary just didn't get it. Mothering and serving seemed all right enough for Martha, but Mary wanted to learn; despite the laws against such, she wanted to learn. Mary heard that Jesus, the Teacher, had accepted Martha's invitation to dinner, and the thought energized her to the point of giddiness.

Still, Martha cleaned. And she cooked. Then she cleaned up after she cooked. All the while Mary swept dust out the door, peeking, waiting, and watching for the arrival of the Teacher.

When Jesus finally arrived and settled in, Martha busied herself about her tasks, while Mary sat at Jesus' feet and soaked in every word He spoke. From Him she heard words of hope, confidence, and authority. He was filling her need, and no amount of dish washing could tear her away. Meanwhile, Martha banged and clanged and splashed through the kitchen area until she could no longer bear the load alone.

"Lord," she complained, "you can see that my sister isn't doing her part. Tell her to come into the kitchen and help me."

But Jesus handled her protest with ease and confidence. "Martha," He responded, "you have chosen to do one thing, and she has chosen another. What she has chosen to do is the better of the two." With those soft words, Jesus kept the peace, mended the relationship, and taught a valuable lesson.

—LUKE 10:38–42

Perhaps as a businessperson you were not aware of the following:

> Ninety-six percent of consumers who experience a problem with a small-ticket product (for example, small packaged goods) do not complain to the manufacturer. (Of these, 63 percent will not buy again.) Forty-five percent of consumers who experience a problem with a small-ticket service (for example, cable television or local telephone service) do not complain. (Of these, 45 percent will not buy again.) Not surprisingly, only 27 percent of unhappy consumers of large-ticket durable products (for example, automobiles, computers) do not complain. (Of these, 41 percent will not buy again.)[1]

One survey group estimates the numbers to run as high as 91 percent not buying again!

Unhappy customers tell their experiences, on average, to ten other people, unless the problem happens to be a large-ticket item. The number then rises to sixteen. However, a small-ticket customer who has had his or her complaint adequately resolved will tell five people, some of whom may become customers of that caring business.

Most organizations never weigh the cost of a complaint. Take the auto industry for example. They estimate that every loyal customer will pass on about $140,000 if they stick with the same company. Why on earth do they quibble over a $15 replacement part or $30 repair bill?

SOME TRUE-LIFE STORIES

As a consumer (and vendor), I have had my share of purchasing horror stories. For the sake of illustration, and because they were all resolved to my satisfaction, I will briefly relate them here. I purchased an expensive mixer-blender-processor. While on, the beast would arbitrarily zoom from speed to speed, spraying the walls with whatever batter I happened to be mixing. Within six months of purchase, the interior plastic gears had stripped and the machine became useless. I called the manufacturer to complain, and without argument they offered to replace the broken part if I returned it at their expense. I did, and a week later I received a completely new and upgraded model.

Another time I had taken my car to the dealership for a tune-up, half hour guaranteed. After nine hours of sitting in a greasy service waiting room, and missing a day's work, I returned home to prepare what has become known at the dealership as the infamous Zabloski letter. Two days later I received apology calls from the general manager and the service manager, and the following day an envelope arrived containing coupons for free car rental during any repair, free wash and wax, free interior detailing, and free oil changes for as long as I owned the car, which was five years old. In some cases, it pays to complain, and to complain to the right people.

YOU GOT A PROBLEM, LADY?

In the story of Mary and Martha, Jesus allowed a follower time to complain. He let her complain high up. Jesus listened, then ferreted out the individual's motives and intentions. In many corporations, the CEOs may not have a clue as to what is going on in the field. Nor do they hear customer complaints unless they are filtered through the customer-service department. In order to get the information firsthand, you must invite customers out to lunch or dinner. Let them see you as a normal person interested in their needs.

Customer complaints can be easily categorized. Both as a consumer and as a businessman who demands excellence, I have narrowed customer complaints to these simple needs not being met and the likely corresponding type of complaint.

Problem	Complaint
Disrespect: rude, discourteous service, ordertakers interrupting, receptionists cutting them off	"This is the third time I've called!" "What is the matter with you people?" "Well, I never!"
Inconvenience: having to return product and/or having to pay for it, portions of a product missing, unreasonable operating hours	"I have to pay for postage again?" "There are three nuts missing from assembly-part C." "Everybody but you guys works till five o'clock."
Misunderstanding: customer's order versus invoice disputes, differing advice from employees, order mix-ups	"What a rip-off!" "What on earth am I going to do with fifty of these things?" "Someone there named Lisa told me it would be OK."
Tardy service: order not received on time, back orders not announced at time of order, inordinate time serving customer	"Why on earth does it take you eight weeks to ship a five-ounce item?" "Why didn't you tell me you didn't have it in pink when I ordered it?"
Disorderly service: lack of proper equipment to process orders, not making procedures clear, returns	"C'mon. Everybody uses credit these days." "Explain again why you need all these forms filled out for a simple return." "I waited here twenty minutes and now I need to go back and fill out what?"
Inferior product: ill-fitting parts, product life too short, quality missing	"Look at the seams on this thing." "I've had dreams that lasted longer than this thing." "This thing is so cheap!"

Customers really expect little more from you than they do anyone else. Except for the fact that money has changed hands for a product or service, customers are still people and deserve to be treated as such. We forget as businesspeople that tomorrow afternoon we will be someone else's customer. We will stop at the dry cleaners after grabbing a fast food meal as we head off to the mall to return a birthday gift. What do we expect from other companies? We want workers to be considerate, interested, friendly, calm, available, fair, and honest toward us. Remember, although you are a businessperson you must think like a customer. How do excellent businesses handle your complaint? My guess is they probably follow this three-step solution.

1. They apologize profusely. They grovel and humble themselves. They agree.

2. They never condemn either the customer or the employee. They'll investigate the situation and resolve it within twenty-four hours, and then will report back to the customer the results even if the customer left satisfied. Customers want to know you have not forgotten about it. Excellent businesses offer something in return for their trouble.

3. They establish ways to avoid repeating problems. Every complaint is an opportunity to find and eliminate a glitch in the operation.

FAR AND AWAY THE BEST

One of the best operating philosophies your organization can develop is to exceed your customer's expectations. Go beyond that. Repair all your errors and make good on your mistakes. Learn from them. Never make excuses for making an honest mistake; apologize for errors, yes, but don't make excuses.

It never ceases to amaze me how many businesses never learned this rule. A friend of mine had ordered chicken at a famous eatery and, having taken a seat near the checkout counter, noticed another customer approaching the cashier with his plate. Apparently, the man complained that his chicken was raw and bloody and wanted another plate. The cashier looked at the plate, declared the food perfect, and said the customer would have to pay for another plate. The man held his ground (and other customers in line) trying to get a resolution to his problem. The manager got involved and took the employee's side. At this point, the customer simply asked for his money back, which both manager and teller refused to do. This, understandably, lit the customer's fuse. At this point, my friend went to the counter and offered to buy the man another plate of food. He thanked her but refused and continued his fracas with the management who in the meantime had called the police! As my friend left, vowing never again to eat in this chicken place, she passed the police entering the store. Imagine! Over a three-dollar plate of uncooked chicken!

I wish I could tell you this sort of example is the exception, but it is not. Here's an example of how complaints ought to be handled. One woman went to a local store to buy some shorts for her father-in-law. After he tried them on, he said he preferred a larger size. So she returned them to the store for a larger size, which they didn't have. She asked for her money back instead, and the manager gave her such a hard time she contacted the owner of the company. She explained the story to him and told of how she argued with the manager but to no avail. The president got the manager on the phone, said a few brief words to him, and hung up. She got her money back, and with a smile! As an object lesson, the president flew that manager to the headquarters where he was asked to hold up those very shorts in question in front of everyone and recite the company's motto of "satisfaction guaranteed." Extreme, you say? That manager and a whole bunch of people were reminded of the reason for being in business that day. The episode changed their lives and their outlook on customers.

IT'S NOT MY PROBLEM

The best method of resolving customer complaints is to remember this: Everyone in your organization is responsible when a customer complains. I realize that many organizations have specialized, trained, and toughened people working in what we call customer service. However, on occasion the chief officers of the organization must make themselves accessible for a customer complaint as Jesus did with Martha. Not every day, but once in a while management needs to sit eyeball to eyeball with customers and hear their grievances. That makes everyone, including the president, accountable. Everyone needs to be accountable because "everyone is the company." It isn't that difficult to do. Start by rewarding any customer-relation actions beyond the call of duty. Be sure that account-ability is explained and understood. Praise the performers publicly. Train the employees causing customer dissatisfactions by making them solve the problems personally.

If a customer tells you that product X has flaws, she wants to know as Martha did in our illustration with Jesus just what you plan to do about it. As with Jesus, you must listen beyond the words and get to the heart of the matter. Is she really complaining that your product is faulty? Then give her another. Also, if you choose to inspect the flaw for future product improvement, for heaven's sake don't ask the customer to pay for it. Let me give you an example. In the business of publishing books, there are a number of misships. The customer may receive the wrong product, or may receive too many. In the first case, I would tell the customer to keep the wrong product we shipped as our gift and then ship the right product (for which they already paid) to them. In the second, likewise. Tell the customer to keep the extras at our expense. This philosophy serves two purposes: (1) the customer is endeared to your generosity and will stick with you if for no other reason than the hope that you will mess up again; (2) it will force you to investigate and improve upon a failing distribution system that is costing you money you could invest elsewhere.

The scenario is the same whether we are talking about an individual customer or a business vendor. When dealing with a business that is dissatisfied with a product or service you offer, consider the principle. What can you give to them? What do they really want? How can you go beyond the standard business practice and win this business for life? Ponder how to do it without being lavish, but then do it. Good intentions are useless. Customers know the difference between words and actions.

Remember that what you think you are selling may be quite different from what the customer is buying. Many businesses buy IBM computers, not for the superiority of the equipment, but because of the follow-up customer service that comes with it. Determine never to let someone enter your door without exiting satisfied.

Jesus undoubtedly knew the Scripture that says that "a soft answer turns away wrath." He allowed Martha to vent her complaint, and He received it graciously. He responded to her with graciousness. He is our best example.

PRACTICAL TIPS

1. Drill home the concept that the customer is always right.
2. When the customer is wrong, refer to number 1.
3. Find ways to overcompensate a customer for their inconvenience.
4. Make yourself accessible to customers who want to complain to higher-ups.
5. Empower every employee to solve complaints.

CHAPTER 7

CUSTOMERS: MAKING THE CUSTOMER NUMBER ONE

The secret of success is to keep the five guys who hate you away from the five guys who haven't made up their minds.
— CASEY STENGEL, PROFESSIONAL BASEBALL MANAGER

A consumer is born every ten seconds.
— EDWIN NEWMAN, JOURNALIST AND AUTHOR

Jesus entered the town of Capernaum worn from the day's travel. As He entered the city gates, a group of Jewish elders approached Him, not to greet Him, but to ask of Him.

"Lord, one of the Roman guard—the head Roman centurion for this district, to be exact—has a servant whom he loves dearly as his own son. The servant is sick and at death's door. We know it is an unusual request of us to ask You to come heal the servant of a pagan Roman soldier, but this man has been a friend of Israel. As head centurion, he has spent a great deal of his own personal wealth helping us build our synagogue. We believe that though he is not a Jew, he deserves to be granted this request."

While Jesus knew the cost of reaching out to a Roman, and the persecution it might bring Him, He had compassion on the man and on his servant. He agreed to follow the elders to the centurion's home, but while they made their way through the dusty streets, several Romans approached Jesus and His band. The Roman messenger greeted Jesus and proclaimed yet another message. "Sir," the messenger voiced louder than necessary, "the centurion sends us with another message, which he scripted in haste. I beg your pardon, but it is difficult to read. The centurion says, 'I did not expect You to come to my home in person to heal my servant. I am not that important. But I believe that if You will but speak the words from where You stand, my servant will rise completely healed. I, too, am a man of authority. When I tell someone to go or to come, they do it. Or if I order a servant to do something, he does it without question. Now, please, speak. I believe.' That is the end of the message, Sir." The soldier rolled the scroll tightly, and he and his friends returned to the centurion's home.

Jesus marveled at the message. Then He turned to the band that had grown to a large crowd and shouted, "Hear this! I tell you that in all of Israel I have not seen so great a faith as demonstrated by this one Roman centurion." Though He would have, Jesus did not proceed to the Roman house. He did not need to. When the band of messengers returned to the home they found the centurion and the servant in perfect health.

—LUKE 7:1–10

There can be no doubt. If you hired Jesus Christ to rejuvenate your stale customer-relations policy, He would spearhead the strongest customer-first program since God called the Israelites His chosen people. There were no unimportant people to Jesus. There were no pains in the neck. Every human who crossed His path felt alive, important, and useful. Every desire seemed pale compared to what He had to offer, and what He had to offer in today's terms was "customer satisfaction" bar none.

LET'S START WITH
PROBLEM NUMBER ONE

The number one problem facing businesses today is not "the economy, stupid." It is not price freezing, low morale, health care, or poor location. The number one problem with businesses today is lack of quality, in-your-shoes, as-you-wish, the-customer-comes-first kind of customer service. Ads declare it. Radios blare it. But walk off the street into any business, and you will experience the truth.

Walk into any fast-food restaurant, and before your hand lets go of the door some teenager is asking you for your order. That is problem number one. Some marketing genius drummed up the idea that speedy service equals quality service. They are not the same. Sensitivity to the customer is more important than meeting a quota. None of us expects to have a long-term relationship with the person behind the counter, but it would be nice if he or she occasionally looked up at you and smiled. Ditto for bank tellers, hotel clerks, parking lot attendants, government office clerks, ad nauseum. The person about to flop over his hard-earned money has needs beyond what he is about to buy, and a personable touch from your employee may mean he'll come back.

Problem number two in customer service is rude, discourteous and/or inadequate service. Been to the food court in a mall lately? The frustrated customer stands at the counter with her wailing toddler, waiting to place an order. No manager in sight. The two folks behind the counter are engaged in a heartrending conversation about last night's date. "Excuse me?" "Yeah, just a minute." She waits another twenty seconds. "I said, 'Excuse me.'" Now they both give her THE LOOK. She's decided the food isn't that great, but this fight is worth it. She pursues it. Tempers flare. In a no-win situation she huffs out, and the duo blithely resume their conversation.

Problem number three. Out with the old and in with the new. Many companies make the mistake of spending so much time adding new customers when times are good that they forget about the customers they have had for years. They want to grow, so they take on more accounts than they can possibly handle well. Eventually the faithful customer of the past loses faith in his supplier because he was left behind for sweeter grass. Inattention is one of the major causes of discontent in customer service. It isn't that customers have a complaint about service or quality; they simply cannot voice that they dislike being treated like stepchildren, so they run away from home.

When was the last time a business called you to see how you liked their product or service? Most businesses take the attitude that they have you and there you will stay. Companies will spend huge amounts to attract new customers while the old customers go unattended. No marriage can stand apathy and inattention for long. Neither can a business-customer relationship.

A sales clerk tells you over the phone that if you will come in, they will have your item ready. After a twenty-five minute drive, you arrive just in time to be told the product is back ordered. "Yes, but the salesperson said not thirty minutes ago that . . ." "Do you have that person's name?" "Well, no." "I'm sorry. I don't know who told you we had that product, but they shouldn't have." Terrific. The salespeople are to blame. The order people are to blame. The computers are to blame, and you still don't have your product. You call customer service, and what do you get? If history is any indicator, you reach the most unskilled employee in the company who may be working only part time to pay his way through college. He can't even tell you where the executive washroom is, let alone solve your complaint. This illustrates customer service problem number four: passing the buck and breaking a promise. They usually go hand in hand, and both feed upon excuses.

DEVELOP A CUSTOMER FIXATION

Which of these problems plagues your business? Look objectively; better yet, ask ten customers to tell you candidly. How can you tell if your business is succeeding in the customer service arena? How do you implement winning strategies for customer service?

First, develop a customer fixation. Become a lunatic when it comes to servicing your customers. Treat every customer as though he or she will become a lifetime patron. Remember that this customer may become one who, through word-of-mouth referrals, generates more business for you than any advertising campaign could. Find some rules to live by, and then live by them. It doesn't matter whether your rule is as cliché as "The customer is always number one," or "If we don't take care of our customers, someone else will," or "Give us your business once and we'll be your friend for life." It is not the rule that makes yours a customer-service oriented company, nor is it great intentions. Customers know the difference between what you say and what you do, and the best intentions in the world do not create quality customer service.

Then set the thing in motion. Don't plan it to death; do it. Ross Perot more than once complained of the comparison between his company EDS, and his stay at General Motors: "The first EDSer to see a snake kills it. At GM, the first thing you do is organize a committee on snakes. Then you bring in a consultant who knows a lot about snakes. Third thing you do is talk about it for a year."[1] Gather your staff together (not just your core management team, but the receptionist, the financial officer, the plant waterer . . . everybody) and explain your new philosophy and strategy. Explain that service is not an option, but that it is your primary goal as a business. Get their feedback. Drive the point home that this must be the number one priority of all who are on payroll, including their spouses, children, and pets. This is the end of mediocrity and contentment with the status quo. Repent big time for the lousy service you've provided in the past, and declare war on inept, discourteous, uncaring customer service. Tell them the buck stops with you, because it does. You will become their role model (like it or not). More about this in a minute.

This new philosophy of customer first will become your competitive edge. No matter what product or service you are selling, there are a dozen just like you who are bidding for your customer dollars. People do not generally care what product they buy or where they buy it; they care about how they are treated in the process. After doing a consulting job for a friend with whom I had shared this concept, he excused, "But Jim, we're already giving fine customer service." "No you're not," I followed. "If you were, you'd be making twice the income you are now." "Oh. So if we were making twice as much as we are now we'd be doing OK?" "No," I retorted, "if you were making twice as much as you are now, you'd still only be making half as much as you could be making." I tell that to every business, because no matter how good the customer service seems, it can always improve.

DON'T SAY IT IF YOU DON'T MEAN IT

So it starts with the boss, the CEO, the big muck-a-muck. The first thing that needs to take place after the strategy and philosophy are laid out is for the president, chief officers, and head managers to get out of their offices and get in touch with the customer. Go wait on someone for a day. Hit the sidewalks and find out what people think of your business. Spend two days on the phone calling up the competition to find out what they think of your business. Go find out what they are doing better than you in the area of customer service. Then go back to the office and tell those folks who hit the road with you that all customer complaint calls will be directed to you and them for the next month. Make no fewer than ten calls to existing customers regarding a purchase or repair they spent money on. After you've assessed the damage, meet with your staff again and hold nothing back. Take the blame for everything. It is your fault. They followed your lead. They will again. You only need to show them how to do it.

Reaffirm your commitment and let the news filter down to your employees. Does the phone system irritate the customer? Change it. Do they hate the wallpaper in the waiting room? Paint it. Are you still playing Muzak? Kill it. Are customers being put on hold? Find out why. Do the rest rooms need cleaning? Does the lawn need manicuring? Does the receptionist's bouffant hairdo make people laugh? Whatever detracts from the best possible customer service, change it, even if it is only a perceived problem on the part of the customer. Remember that their perception is their reality. If you or your staff thinks a product or service is superior, but the customer doesn't, change it. Remember, customers don't care what *you* think about your product; they only care what *they* think about your product, and what they think about your product is in direct proportion to the amount of hassle it took to get it.

Your staff must see you mean what you say. Put your feet in the fire and put meat on the bones of your words by rearranging your budget to allocate more funds to customer service. I'd recommend you go further than that. If your company is large enough to have a director or vice president of marketing, you ought to also have a director or vice president of customer relations.

It is important to follow through. Do it, don't just say it. Mean it. To do so may mean some loss of revenue for a time. If the survival of your business is at stake, that is all the more reason to implement a customer fixation philosophy now. Your company may die if you do; it will certainly die if you don't. Change is never easy. Some companies learned over a period of time that service to the customer pays off in the end, even if it costs you in the beginning.

Tom Peters, in his book *Thriving on Chaos*, gives the illustration of a man in one of his seminars who stood to give testimony to great customer service. It is such a great lesson that it bears repeating. At the urging of his wife and daughters, a guy reluctantly went to Nordstrom's to buy a suit, though he thought Nordstrom's charged too much. Being a businessman on the run, he really needed some suits, and fortunately Nordstrom's was having a great sale. He went, reluctantly, but he figured he had nothing to lose.

He found the service and treatment by his sales assistant exemplary. He found two suits he liked, one on sale and the other at full price. He asked about Nordstrom's same-day alterations policy, but he discovered this only applied to non-sale items. The suit on sale would be delayed another day. He could wait another day to pick up both suits, which he did.

When he returned to Nordstrom's at fifteen minutes to closing the next day, the salesman greeted him by name though they'd only met briefly the day before. He told the salesman he needed the suits to go as he was heading for a plane that night. The salesman went to get the altered suits, but returned empty-handed. After accepting a number of apologies from the salesman, the man left for his business trip first to Seattle and then to Dallas.

When he got to his hotel room in Dallas, he noticed the message light blinking. He asked the front desk for his message. No message, they told him, but he did have a Federal Express package waiting for him. The bellhop brought it up, and the man gasped at the postage—ninety-eight dollars! Nordstrom's sent the package. Inside he found not only his two altered suits, but three twenty-five-dollar silk ties as well thrown in for free for the inconvenience. Finally, he found a note from the salesman at Nordstrom's who again apologized and explained that he had called the man's home and had spoken to one of his daughters to learn of his travel plans. That day the businessman became a believer and faithful customer of Nordstrom's.

How has Nordstrom's fared from this kind of wild frivolous spending to get and keep a customer? They have grown seven-fold since 1978, from $225 million to $1.9 billion in sales.

Any wonder why? Some businesses only dream of perpetuating that kind of customer service. Some are actually doing it. Like the centurion Jesus dealt with, making believers out of people takes very little, really.

PRACTICAL TIPS

1. Teach your staff that courtesy keeps the customer when all else fails.

2. Work harder at keeping the customers you have than adding new ones.

3. Develop a whole-house customer fixation.

4. Find ways to get every employee to rub shoulders with customers.

5. Allocate more funds in your next budget to customer service.

CHAPTER 8

DELEGATING: GIVING ORDERS AND RESPONSIBILITIES

People who row the boat usually don't have time to rock it.

—ANONYMOUS

Never learn to do anything. If you don't learn, you will always find someone else to do it for you.

—MARK TWAIN, AMERICAN AUTHOR

Jesus sat on a roughly hewn bench with His back against the clay wall. In front of Him on the floor sat His twelve disciples. Jesus spoke.

"I cannot do all that needs to be done in the amount of time I have left. So I am sending you. You've seen how I healed the lepers? You watched Me make lame men walk and blind men see? For three years you watched. Now you must do."

The men mumbled among themselves as to the meaning.

Jesus continued. "There are two dozen cities I must visit, and I cannot. I must let you do it in my stead. Here are your instructions."

James shuffled his feet and kicked up dust. Thomas sneezed, and Peter glared at him with a "pay attention" frown.

"Do not go among the Gentiles or enter any town of the Samaritans. Go rather to the lost sheep of Israel. As you go, preach this message: 'The kingdom of heaven is near.' Heal the sick, raise the dead, cleanse those who have leprosy, drive out demons. Freely you have received, freely give. Do not take along any gold or silver or copper in your belts; take no bag for the journey, or extra tunic, or sandals or a staff; for the worker is worth his keep.

"Whatever town or village you enter, search for some worthy person there and stay at his house until you leave. As you enter the home, give it your greeting. If the home is deserving, let your peace rest on it; if it is not, let your peace return to you. If anyone will not welcome you or listen to your words, shake the dust off your feet when you leave that home or town."[1]

Peter whispered to James, "Brother, that's when you kick up dust."

James replied, "I can't believe He's letting us do all this for Him. Why?"

Thomas interjected, "He just told us. He can't do it all. He needs us to help Him. Now will you two be quiet so I can hear? I don't want to miss anything."

Jesus finished His speech and stood. "I am sending you out like sheep to a pack of wolves. Beware. Be wise. Be as cunning as snakes but as gentle as doves. When in doubt, do what you think I would do. Now go."

—MATTHEW 10:1–14

Jesus sets the classic example of the mastery of delegation. He did it right.

He understood the three aspects of delegation, which is giving someone else the responsibility, accountability, and authority to carry out part of one's own job. Managers and leaders have had problems delegating since the days of Moses, when Moses' father-in-law told him that he was in over his head and needed to find men who could take part of his responsibilities away so he could manage the unruly Israelites. Once Moses followed that advice and delegated his tasks away, things turned around for him.

BLOCKS TO DELEGATION-GATE

For some strange reason, despite years of discussion in business courses and books, managers still don't delegate correctly. There are four major reasons.

1. Their tasks become their security blankets. For the insecure manager, there is always the fear that if they delegate some task, then their subordinates will outshine them. They also may feel insecure about their ability to teach or train their staff, a problem that will ultimately drift back to them if the job goes awry. Some insecure managers fear they'll run out of things to do and be caught reading a magazine instead of pushing a pencil when the boss comes in.

2. Distrust and skepticism from outside have crept into the office. Managers may look over their staff and consider them adept enough at making coffee or sending faxes, but they may consider employees inept at negotiating contracts or issuing check requests.

3. An ego the size of Godzilla runs the place. Pity the employees who work for a manager who leans toward the I-might-as-well-do-it-myself attitude. This kind of manager is convinced that if he or she dies, the world as we know it will cease spinning. No one can do it as well as they can. They are irreplaceable. Little have they learned that being irreplaceable is not a compliment but a curse to an organization.

4. The very overactivity they need to delegate keeps them from doing so. The manager runs from sunup to sundown trying to manage as he or she ought to. Proper delegation takes time; so does nondelegation.

ITEMS NOT TO DELEGATE

Not everything you do can or should be delegated. If it could, then why on earth does your organization need you? Each of these is open for criticism and disagreement, and may be considered on a case-by-case basis, but as a norm I would not delegate the following items:

Items that could affect the very life of an organization ought not be delegated to others. Recently the city of Los Angeles declared bankruptcy because those in charge delegated the lifeblood of the city (money) to someone who speculated it away on risky investments. Jesus did not entrust the preaching of the gospel to His men until they were ready.

Items of great confidentiality. Of course you need to trust people. Delegation is largely based on the trust factor, but let's not be stupid about it. If your organization is setting a proto-type in motion that could effectively change the way you do business, the fewer people who know, the better. No sense tempting someone with information, or with risking an unnec-essary leak. Better to handle superconfidential matters yourself.

Items only you are trained to do. You are responsible, for example, for disciplining a wayward but salvageable employee. Do not delegate the disciplinary interview to someone else just because you don't want to handle it. Some responsibilities are job-title specific and require a great deal of expertise or experience.

Items you want to pass the buck on. You know the Weider-mayer deal is a dud, and you'd rather not have to watch it die a slow death. The temptation is to pass it on to someone else who will be responsible for its burial. That is not delegation; it is irresponsibility, and any manager worth his salt will soon recognize it.

Items of legality. The last area I would avoid passing on to subordinates concerns matters of the law. Be careful passing the responsibility of signing or negotiating contracts. Seldom will subordinates take it as seriously as you will, nor will they have the level of expertise it takes to handle it on their own. You might want to walk them through it, but avoid handing the whole baby over to them.

IT CAN BE DONE

Successful delegation looks very different from ordinary delegation. It can and must be done. I cannot understand this "holding on" attitude some managers have. The day I first became a manager, I held a meeting and divvied up a bunch of tasks I knew I couldn't handle. Not just items I didn't want to do. I liked some of the things I delegated away, but common sense told me that if I planned on succeeding as a leader and manager, I had to help my employees succeed, and to do that I had to give them responsibility. I followed an eight-step process.

First, pick out the tasks that can be delegated. You must go through your job description and all the footnotes, addendums, and unwritten "as requested" tasks and consider which of those could easily and/or better be done by someone else. Write them down and then prioritize them. Decide which of those tasks to unload first. If you are guilty of not delegating, then I recommend listing all of your tasks on a piece of paper first, numbering them, and selecting no fewer than one third to delegate away.

Next, spell out what needs to be done in clear, simple language, and write out briefly how much responsibility you plan or need to give to the person you choose to get the job done. While you're at it, save yourself some headache and include any responsibility or authority you are not giving. The amount of authority and responsibility can be defined in one of four ways or levels. At the end of your delegation speech, you will say one of these four things:

"Do it, and report back to me with information so I can make a decision."

"Do it, and recommend a decision to me. I'll still decide, but I'd like your opinion."

"Do it, and let me know how it's going now and then."

"Do it, and don't bother me with the results."

Jesus took His staff right to the last level in the opening illustration. The success of the operation centered around His giving responsibility and authority to His men. Responsibility without authority is self-defeating. It ruins morale. It forces people to work with one hand tied behind their backs. It causes people to look like incompetent fools when they have been instructed to carry out a task, only to hit a minor snag that they cannot resolve but would if they had the ability. Look at the authority level Jesus gave His staff. They could virtually do anything and everything He did. They had to in order to get done what He needed them to do. If you are willing to delegate, you must likewise be willing to give away some of your authority.

Third, pick the appropriate person to whom you should delegate. Usually a manager's natural inclination is to delegate to the most responsible—and often the longest employed—person. Remember that "old reliable" may be reliable, but she is probably overworked already. Don't be shy to give tasks to newer employees. They should be delegated less than a senior staffer, but as they grow responsible, so should their responsibility level. Place fewer limitations on senior staffers than you would on the new guy. If people don't succeed at tasks you delegated, it is a reflection on your leadership, for you selected them.

Clarify the assignment without telling what steps to take. This is the most difficult part of delegation. Look at Jesus again. On the surface it appears He was telling His men exactly what to do and when to do it. But a deeper investigation reveals a number of things every manager must consider to successfully delegate. Jesus was merely explaining to His men exactly what His own plan of action had been for the past months. This is how He did it, and this is why it succeeded. For the first time, He took His mental strategy and verbalized it for them to see. Once He did, the disciples undoubtedly realized as the light came on that this is what they'd been doing all along. It gave them the confidence to do the same. Jesus also leveled the playing field for this delegation order. He did not say, as He later would, to go into all the world. No, He instead limited the terrain these men could work under. By doing so, He virtually guaranteed their success. He knew the danger of spreading His resources and those of His staff too thin. He delegated in increments. He set a specific circle of parameters. As long as they stayed inside that circle, they were free to do whatever they wished.

The Bible does not say so, but I suspect Jesus established deadlines for His staff. Eventually, He would let them have full and free reign to carry out larger tasks, but on this, their first delegated endeavor, He needed to hear of their success. Indeed, we are told of one occasion when a disciple tried to exorcise a demon for Jesus (as he had been delegated the authority to do), but he was unsuccessful. It may have likely occurred during this trip, at the end of which the disciple brought the demonized boy to Jesus to cure. This test told Jesus that these men were not yet ready to head out on their own into more hostile regions.

Tell the individual why you selected her or him. People need to know that you think enough of them to give them one of your jobs. Tell them why. It will boost their confidence and increase their motivation to succeed and please you.

Next, be certain to discuss any potential traps or problems. Jesus told His men later on in the illustration that they would be taken into prisons and beaten for doing this. They were not unaware. It is unfair to make people go the hard route without warning them. Help them be successful by warning them of the pitfalls and pit bulls that might stand in the way of their progress. Tell them who they are likely to encounter and what their reaction might be. Let them know by whom, what, when, where, why, and how they may encounter interference or delay.

Finally, evaluate the final results. If the task you are delegating is close ended, look at the entire job and discuss it with the delegate. If the results were successful, praise the employee for a job well done. If the results were less than you expected, be kind but honest. Help them see through the rough points, offer recommendations for next time, and unless they completely blew the experiment, assure them that there will be other opportunities to do your work again. Remember, you are training your replacement.

You probably realize that the higher up your position, the less time you should spend on tasks. Presidents may not make photocopies. They simply don't have time. They need to deal with people—people who are working on tasks. If you are spending the majority of your time as a manager still working on tasks, reevaluate your situation quickly and begin to set a plan in motion to delegate some of it away. Then go through the major steps to successful delegation listed in this chapter.

As Jesus discovered, if you give people the sweet taste of responsibility, they'll come back for more. Once people see what they can do, they will be willing to do it. Once they are willing to do it, the job of delegation has been successfully completed.

PRACTICAL TIPS

1. Tomorrow make a list of all the items you could delegate.
2. Sift through your staff and select appropriate tasks for appropriate abilities and talents.
3. Force yourself to take the time to explain every task you delegate.
4. Praise people immediately once a delegated task is completed.
5. Work toward the highest level of delegation so you can have time to manage.

CHAPTER 9

FAILURE: HOW TO SUCCEED BY FAILING

There are a lot of ways to become a failure, but never taking a risk is a sure bet.

—ANONYMOUS

Measure twice; cut once.

—WOODWORKERS' SAYING

The darkness surrounding Peter was thick enough to be felt. Huddled alone in a corner, balled up as small as he could make himself, he hid. The authorities had put out a search for any and all of Jesus' followers. Anyone could be looking for them tonight with the bounty the authorities had offered. Peter pulled his knees up and laid his forehead on them. His mind replayed the events of the last six hours.

He recalled standing with Jesus in a room. He and Jesus argued.

"Jesus, I'm telling You to Your face. I will never, *never* deny You. I will die for You first."

Jesus replied, "You will deny Me, My friend. This very night, and not once but three times, before the rooster crows at dawn."

The ruse of a trial had taken place. He watched as Roman guards defleshed Jesus' back with whips. He watched as men slapped Jesus, spit on Him and smeared it into His beard, shoved thorns into His skull, kicked, punched, and kicked again.

"I said nothing," Peter whispered to himself. "Is that denying Him?" He looked up as someone approached him.

"Excuse me," a Judean woman inquired. "Weren't you with that Jesus tonight?"

"No, no, not me. It wasn't me," Peter said as he ran to another secluded wall. He watched the Judean woman and her friends cluster around a fire they'd built in the courtyard. Its warmth beckoned him after a while to leave the cold shadows. He stood with his hands outstretched toward the warmth.

"It is him. Miriam, look, it is one of the followers of that Nazarene they are executing tonight."

"I tell you, it wasn't me!" Peter ran again, fearful for his life, fearful they were spies. They eyed him suspiciously as he sought shelter inside a horse stall. The cackle of chickens, the snort of a pig, a horse stomping, all gave him some sort of strange comfort that humans could not. He closed his eyes. Sleep finally came, but not for long. He awakened to find a group of twenty, maybe thirty women surrounding him. They smelled of smoke from the fire. Peter stood to run again, but they trapped him in the back of the stone stall. One woman, leathery skinned and nearly toothless, pointed a crooked finger and cawed an accusation.

"It was you. I saw you. It was him. He is one of Jesus' own followers. I say he is."

"Stop it! Stop! I'm not, I tell you. I never saw the man. I never knew the man. I deny . . ."

Every eye turned as a black rooster on the wall near Peter flapped its wings, stretched its neck and crowed. One crow, then another. The women's gaze returned to the man in the stall. They covered their mouths as they watched this strange one crying. He dropped to his knees, weeping harder. They returned to their dying fire unaware that he dropped in the straw. One woman peeked back out of curiosity.

She saw a broken man, lying with his face down, sobbing uncontrollably. He pulled himself into a fetal position. He had hit bottom.
        —Matthew 26:33–35, 69–75; John 20:25–28

It is one of the saddest scenes in recorded history. Peter's mistakes were many, but this was his biggest failure yet. Few of us have made such a royal mess of our lives. A few have.

Everyone Fails

Many people truly believe they should never make mistakes. That is perhaps the greatest mistake of all. Everyone fails. Life is a casket of failures we collect and bury; at least we should. Some people never let go of their failures, so they themselves become one. Yet what they truly fail at is understanding what failure is and how to do more than just live with it—how to overcome it, embrace it, and even welcome it.

The problem with failure does not lie with getting knocked down by life's bully. The failure is in staying on the ground. Making a success of failure means we not only have to get back up, but we need to get up with a resolve to do better next time.

The world is ripe with examples of failure. An August 24, 1994, *Wall Street Journal* article highlighted the failure of one successful man, Larry Dean. Mr. Dean made a fortune selling his computer software company for $68 million. He and his wife decided to leave a legacy to their four children. So Dean built a house. This was not just any house, but a 32,000-square-foot home with 24-karat gold sinks, fifteen bedrooms, bathrooms built like Egyptian tombs, a dance hall, thirteen fireplaces, a 24-seat dining room with a wall-sized aquarium, and an 18-hole golf course all on sixty acres in Atlanta. Upkeep and taxes on the property are more than $100,000 a month. The success story doesn't end there, however.

The six Deans lived in the house about a year and a half after it was completed. Mrs. Dean then left with the four children and filed for divorce. With the echo of his own voice to keep him company, Mr. Dean moved into the apartment above the garage. His assets dried up faster than he anticipated, and at the time of the article, Dean sought a buyer for his $40 million estate. Alone, dejected, and beaten by his own success, Mr. Dean ends his interview stating, "Maybe there's a purpose to all of this that I just don't see. But right now, I'd say this was a big mistake."

Success and failure seem to blur the longer we look at them, and the chasm between the two is very narrow indeed. Seventy years ago, five of the wealthiest men in the world held a meeting of minds in Chicago. The meeting included the president of Bank of International Settlements, Leon Frasier; president of the largest steel manufacturing company, Charles Schwab; a member of the Coolidge cabinet, Albert Fall; head of the world's largest monopoly, Ivan Kreuger; and Richard Whitney, president of the New York Stock Exchange. Within twenty-five years of that historic meeting, two of them were imprisoned, two committed suicide, and one was completely broke.

MURPHY WAS A FAILURE

Failure is no laughing matter, unless you happen to read Murphyisms. You know, those pithy little statements about life that ring true and make us laugh at our failures and disappointments. Here are several that touch my heart.

> Leakproof seals—will.
> Self-starters will not.
> Interchangeable parts—won't.
> If it jams, force it. If it breaks, it needed replacing anyway.
> All warranties expire upon payment of invoice.
> There's never time to do it right, but there's always time to do it over.
> The light at the end of the tunnel is the headlamp of an oncoming train.
> The other line always moves faster.

A shortcut is always the longest distance between two points.
When in doubt, mumble. When in trouble, delegate.
And the classic, Anything that can go wrong, will go wrong.

I suppose laughing at our foibles helps us handle them. Another way we can endure them is by sharing them with others. This is difficult because human nature and instinct teach us to cover our mistakes, not display them for the world to see. It started in the Garden of Eden when Adam and Eve sewed fig leaves together to cover their failure, and it continues today with financiers covering up their errors by creatively juggling numbers. Showing your disappointments has a healing effect on the soul. During those times when Jesus became weak and discouraged, He revealed Himself to His staff. Leaders who never show emotion or never reveal their mistakes may come across as perfection personified to their employees. All that does is discourage the rest of the group. People truly do not like such perfection. They cannot relate to it. If you don't reveal your flaws to your employees, they will seek them out for you, and once revealed, they will gleefully gloat about them. If they still cannot find any failures or mistakes, they will take the liberty of making some up.

HOW FAILURE WINS

Failure is a natural course of events. It is bound to happen now and then, but sometimes we do things to help it along a little. How?

1. By second-guessing the outcome of a decision or a problem. How often do you find yourself sitting at your desk sweating the outcome of a proposal or a decision? One major corporation built an entire marketing plan around the two words, *what if.* Those two words can have a positive impact or a negative one. If the brain leans toward the negative, you will say, "Yeah, but what if Johnson hates the proposal? What if my spell checker missed a key word? What'll the boss say if I fire his best friend? What if . . ." Tied right in with all the "what-if" questions is the "if-then" clause. "If I give my secretary more work, then she might quit. If I ask the staff to work an extra hour, then they'll think I'm an ogre. If I park in Bob's spot, then he'll punch me in the nose." "What ifs" and "if thens" are our vain attempt at fortune telling. Unless you happen to be a psychic with a flawless track record, give up this habit.

2. *By taking responsibility for everything.* Do you want a sure-fire way to failure? Do everything. Sign up for the whole bus-load and go along for the ride. I have a friend who not only thinks he can do everything, he vainly tries to do so. As a result, many of his tasks end up either on the cutting-room floor or end in disaster because he takes them into his heart and home as if they were his children. He has not learned that he cannot do it all.

3. *Through too much positive thinking.* I firmly believe that a positive attitude is critical in business, but I also have seen positive attitudes become clinical denial. There is merit in finding good in bad events, but there is also as much merit in finding bad in bad events. Failure and disappointments have their good points, and they have their bad. I believe you will learn more by focusing on what went wrong than what went right. Positive mindbenders teach us that everything looks bright. Nothing is wrong. Sorry, but life has taught me that what I can improve upon is what I fail at. To continue to extract the small seeds of good to the complete exclusion of the bad is not only unhelpful, it may even be damaging. It may perpetuate more failure.

4. *By looking at others' successes only.* Another sure way to meet with failure is to look outside yourself. Let's take money, for example. Our society says the more money we make, the more of a success we are. The less money, the bigger the fail-ure. Actor Sylvester Stallone makes an average of $16 million per film. Most major league baseball players earn around $400,00 a year. The United States president hauls in an even $200,000; the Pope's salary is zero. So where is the failure? The failure is in looking at others for your self-fulfillment.

Doing so virtually guarantees that you will not be fulfilled. There will always be someone greater, more popular, richer, and more beautiful than you.

5. *By listening to criticism.* I'm sure society has a place for professional critics though I've never seen a statue erected to one. Every time I read a film critic's review, I ask myself then why doesn't he go do it better? The answer? Because he can't. He knows if he tried he would fail miserably, and he would open himself up to the critics-in-waiting. People will criticize you for everything: from the color of wallpaper you choose, to the brand of coffee you drink, to the choice of car you drive, to the name you gave your second child. Ignore them. Critics are faultfinders. They have no idea how to improve the thing, only how to slam it. There is no such thing as constructive criticism; it is an oxymoron. I prefer to receive constructive recommendations from people who come not to complain, but who come with solutions to making it better.

6. *By giving in to excuses.* Your failure rate increases proportionately to the number of excuses used to cover it up. Think about it. What purpose does an excuse serve? Like the farmer who asked another if he could borrow some rope. "Sorry," the neighbor replied, "I'm using it to tie up, uh . . . my milk." "Your milk?" asked the other. "Rope can't tie up milk." "I know," said the neighbor, "but I figure if you need an excuse, one's as good as another."

Everyone has an excuse as to why they don't, why they aren't, why they haven't, or why they can't. We blame our lack of education, our poor health, our young, middle, or old age or our rotten luck. Whatever excuse we can find, we use. Stop making excuses for your failures. A failure is a failure. For whatever reason, something failed. Learn from it and go on.

7. *By trying to please everyone.* Remember the saying that you can please some of the people all of the time, and you can please all of the people some of the time, but you can't please all of the people all of the time? You're doomed to fail if you even try. When I look over my staff and the variety of needs

and personalities, I would have to be a multiple personality to satisfy them all. Even Jesus, for all of His perfection, could not make everybody happy. He knew better than to try.

HOW TO WIN AT FAILURE

Failure is part of the human experience. We all face it, and we all must deal with it. Some overcome failure by pulling up their bootstraps and trying again and again as Thomas Edison did with his lightbulbs. Too many unresolved and unconquered failures can bring complete ruin. Learn how to overcome your failures and disappointments. You can defeat failure and disappointment:

1. By knowing your strengths and weaknesses. The chain of your character is only as strong as its weakest link. It is there that you are most likely to fail, and it is there you should put your efforts to overcome. A man with an eye for the women is destined to fail in this area unless he acknowledges it as his weakness. A woman with a nasty disposition will fail to make friends and wonder why. An employee with a bad attitude will be passed up time and time again for a responsible position. Take time for self-examination right now. Look at your life, at your character, and at your career. Find the areas you feel most prone to fail. Then, imagine every possible situation that might cause you to fail there. The more you know about your weakest link, the better prepared you can be to repel failure when it tries to crash through.

2. By taking more risks. This seems to be the opposite of what your natural inclination will tell you. "Oh, no. I'm not taking another risk. That's what got me into this mess in the first place," you might say. However, the longer you take to bounce back from a risky venture, disappointment, or failure, the longer the dragon holds you down and the stronger he grows. Blow after blow, you must jump back into the fray immediately. This builds your resiliency. In the world of failures, only the strong survive.

3. *By reading of other successful failures.* Aren't you inspired by reading how other failures succeeded? I am. You've probably read about the guy who failed in business in 1831, lost in a legislative race in 1832, failed at another business in 1833, suffered a nervous breakdown in 1836, lost the House Speaker race in 1838, lost the electoral race in 1840, lost in a race for congress in 1843 and again in 1848, and lost in senate races in 1855 and 1858. After all his failures, Abraham Lincoln was finally elected president in 1860. What an inspiration!

There are more. Alexander Graham Bell failed to sell his telephone idea to Western Union. Chester Carlton tried to sell the idea of his xerograph machine, but every major corporation rejected it as useless, so he created his own company called Xerox. Tom Watson, head of International Business Machines (IBM), saw computers as a limited tool and estimated total sales for them to be around (are you ready for this?) five units. The stories go on and on. Did you know Walt Disney was fired from his job at an editorial house because the managing editor accused him of having no creative ideas? And R. H. Macy failed seven times before the store bearing his name caught on in New York. Western novelist Louis L'Amour had more than 300 rejections before he sold his first manuscript, and English novelist John Creasey had 753 rejections before he published 564 titles. Even Babe Ruth struck out 1,330 times on his way to 714 home runs. Use these stories as your inspiration. Find some of your own. Just look around your office tomorrow. That place is one big failure after another. Write down the good ones and keep them handy for the next time you fail.

4. *By finding your purpose in life.* Most people fail because they wander through life without goals. They achieve nothing because they don't know what they are on earth to achieve. They stab at life, hoping to pull out one or two successes they can call their own. They are never sure who they are, or why they are where they are, and so they are destined to fail. One

man tried job after job, but nothing satisfied him. He failed at each one. He tried teaching school. He tried preaching, but the ministerial association dismissed him because of his over-zealousness. Tired of living off his brother's income for so many years, he tried selling pictures he had painted later in life. He sold only one painting for five francs. He tried all varieties of painting to find himself, as most struggling artists do, but this lack of purpose and meaning meant complete and total breakdown for this failure of a man. Committed to a mental institution, Vincent van Gogh finally ended his life. Years later, in 1988, the work of this failed artist set a world record at an auction where his painting *Irises* sold for an unprecedented $53.9 million. Imagine how different the world might have been for van Gogh if he knew early in life that his purpose was to be an artist.

5. *By considering your failures as experiments or hypotheses.* Scientists and inventors get all the breaks when it comes to failure. When scientists fail to find a cure for something, they call it an experiment that didn't work. They may call it a hypothesis. In either case, they go on their merry way, failure after failure, without the least bit of frustration or depression the rest of us feel. Rather than looking at your failures as devastating blows, why not look at them as experiments in life. It will change your attitude about them completely.

6. *By learning from failure.* You will learn more from failure than you ever will from success. A baby walks by handling failure after failure. A child rides a bike one fall at a time. So it is in business. Contrary to popular belief, I consider failure a necessity in business. If you're not failing at least five times a day, you're probably not doing enough. The more you do, the more you fail. The more you fail, the more you learn. The more you learn, the better you get. The operative word here is *learn*. If you repeat the same mistake two or three times, you are not learning from it. You must learn from your own mistakes and from the mistakes of others before you.

7. *By heeding a stronger voice.* I recall as a little child watching the movie *Bambi*. Remember the scene? A raging forest fire has all the animals running for their lives. Bambi and his father jump from stream to rock, dodging the flames. A flaming branch slams Bambi to the ground as the fire rages closer, and Bambi's father orders him, "Get up! Get up, Bambi. You must get up!" There, in my theater seat I remember saying out loud with tears in my eyes, "Please, Bambi. Get up. Get up."

We all need a strong voice to push us along when we fail. Most of the time we have to talk to ourselves, pick ourselves up, dust ourselves off, and try it again. Sometimes, though, the load is simply too much. Friends and family can't seem to help. We need someone greater than all the world's failures to see us through. We need God. When Peter abandoned Jesus there in the courtyard, he had exhausted all his resources. He reached the point where life didn't matter any longer, and at this tragic time of failure he cried out to God, and God answered his cry. God changed Peter's life forever. For all the ways man can think of to rise out of the mire he has created for himself, none are as sure as calling on God. The unfortunate thing is that we tend to save this one for last instead of doing it first.

Peter went from being a broken, humbled failure to become one of the founders of the Christian faith. His failure record was among the highest in his group, yet Jesus had placed enough confidence in him to set him up as a major player in the world of religion. Jesus took failures from all walks of life and turned them into successes. He's still doing that today.

PRACTICAL TIPS

1. Set a personal policy to reveal your mistakes as soon as they happen.

2. Take all criticism with a grain of salt.

3. Right now write down your known strengths and weaknesses.

4. Go to the library and check out only biographies and autobiographies.

5. Appeal to God before you are at your lowest for strength.

CHAPTER 10

FAMILY: FRIENDS, RELATIVES, AND THE WORKPLACE

Not much more can happen to you after you lose your reputation and your wife.
— JOHN MITCHELL, FORMER MEMBER OF THE NIXON ADMINISTRATION

Women are told they can have it all—career, marriage, children. Take a look at your child. He will be the one who pays the price for your wanting to have it all.
— BEVERLY SILLS, OPERA SINGER

"Wake up, men," Jesus said as He shook Peter, "we have a wedding to go to."

Peter groaned and tapped his brother Andrew who was lying next to him. The sons of Zebedee, James and John, awoke together. Each of the other men—Philip, Bartholomew, Thomas, Matthew, James, Thaddaeus, Simon, and Judas—all awoke, rolled up their woven mats, and laid them neatly in a corner.

"We're going to a wedding feast at this hour of the morning?" asked Andrew.

"Yes," Jesus answered. "You know those people in Cana will celebrate a wedding for a week if you let them. We can stay but one day, so let it be the first."

"Who are these people?" James asked of Jesus.

"Friends of the family."

James said, "But we're strangers."

Jesus answered, "To each other perhaps. And in time you will become friends and brothers. You will become My family.

But for now, I want you to meet and be a part of My other family. No man is a stranger in My family, James. Now, let us go."

Later that day as Jesus sat around the family courtyard, listening to the joyous wedding music playing, hearing the laughter of adults and the running sandals of children, His eyes turned toward His new followers. A few days ago, except for the two pairs of brothers, these men were strangers. Now they were engrossed in conversations with wild-eyed uncles and merry cousins. They had become His family. And now as the wine was running low, Jesus knew that in a few moments His family would become His work.

—JOHN 2:1–11; JOHN 19:25–27; MATTHEW 10:1–5

Jesus had many friends at the start of His ministry, as is evidenced by His invitation to a wedding feast at Cana. It is believed that He also had numerous brothers and sisters and that He was not an only child. With that in mind, why did He deliberately choose not to have personal friends or relatives involved in His work? What can we learn from His example today? Is this a pattern for us to follow? How did His family accept this shunning? Did He in effect forsake His family duties?

FRIENDS AND FAMILY
INSIDE THE WORKPLACE

It is easy to overlook the shadows in a da Vinci painting. Having been a student of art for many years, I am learning to appreciate what made so many artists great. In da Vinci's case, his greatness does not lie in the bright colors he revealed, but in his mastery of light sources and shadows. Up until his day, Italian artwork for the most part seemed flat and two dimensional. But when he introduced shadows, the still world of the canvas came alive. Critics marveled for years, pondering his genius; yet little did they realize that the genius of the man was not in what they saw but in what they overlooked.

So it is with many of the things in Jesus' life. He never said, "Thou shalt not hire thy mother or thy brother or thy best friend," but those are the very ones who probably noticed that He didn't. Ever wonder why?

Perhaps Jesus knew what so few managers today seem to know. Maybe He understood that to be personally involved with subordinates means losing your objectivity. In some cases this is difficult for a manager to understand. She wants her brother-in-law to join the sales force because he is her brother-in-law, not because he is a great salesman. Another hires his sister because she's a good kid and needs a break; but when the time comes to lay off a relative or friend, or worse, to fire them for poor work habits, the manager who lacks wisdom in this area makes an already difficult job twice as hard. That is not to say that Jesus did not have friends or relatives involved in His ministry. I believe He did, but much later. The key to understanding Jesus' policy regarding nepotism and cronyism is that He did not hire friends and family.

For all His opposition, Jesus also had a number of friends as well. Many people invited Him to dine, and one doesn't send out an invitation to someone they hate. So Jesus had no problem making and being friends with those He considered His peers, but staff friendships was a different matter altogether.

Why avoid nepotism and cronyism in the workplace? What's the big deal about hiring a friend or family member? I suppose the answer has more to do with common sense than with laws laid down in stone.

First of all, nepotism (favoring family) and cronyism (favoring friends) breeds discontent among other employees. The guy who has been trying to win your favor is constantly struggling against the thought that so-and-so is also trying to get your attention, and he is a friend of your brother. It may be that your brother thinks poorly of the guy. That is not important. What matters is what the guy thinks your brother thinks. It breeds political games, back patting, and back stabbing among staff members to maneuver each other to gain favor in your eyes.

Another thing nepotism/cronyism does is minimize your authority and strength in time of need. Let's take the firing example. I have seen this scene played over and over by other managers, until one wonders if maybe the Florida sun didn't give them brain damage. Boss hires friend. Boss hires relative of friend. Boss hires another friend. Friend #1 begins to sour on the job that boss promised him. Friend #1 shares his concern with relative, who believes that blood is thicker than water. Boss gets ticked off at all the bickering and snickering and tries to head it off. Friends #1 and #2 and relative go out for lunch.

"Who does he think he is?" one murmurs. "I knew him when he was a runny-nosed punk. He's just trying to pull rank on me, that's all."

"He forgot that we know about the letters. Maybe one of us ought to remind him of what we know and what his wife doesn't."

"Maybe he'll apologize, but I'm still not going to let him forget it. He embarrassed me in front of everyone."

"We'd better get back. We don't want the almighty one to pitch a fit again."

Meanwhile, back in his office, Boss calls his wife and pours his heart out over the phone. "I don't understand it. I give these guys a break, try to help them out in their careers, and what do they do? Stab me in the back the minute I turn. I can't even ask them to work overtime without their reminding me of my past. I'm sick of it. I ought to fire the whole lot of them. Yeah, you're right. His mother would call mom and . . ."

As a manager you must be a leader. Nepotism and cronyism are guaranteed to strip you of any authority you have. Guaranteed.

This practice also weakens your objectivity. Few humans could stare a friend in the face and fire them. Few men and women can look at the poor work of a relative or friend and call it what it is. Fewer still can follow through and do something about it. Our natural inclination is to value the friendship above the work. This is paramount in a marriage, but it has no place in a business setting. When you read some of the scathing comments Jesus made to His staff at times, it is clear that He had solid objectivity and keenness of mind when He said them. His comments were not muddied by relationships.

One sure way to keep friends and family from succeeding on their own is to hire them to work for you. I always feel bad when I see the son or daughter of a famous actor get a role in a movie. I wonder if they also wonder if they could have made it big without the help of the family name. By hiring friends and family, you deny them the opportunity every human deserves to seek and find themselves. It diminishes their ability to know they can prosper without your help. It cripples them and handicaps them; it doesn't help them.

If you lean toward favoritism, really good people won't want to work for you. When some sharp executive-to-be sends in her resume, she doesn't know about cousin Kandy sitting next to your office. When she finds out you have family under your wing, exec-to-be will look elsewhere. She knows what you fail to know: she has no equal chance available to her to succeed so long as you have a favorite card to play. She wants to compete on a level playing field.

Word of nepotism/cronyism spreads quickly. You must decide whether your friend or relative is worth the price of losing some of the brightest people in the field. Please understand that I am not inferring that all your relatives are dolts; indeed, they may be among the brightest in their field. If so, what do they need you for?

Executive-to-be also knows what perhaps you do not: family and friends will monopolize your time. Somehow these people manage to override every major corporate policy concerning chain of command and private time and closed doors. If brother Bob can just walk into your home, why not into your office? You will be harangued with calls, notes, and questions that other staff members would never dare put forth.

Hiring friends and family members creates cliques and divisions. It destroys the concept of teamwork. Who on earth wants to be a team with cousin Harold sitting around the table ready to report everything that goes on? How can you expect people to exchange ideas freely if someone in the group is favored and likely to get the credit for them?

I cannot voice strongly enough the idea that nearly everything you read in this book can be undermined if you disregard this advice. It was solidly practiced by Jesus. He had every opportunity to make His brothers members of the chosen twelve, but He deliberately chose not to. He had a cousin named John the Baptist who would've made an interesting addition to His staff. Jesus hired strangers. Through time, these strangers among themselves became friends. That is how it should be. Jesus created an aura of family around His staff. True, Jesus hired several pairs of brothers, but to Jesus these men were strangers at the start.

What about Jesus' family then? Did He forsake them? Apparently not. We are introduced to Jesus, in terms of His first miracle, at a wedding feast where urns were churning out wine and where laughter and family abounded. This is also an example for us. Jesus valued His true family until His dying day, literally. As He hung dying on a Roman cross, He told one of His men to accept and take care of His mother as He had. Though He traveled from home, though His life turned rough, though everything around Him lay in heaps, Jesus never gave up on His love and commitment to His family.

FRIENDS AND FAMILY
OUTSIDE THE WORKPLACE

Day after day I drive forty minutes on the interstate watching men and women in ridiculously priced cars racing by me while completing some deal on the car phone. I wonder how many of them are racing home to lushly landscaped yards or plushly decorated condos, only to spend the evening with their portfolios. Do these people know what it is to come home to the squealing delight of a child rather than the blaring declaration of a television commercial? Do they understand the value of maintaining a loving, committed marriage in a society of split-ups? And if they are single, do they seek out and maintain friendships as passionately as they pursue their career goals?

I cannot speak to them. I can speak to you. As I write this page, I am staring out the window across the street to my neighbor whose house now has one car and one parent instead of two. Last Thanksgiving I watched as the dad drove up in his pickup and he and his sons dangled their feet from the back of the truck bed before the boys went in to celebrate the holiday with their mom. Thirty minutes is all he got. And I wondered, what on earth did he do, what on earth was valuable enough to him to forsake his family? His career? Who knows.

In the world of business, family and friends can easily become a commodity or a convenient piece of luggage you carry around with you. Like luggage, you carry them around from place to place, using them when it's convenient until one day someone asks you what you're carrying all that baggage for, and you drop it to head off to a carefree life. You never looked inside, for if you had, you might have seen that the baggage you carried contained precious jewels beyond price.

There are hundreds of ways to help maintain healthy families and friendships. Let me list a few of my personal favorites.

Send flowers or dinner coupons to someone else's spouse. Every time I suggest that to a manager, they think I'm a marriage wrecker. This is intended to keep marriages together. If you, as a manager, find that one of your staff is spending a lot of time away from home working on projects or traveling, why not send a basket of flowers, fruit, or perhaps a gift certificate to the employee's spouse with a note saying, "I know how hard it is on everyone when ———— has to put in some extra time. I appreciate your sacrifice. Thanks for your understanding."

Work like crazy during the day to avoid taking work home at night. According to an April 23, 1990, article in *U.S. News and World Report* titled "Piece Meal Dinners," the average American couple spends only four minutes a day in meaningful conversation. If you think this dilemma affects married couples only, how do you explain some titles in your local bookstore like *The Friendless American Male* and *Women Who Do Too Much?* Singles need a social life too. If you must bring work home, don't bring it home at 8:00 P.M. Come home earlier and spend time with friends and family and do the work later in the evening if you must.

Several weeks ago I had done some introspection (again) on this area in my life. I announced to my staff that no matter what, my company would always take second place to my family and that I intended to keep it that way. I asked them to hold me accountable to my wedding vows. I told them that I would never apologize for leaving work at a decent hour to go spend time with my wife and two children. I paused and looked at faces with mouths open. They looked like dazed cows who'd just been hit upside the head with a board. It occurred to me that perhaps they had not heard management say this enough.

Date your spouse once a month, or if you're single, treat a friend to dinner. Put it on your calendar as a regular item to be done each month, or you won't do it. My wife and I trade off months to make it easier. One month I find a sitter and organize an activity, and the next month is hers. A number of family counselors will tell you to do it weekly or biweekly. Ideally, I agree with them. I wish I could. But you and I both know that the corporate world is more demanding than that, so I think once a month is a more realistic goal. To do less than that is inexcusable.

Take a loved one with you on business trips. Add to that statement, *when possible.* I realize no company will tolerate paying for two all the time, but if you travel very often they will occasionally slide in a free ticket for you. Consider doing this for any of your staff on the road too much. Neither you nor your staff will be very productive if there is turmoil in the home. The price of a plane ticket now and then is worth the keeping of a productive employee.

Call your spouse daily when on business trips. Make it a personal and company policy that every staff member must call home every night (on the company's tab) while away from home. No excuses. Check the hotel bill to see that they do. Set the example yourself. Obviously, you may wish to set a minimum payment plan for the first ten minutes and let the employee pay the rest. This little effort will be appreciated by staff members and spouses. If you're single, don't let the company cheat you out of the right to stay in touch with someone at home. Insist on one personal call a day too.

Build social relationships around friends. If you're married, focus on your spouse's friends, not yours. Experience has shown that corporate workers often make friends at work but have few friends outside the office. What happens to the spouse? He or she gets dragged into conversations and social gatherings with people they only know by name. They become only a part of your life. You must become part of theirs.

Explain to your children and friends what you do and why. For thirty-two years my father worked in a steel mill in Youngstown, Ohio. To this day if you ask any of his five children or his wife what he did for a living, they'll tell you, "He worked in the mill." Maybe one will go a sentence further and say something about working on the paint line. For thirty-two years my father spent 63,520 hours away from his home, and for all that time we still don't know exactly what he did. And I'm not alone in that cry.

Author David Thomas confesses in his book *Not Guilty: In Defense of the Modern Man*, "Every man grows up watching what work has done to his father. In my own case, I was profoundly affected by the knowledge that my father, whom I idolized, went off every day to work at a job which, to my young eyes, he did not appear to enjoy, purely in order to meet the needs of his family. I always swore that I would never be in the same position myself. Yet, as I lived through my early thirties, I found myself doing exactly what Dad had done."[1]

It is critical that your friends and family know and understand what you do, why you do it, and how it brings in money. The more they understand, the less likely they are to resent your work.

Do your part to help around the house. This shoe fits both pairs of feet. Men, you need to do something for your wife that she could probably do herself, but it would be nice if you did it once in a while. Bring in the laundry and fold it without being told. Empty the dishwasher (my wife's favorite). Offer to cook dinner. Take the kids out so she can have some quiet time alone. And ladies, lest you get left out, why not help your husband in areas outside the norm? Mow the lawn; tell him you checked the oil in the car and it was all right. Change the furnace filter. Do something that'll tickle his or her socks off. If you are single, give of yourself by helping out a single mother with children. Offer to clean her floors, windows, or bathrooms. If you like kids, offer to baby-sit so she can do the laundry or just read a book uninterrupted.

Maintain consistency and undercommitment. Nothing can kill marital (or single) bliss faster than inconsistency and overcommitment. They both place undue stress on the bonds of friendship and marriage. The spouse who must deal with a moody partner walks on eggshells, never knowing whether this is a good time or not to talk. Broken promises to your friends or children lead them to believe that your word is worthless, and if your word is, what about the person speaking them? If one or both of the partners in a marriage is prone to overcommitting themselves, the marriage is destined for rough waters. Learn to say no to others and yes to each other. Try becoming a homebody for a change. You might like it.

Give your friends and family three irreplaceable gifts: commitment, time, and love. Before you know it, the baby won't need rocking; he'll be a toddler. Then the toddler won't ask why every minute; he'll be out playing ball. Then the little boy won't need help with his bike; he'll be dating a girl. Then he won't need money for college; he'll be a married man earning his own way. Time is a precious gift. It comes. It goes. It can never be replaced.

The same goes for love and commitment. When I married my wife I told her that no matter what horror she may go through, no matter whether my feelings of love diminish, no matter what walls may try to separate us, I would be committed to her forever. You may say, "Oh, how Victorian." I prefer to think of it as maturity. Love will never see you through every detail of marriage; only commitment can do that. The company that manufactured my lawnmower gave me a longer warranty than some husbands give their wives at the altar. Stay committed and work at the love part.

These wonderful words I think best sum up what love in a relationship is.

Money, of course, can build a charming house, but only love can furnish it with a feeling of home.

Duty can pack an adequate sack lunch, but love may decide to tuck a little love note inside.

Money can provide a television set, but love controls it and cares enough to say no and take the guff that comes with it.

Obligation sends the children to bed on time, but love tucks the covers in around their necks and passes out kisses and hugs (even to teenagers!).

Obligation can cook a meal, but love embellishes the table with a potted ivy trailing around slender candles.

Duty writes many letters, but love tucks a joke or a picture or a fresh stick of gum inside.

Compulsion keeps a sparkling house, but love and prayer stand a better chance of producing a happy family.

Duty gets offended quickly if it isn't appreciated, but love learns to laugh a lot and to work for the sheer joy of doing it.

Obligation can pour a glass of milk, but quite often love will add a little chocolate.[2]

I am not of the opinion that corporate success necessarily means alienation from family or friends. I believe Jesus' principles stand true for those of us in business today as much as they did in His day.

PRACTICAL TIPS

1. Set a policy that any employee exceeding thirty thousand flying miles takes the spouse next trip.

2. Set another personal policy to not hire family and friends.

3. Send gifts to the spouses of employees who are putting in extra time away from home.

4. Work out a deal to take your spouse with you on business trips.

5. Set a policy that all employees away from home must call home nightly.

CHAPTER 11

FINANCE: HANDLING MONEY

Farming looks mighty easy when your plow is a pencil and you're a thousand miles from a cornfield.

—DWIGHT D. EISENHOWER, 34TH PRESIDENT

In God we trust; everyone else pays cash.

—AMERICAN SAYING

Jesus sat with His disciples near Him. Listening in the crowd were a group called the Pharisees, who loved money. Knowing the influence money could have on a soul, Jesus told this story.

There once was a manager, shrewd and dishonorable, who continually stole from his employer's pockets. He did this for quite some time, until the owner finally caught up with him and called him into his office. "What is this I hear about you? After all I've done for you? How do you answer to these charges? I'm sorry; you can no longer be a manager in this business. And to think I trusted you."

So the manager, too weak to dig and too proud to beg, set about a plan to make his future worthwhile. He looked through the journals at the accounts receivables. He made a list of all those who owed his employer money and called them in one by one.

"What do you owe us?" he said to the first.

"I owe you eight hundred."

And before the debtor could offer an excuse, the shrewd manager said, "Take the eight hundred you owe us and make it four hundred." To the next he said, "So you owe us a thousand? Then make it eight hundred." And on it went, until his boss discovered his tactic. He could not help but be impressed at the manager's ingenuity, and so he commended him. He knew that when the manager finally left, he could walk into any one of those debtor's offices and be handed a job.

Jesus concluded his message by saying that those who are trusted with little will later be trusted with much, and those who are dishonest with a little will also be dishonest if given more.

—LUKE 16:1–14

People are amazed (or appalled) to find that the Bible speaks of finances and money. The issue, to them, seems to be a rather unspiritual one. The Bible speaks about prayer over five hundred times. The same number applies for the subject of faith. But when it comes to talking about money, the Bible mentions it more than two thousand times. Sixteen of the thirty-eight parables Jesus told directly or indirectly dealt with the subject of money. In the first four books of the New Testament alone, money is mentioned 288 times, or once every ten verses. Jesus knew that where mankind is, there money is; man and his money are inseparably linked.

Jesus also knew that everyone, whether at home, at work, or in government, has to live within his or her means. He also knew the age-old secret that homes and businesses must budget their incomes so they can pay taxes to a government that doesn't budget its income. Of all the principles Jesus taught, this one stands out as the most prominent, but also as the most controversial.

After looking at it more carefully, I believe the lesson Jesus wanted those of us in business to learn is this: pay your bills, be fiscally responsible, and be creative in your approach to getting and giving money. But most of all, be trustworthy with it, even when times get tough.

YA GOTTA CUT BACK ON CUTTING BACK

Most companies face layoffs at one time or another. If your company finds itself in this position, rather than cut costs across the board, cut one area heavily, if not altogether. Look for what you shouldn't do rather than doing everything cheaply. I can honestly say I have never worked for a prosperous company. All of them were in a constant cutting-back mode, and it gets old after a while. It destroys morale to ask everyone in the organization to skim down. Look creatively for alternatives.

It has been my experience that every organization and home can do with less. We must develop an attitude of not "Can we operate on less?" but "Are we willing to?" Everyone can, and does when they have to. The difficulty is getting minds to think about saving costs or increasing profits on a day-to-day basis as a matter of course.

The story is told of a muscular circus performer who challenged his audience to defy his great strength. He would take an orange and squeeze it until every last drop could be extracted from it. Then he would challenge anyone from the audience to come and extract more juice from what was left. If they could, he would pay a thousand dollars. From city to city he traveled, and not a single man could extract another drop.

One day he went to a little town called Riverside and performed his feat and offered his challenge. He bellowed, "Is there a man alive who can squeeze more juice from the orange? Him will I pay a thousand dollars who can surpass my great strength." Just then a bony, frail, five-foot, gray-haired man shuffled from his seat and approached the muscle man. He grabbed the smashed orange rind between his palms and squeezed and squeezed until six more drops of juice fell from the orange. The muscle man stood aghast with his eyes wide. He asked the old man how he could possibly perform this great feat. "Oh, it's not that hard, really," said the old man. "I'm the treasurer down at the Riverside Baptist Church and we do this all the time."

One of the most difficult tasks of saving company money or of increasing company profits lies in the area of ethics. Anyone can do both with a measure of Rasputin in his veins, but it becomes nearly impossible when morals stand in your way. Churches and nonprofit organizations have had a set of guidelines to follow for years, and until only recently have the ethical walls fallen down around a select few. But the business world is now facing the fact that business without ethics leads to chaos and disaster. John Shad, former SEC chairman, recently gave Harvard Business School $20 million to establish a program on business ethics because the problem is becoming so pervasive.

Find ways to cut costs and increase profits while maintaining a level of ethics that allows you to hold your head high knowing you treated people right in the process. Let's look at a number of creative alternatives. Some of these ideas may not apply to your situation; some will. Take what you can use, change them, and use them however possible. Better than that, think up some of your own.

WAYS TO CUT COSTS

Be an example by being one of the crowd. I know of one corporate boss who asked his entire staff to consider taking a cut in pay, with the threat that some might not even get a paycheck if things didn't look up, and then he had the gall to get into his high-end luxury car and head off to his palatial estate. Don't expect people to pitch in to help the organization if you aren't willing to visibly lead the pack. People are more apt to follow than to be steered. A man or woman making $100,000 and a man or woman making $30,000 suffer very different consequences when asked to forsake 10 percent of their weekly income. If you ask your people to take such drastic measures during hard times, be sure that the cut is proportionately fair to all. You need to start the ball rolling.

Spend money on modern equipment. "Wait a minute," you say. "Spend money to cut costs? Isn't that like going to a sale and buying up the place with the attitude that you're saving by doing so?" Well, sort of. The idea is to modernize your facility to the point that time—which equals money—is used wisely. When people sit around flying paper airplanes because the computer equipment has gone down again, multiply the number of staff people times their people costs times the amount of time spent down, and my guess is you'll more than pay for the cost of newer equipment. Modernization means speed and convenience. People standing around broken, clunky copiers, fax machines, and phone systems are eating up your personnel costs, and most of these costs are difficult to capture on a ledger.

Make individuals responsible, not groups. Continue to emphasize the concept of teams and teamwork, but during the interview process and again during a financial downturn, I recommend clearly explaining to employees just how much they are costing the company to keep them on the payroll. Go beyond just salary. Show them the dollars you spend for benefits, insurance, social security, disability, unemployment, and the rest. Knowledge equals responsibility equals accountability. People are more likely to contribute to the cost-cutting endeavor if they know their contribution matters.

Let employees make suggestions. Generally, the frontliners know where the money is being wasted. After all, they talk about it every day at lunch. Even under the best of management conditions, the ones doing the work are more sensitive to expenses than are managers. They'll be more than happy to show you where the ridiculous wastes of money are, but managers have to be tough enough to endure the suggestions. A thorough housecleaning may be in order, but welcome it. Look at it as an opportunity to improve rather than taking it as a personal criticism. Your employees only want to help, and they may know how. Up to this point, management has been too wrapped up in itself or too dumb to listen.

Regularly repeat the need to keep costs down. This can be done positively, and must be. Harping about costs, costs, costs will drive your people to seek employment elsewhere. "If things are this bad," they muse, "I'd better get out before the whole ship goes under." Don't make the problem sound worse than it really is, but be honest. Publicly praise efforts staffers make to reduce company costs. Let everyone know when a targeted cost is reached, who did it, and how. The same goes for innovations that cut costs.

Share the achieved savings with the innovator. When one of your staff members comes up with a great cost-saving idea, calculate the amount of money saved from it and give the innovator a piece of the pie after the savings actually come in. You don't want to pay for an idea that flops, even if it is good, but you should pay for the winners. It will motivate them and those around to seek out money wasters.

Bosses seem to be of the opinion that managers are getting paid to cut costs, while on-clock employees are not. In some industries, it is not unusual to give on-clockers a bonus or commission, while denying a salaried member the same privilege. I'll grant you that salaried personnel are probably paid higher to begin with, but that does not necessarily invalidate a good idea and make it worthless. If a cost-cutting (or income-increasing) idea is worth implementing, someone ought to receive credit. If you plan to reward on-clock staff, be sure to reward salaried people too. You will demotivate your brightest people by throwing their ideas on the altar of sacrifice. Perhaps an option to consider is to pay managers and salaried people 5 percent of savings realized instead of the 10 percent paid to on-clock people.

Give employees a shot at large corporate orders. When your company orders bulk items such as technical equipment, airline tickets, office furniture, or supplies, why not let staff members get in on the buy? When Jesus fed the five thousand, His own staff fed off the same fish and bread. If your company gets a break on computer equipment, why not pass those savings on to them in return for their passing savings ideas on to you? Just remember to maintain a standard of ethics, and don't claim all the purchases toward capital expenditures if indeed they were not.

WAYS TO INCREASE PROFITS

It is much more painful to cut costs than to increase profits, and it is much less fun. Once a business starts putting more emphasis on cutting costs than on increasing income, red flags should send a warning that the place is in serious trouble.

Lest you think that making money or increasing profits is somehow anti-Jesus, you should recall the parable of the talents as told by Jesus. Briefly, Jesus told of a master who gave to one servant five thousand dollars, to another two thousand, and to the last one thousand dollars, to keep in trust until he returned. When he returned, he discovered that the servant with five thousand had doubled the master's money, and the one with two thousand dollars likewise doubled his. The one with the least amount unwisely buried his thousand in the ground until his master returned. The master looked at the dirty money and chided the servant for his ignorance. At the very least, he scolded, he could have put the money in the bank and collected some interest. With that in mind, below are a number of ideas to help increase profits.

Hold a fire sale. If your inventory is great enough, you can't afford to spin your wheels selling products whose life has ended. You must consider which items are your greatest moneymakers, or have the potential for becoming so, and concentrate on those. To do that, you will have to eliminate all the little items that invariably seem to take up so much of your time and effort. Many companies spend countless hours trying to promote their dogs while at the same time sacrificing their cash cows. Get the slow sellers out of your hair once and for all, and pack all your punches into the profitable items.

Try offering postponed bonuses. Rather than offer bonuses every year, then lose your best performers to some other company after three years, consider offering a bonus plan whereby a bonus is calculated and kept in escrow at a high-yield interest program for five years. Each of five years you will add another year's achieved bonus. At the end of five years, you will have kept a major player on your staff, and he or she will have received a larger bonus check than if you had divvied it out each year. Here's the catch. You will have to offer a larger than normal bonus plan to make it enticing, and it will have to be an all-or-nothing agreement. If they bail out in year four, then you keep the money. But if you can find a high enough yielding interest account, some enterprising salespeople might just see the value in it.

Acknowledge nonsales-staff sales. Many companies take it for granted that everyone on staff generates sales. When a secretary encounters a friend who needs water coolers, she tells her friend that she works for a company that supplies them. The same goes for sneaker companies, record companies, or wallpapering services. But it has always irked me that companies fail to reward nonsales salespeople. If some warehouse man or manager has the bravery to open his or her mouth and initiate a great sale, why should a telemarketer or salesman get all the commission on it just because he closed the deal? Work toward ways of paying off your "other" sales staff, and they will in turn generate more sales for you in the long run. Look beyond your salespeople for sales.

Give salespeople an extra percentage commission for selling to a new customer. Most industries, with the exception of Spam, make their living selling new, improved, or innovative products. Most industries also put a large portion of their funding into new products. Most salespeople, however, float on commission sales from old consistent products. Check their sales record and see. You need to motivate people to push the expensive product into which you have laid your fortune recently. Consider giving a 1 percent increase on commission for sales on new products for a limited amount of time.

Call customers who haven't ordered in more than twelve months. Forgotten customers are just pining away, sitting by the phone waiting for your salespeople to call. Well, probably not, but you ought to take the notion that they are waiting, and set a plan in motion to touch base with all customers in this group. It's a good time to ask how sales went on their last order and to encourage them to order again.

Give salespeople an extra commission for selling a new product to old customers. I hesitate to offer another increase in commission for such sales, but you might cluster them together and give a one-time bonus for new-product sales made to, say, fifty, past customers.

Set award levels for sales quotas. One supply company I deal with offers bonus prizes for purchases: the more I buy, the bigger the prize. Remember Green Stamps? The more groceries you bought, the more Green Stamps you got. The more Green Stamps you got, the bigger the item you traded in your stamps for that year. Why not use the same idea in place of commissions? Set achievement levels for a period of time or for a hot sale. Everyone wins even if they do the minimum expected selling, but the big performers can reach for the stars or combine several smaller prizes.

Give away a dying product with a new release and increase cost of new one. Despite the old adage that nothing comes for free, people still flock to a FREE sign like a moth to a flame. Look at your product line. Is there a new product that complements another older, poorer selling product? If so, tag the two together, increase the cost of the new product enough to make up for the sales on the poor product. Mark each package with a sticker saying something like "Free $7.00 value with this purchase!" and watch sales on new products run. To further capture sales, consider putting a "For a limited time" notice on it also.

Take advantage of the Duty Drawback law. Millions of dollars are unrecouped each year because industries are unaware of the Duty Drawback law. Here's how it works. If the product you make requires that you import some goods to create it, then you can possibly get a refund of up to 99 percent for any duty you paid to import that product, and you can recapture those fees even if someone else did the importing. One company in Ohio reportedly recouped $50,000 in one year simply by following through on this 1798 law. Ask your local customs department about it.

Turn your salespeople into mini-collections departments. I do not believe that a sale is a sale is a sale. In business, a sale is only as good as the cash received to close the deal. If accounts receivables are running slow, hold sales-commissions payout for 120 days. Reduce commissions 5 percent for every thirty days a sale is past due. If a customer hasn't paid in 120 days, the salesperson gets no commission. Even if you pay your sales reps a ridiculous 20 percent commission, their take would equal zero if their customers, whom they know by name, fail to pay up.

You can initiate any of dozens of other plans to cut costs and increase profitability. Whatever program you begin, keep in mind that creatively earning a profit and ethically cutting costs are in keeping with the teachings and practices of Jesus. Planning for your financial future is also.

PRACTICAL TIPS

1. Take seriously every staff recommendation for cutting costs, and reward those implemented.
2. Sell ten things well instead of thirty things poorly.
3. Hold an all-day cost-cutting brainstorm session with all staff.
4. Review your commission structures and policies immediately.
5. Investigate the Duty Drawback law if it applies to your business.

CHAPTER 12

GOALS: MEETING YOUR DEADLINES

It is not enough to be busy. The question is what are we busy about?

—HENRY DAVID THOREAU, POET AND ESSAYEST

If you start to take Vienna—then take Vienna.

—NAPOLEON, FRENCH COMMANDER

Jesus taught many things during His brief stay here on earth. As with any great teacher and leader, when one message comes repeatedly, it bears listening to.

On several occasions Jesus had gathered His followers around Him to repeat one message, one goal. He said it was for this reason He came. Again and again Jesus seemed to keep pointing Himself to His tortured end, His crucifixion, and His resurrection. Perhaps His followers could not comprehend that this could be the goal of any sane man. Who in his right mind would set as a goal these words: "The Son of Man is going to be betrayed into the hands of men. They will kill him, and after three days he will rise"? They could not comprehend what He meant, and lest they misinterpret the message, they were afraid to ask Him.

Jesus received tempting offers that could have turned Him from His goal. Satan offered Him bread after a forty-day fast. He offered Jesus all the kingdoms of the world. He offered Him safe passage from the top of the temple pillar to the hand-cut stones below should He decide to jump. Men tried to crown Jesus a king. But through it all, He kept His eyes on the goal, and because He did, the world has never been the same.

—MARK 8:31; 9:31; 10:33–34

Ask the average person on the street if Jesus set goals for Himself. Go into a church or synagogue and ask the same question. The response will be nearly the same. Most people believe Jesus had goals, but few can identify them. There seems to be a hesitancy to accept that a man of such spirituality could be so callous as to set calculated goals for His accomplishments. Yet the pages of the Bible reveal goals set and goals achieved. There is nothing mystical about setting goals, nor is it only for corporate businesspeople seeking wealth and fame. Goals are merely dreams that are acted upon.

HERE, HAVE A GOAL

Dave Mahoney, one-time president of Good Humor Ice Cream Company, wanted the position so badly and set goals so precisely that he rose from mail-room clerk to president by age thirty-three. John F. Kennedy became the youngest U.S. president because he decided to be. They both realized that goals need not be lofty or complicated. They both wanted to be presidents of something. They both had a dream and acted toward reaching it, and they both managed to keep the goal simple enough to achieve.

One of my favorite examples of this is in the radio message U.S. Navy pilot David Miller sent to his commander on February 26th, 1942. He had been sent out on a search mission to find German submarines and plot their course. It seems Miller had a different set of goals, which came to light clearly and simply in his response to the commander's inquiry as to the location of the German sub. Miller simply radioed back: "Sighted sub. Sank same."

Not every goal is that simple. There are different types of goals for different types of people. Some of Jesus' goals were complex (such as revealing the hypocrisy of the Pharisees without losing favor with the people), and some were relatively simple (such as raising His friend Lazarus from the dead). What is simple for one may be incredibly complicated for another. Every goal is a step-by-step process. Buildings are made brick by brick. Football games are won play by play. Smokers and drinkers give up the habit hour by hour. Companies are built customer by customer.

Human beings require goals for self-fulfillment. Remember the old saying "Nothing ventured, nothing gained?" When Lewis Carroll's Alice asked the Cheshire-Cat, "Would you tell me, please, which way I ought to go from here?" The Cat replied, "That depends a good deal on where you want to get to." When Alice said, "I don't much care where—" the Cat interrupted with, "Then it doesn't matter which way you go." We are a goal-oriented species. We must have a purpose. Even if we determine not to set goals, and we do so quite emphatically, then that becomes our goal. Since we cannot survive without them, we should learn all we can to get along with them and to utilize them as best we can.

Goal types vary. The most obvious goal is the time-related one. Most companies set two-, five-, and ten-year goals. Often those yearly goals are divided into even smaller three-, six-, and twelve-month goals. My wife and I set goals from Monday through Sunday that need doing. In addition to time-factor goals, there are people-related goals. Perhaps you want to be the next company president. Perhaps you want to spend six more hours a week playing with the kids. You may want to set departmental goals for your company. Those are different because of the number of people involved. Yet they are easier to implement than organizational goals that include everyone and all stages of the operation.

Whatever goals you may set, review them with superiors, peers, and subordinates as they relate to them. It not only will help clarify the weak points, but it also will help hold you accountable. Others not involved directly in achieving a particular goal with you will be more apt to point out the impossibility of traveling from Los Angeles to Taiwan in three hours, or of writing a book in one week. They'll also be the ones to keep you at bay and to remind you when you stray from your goal or fall behind in achieving it.

SUCCESS COMES TO THOSE WHO PLAN FOR IT

Jesus knew that implementing goals successfully requires a number of steps. These steps apply whether we are talking about personal or business goals, but for now I will focus on business goals. As a manager, it is your task to take the goals you have in your mind and make them become the goals your staff embraces. In that case you must remember that a good goal is an "our" goal, and changing a "my" goal to an "our" goal requires planning, implementing, and considering the following twelve details.

1. Announced and unannounced goals. I believe that most everything should be shared with your staff and that secrecy is the bane of an organization, but time and wisdom simply do not allow you to tell your people everything. For example, if you schedule a planning retreat in which you set as a goal that you want your staff to feel encouraged or energized at the conclusion, it is not necessary nor is it wise to state that openly. You will know whether you achieved the goal, and probably ought to be the only one who does.

2. Find small common goals first and add to them. Most organizations are goal oriented. As simplistic and silly as it sounds, find and set small goals that can apply to everyone involved, such as clean desk areas at the end of each day or returning all phone calls the same day. Set goals that the entire group can carry, goals they can see being accomplished by everyone. As they feel a sense of accomplishment, they will accept the next step up in the hierarchy of goal setting.

3. Take time. This is difficult for managers. We want goals achieved now, but people must adjust to the idea of goal setting. When you begin setting goals, build in more time up front to explain the details and stages for accomplishment. Give yourself and your staff more than normal time to accomplish the goal. It will tighten itself later on once the mental adjustment of having and needing goals is made.

4. Set dates: an open-ended, nondated goal is not a goal. In the illustration from Jesus' life, He knew the date of His death: Passover. Prophecies gave clear evidence of how Jesus would die, and lest someone think Jesus manipulated His death around those words, many more prophecies concerning His death were out of His control, such as the exact words individuals would say and actions they would take as He hung dying.

You must avoid open-ended goals. They breed disaster and frustrate the sense of accomplishment you want to build. How on earth will you know you've reached your goal if you don't set a deadline for it? Yet I have seen case after case where an organization or manager will assign a task to a department or staff member with no target date in sight, hoping the parties involved will be self-motivated enough to accomplish it without setting rigid dates. The only place where time does not exist is Peter Pan's Never-Never Land. Unless you want your projects to never-never get done, you must set deadlines.

Some people abhor setting a deadline for fear of not meeting it. Consider this: no one ever missed a deadline all of a sudden. Even the greatest of long-range plans can fail because of poorly administrated short-range plans. The better your short-range plans, the more likely you are to achieve the final plan.

5. Work backward from set dates to present. Jesus knew the end. He knew that He had a great deal of work to do before the end came. He could not sit in the desert and hope to be recognized as the Messiah. He took strategic steps, went to specific places, and followed a set path before achieving His ultimate goal.

I work in publishing. For years publishers followed the concept of getting a manuscript and pushing out toward the future rather than setting a date by which they needed a specific product and working toward the present day to secure such a product. You and I have the propensity to start from today and work toward the future, but goal setting is generally the opposite. More often than not, you will need to set the date of the product or project first, and work backward in steps to the present. This is an effective gauge to tell if you are in trouble. Beware of the first signs of failure: postponed target dates.

6. Set achievable goals first. Many new managers tune into the idea of goal setting and then hit their staff with huge, unachievable goals. The idea of goal setting takes some doing. It is a growth process. Just as a newborn cannot handle lobster, your staff must grow into some of your loftier goals. As each person sets their goals with you, it is your responsibility to bring him or her down to earth at first. I have no objection to setting high performance goals, but not until the people involved are ready for them.

7. Plan for failure in your goals—plan A and plan B. I have been involved in planning for twenty years. I have taught others how to plan and set goals over the years, yet the hardest thing I have had to explain is that goal setting includes failure. It must, because we are not omnipotent. Theologians have argued for years about whether Jesus had control over His destiny or not. For that, I have no answer. We humans can strategize, but we do not control destiny. Accidents happen. Staff members die in car accidents. Computers gobble up years of work. Mail doesn't deliver. You name it, and it can happen. The common failure I have seen in planning by both organizations and individuals lies in the area of leaving no fluff room, no margin of error. Planning involves planning for the unexpected. When plan A falls through, you need to be able to open your drawer and pull plan B, which takes over to compensate for all the "what-ifs" you built into plan A.

8. Prioritize goals. You cannot accomplish everything at once. Even God took six days to create the universe. Once you have set down on paper your list of goals, deadlines, and other details, you must prioritize them or you may find yourself sacrificing the important for the immediate, and you'll find yourself getting a lot of fluffy stuff done to the exclusion of the important, critical tasks.

9. Estimate costs: dollars and people and resources. Step nine in the packet of goal details is the least exciting part. It may even be painful, but it will be necessary to consider the cost involved. Everything costs. There will be a price to pay for each goal set, and this exercise will help you determine if you really want to go through with it, or if you can. Millie Laurenzo, a dear friend, a wise entrepreneur, and an astute businesswoman, once offered a bit of advice from her forty years in business. She said, "Jim, if there's one thing you need to know about business and life in general, it's this: No one is who they say they are; no one can do what they say they can do; no one can do it when they say they can do it; and everything costs more than they say it will cost."

10. Assign specific tasks to each person. As your goal setting grows beyond the initial stages, you will want to subdivide and consider each portion of the goal as it relates to individuals. Who is best to carry out each step? Who would balk at the idea? Who is more likely to carry a bigger load than the others? Who do I need to keep out of the loop?

11. Communicate it and repeat it often. Once your goals are set, they must be remembered. Say them orally. As the opportunity arises ask your staff how they are doing with their tasks or goals, but please don't post the goals all over the office. You don't want people to get sick of the goals. The goals will be set in writing somewhere and can easily be pulled when needed. It is more effective to deal with the cognitive than the subliminal. Some will say, "Yes, but if people see it in print, they'll believe it. It will remind them every day and become a part of them." To that statement I would reply, "How many ads on billboards can you repeat? Of those, how many did you embrace as your own?" Remember that you need to make a "my" goal become an "our" goal, and the best way to do that is for your people to see you achieving your goals and believing in theirs.

12. Celebrate. Little victories can go by with no applause. It happens with our children. It happens with our staff, and it shouldn't happen with either. When a goal is accomplished, it needs to be celebrated. I am not saying you throw a party every time someone cleans his desk, but individually or collectively you can determine when, where, and how to celebrate the completion of a goal. The bigger the goal and the more people involved, the bigger the celebration. If too many goals go on unrewarded, people will soon develop a "so what" attitude about them, and you will have ended any chance at goal setting or goal achieving.

WARNING!

All of the positive aside, you need to be warned that there is a downside to all this goal setting. Send up a red flag when you spot one of these.

1. Quantity versus quality goals. It is easy to get into the mode of setting quantitative goals. Sales are up 17 percent. You can see that. Costs are down 4 percent from last year. Quantitative. Easily achievable. No problem. However, any organization that puts emphasis on quantity to the exclusion of quality is headed for disaster. You may sell several billion hamburgers a year, but if they start tasting like shoe leather, you will see your quantities plummet before you can adequately recover. Stay focused on both quantity and quality, and I would even lean more toward the direction of quality goals above quantity. If you perfect the quality, the quantity will come.

2. Goals that only flow down the organization. The temptation management must face is to determine the fate of each organization or individual without ever hearing from the parties involved. It is entirely possible that your staff's individual and collective goals are the same as yours, and the preference is to let them set their own goals. Those they will embrace first, but those you must also hear first. The effectiveness of your goal setting multiplies exponentially if your staff says that they would like to see a drop in tardiness by 50 percent and will work toward that end than if you told them to do it. Also, you might be brave enough to ask your staff to set some goals for you. It would be interesting to see what they would like to see you achieve.

3. Adding projects without dropping others. The tendency of management is to overstuff the bag until the seams rip. Goal setting for an organization has its limits. Even Jesus had transportation problems and could not be everywhere at once. Little by little, events fell into place. When He cured an infirm man, He went on to the next goal. You must learn to see goal setting as a tube rather than a tub: with a tube, you put some marbles in and some drop out the other end. There is a constant flow. With a tub, one marble piles on top of the other; those at the bottom get lost in the mix and crushed beneath the most recently placed ones that rise to the top, until the whole mess finally comes crashing down. Are you piling too much on and not letting enough go?

4. Business goals that exclude family members. This chapter is primarily about company goals, but even those should never take priority over your personal life. Goal setting must be tempered. We must learn to be as responsible for our relationships as we are to the company. One author wrote in his best-selling book, "The attitude of 'It would have been wise for me to change over five years ago, but now I've got a family and I can't change,' illustrates this kind of desire murder weapon. Throw away those murder weapons! Remember, the only way to get full power, to develop full go-force, is to do what you want to do."[1] This is sad advice, but true to our time. Richard Haayen, CEO of Allstate Insurance Company, wrote in the March 1988 *Nation's Business* magazine that "there is something sick about a person whose only interest is money. And the same can be said, I think, for the company whose sole goal is profit." I, too, find the philosophy of money at any cost just a little bit sick. Goals must be in balance with real life.

5. Operating only on management by objectives. I entered the business world when Peter Drucker's Management by Objectives (MBO) became popular. The concept is that management and individuals set goals, and the organization's achievement of those goals determines its success or failure. We, as managers, must watch that the good of MBO does not become evil. The greatest weakness of MBO is that it reduces organizations and people to calculated, definable machines. Again, keep the goal setting in balance and beware of overdoing it.

6. *Excess verbiage in writing goals.* I have seen pages of goals as set down by incredibly gifted grammarians, and having read them found myself wondering what on earth they were saying. Guard against verbiage. The fewer words that can express a goal, the clearer it will become.

7. *Aim high, but not too high.* At first, you must let your people crawl. Once they establish the habit of goal setting, let them leap to heights. They will often leap a bit beyond what they can reach, but it is better for them to do it than for you. Overly optimistic goals will either cause management to pull out all the stops to achieve them, and thus take wild risks, or it will cause people to underachieve because they know the goal is unattainable anyway.

With all the modern business jabber over the years regarding goals, one thing stands clear: Jesus of Nazareth knew goal setting. It is not a new phenomenon. Whether great or small, personal or business, our lives are structured by goals. We should learn to master them and not fear them. They increase our productivity, reduce wasted time, improve our quality of life, and raise our chances for success. They encourage us and help us see our weaknesses. They can be a friend or foe, a master or servant. If He who claimed to be the Son of God lived by them, who are we to think ourselves better?

PRACTICAL TIPS

1. By the first of next month, set in writing five new personal and business goals.

2. Divide each goal you set by a minimum of five substeps.

3. Plan for failure by establishing a plan B for each goal.

4. Celebrate with those who achieve goals.

5. Run your goals by your family for a cross-check to keep things in balance.

CHAPTER 13

GOALS: STRIVING FOR EXCELLENCE

The value of a man's life is in direct proportion to his commitment to excellence.
—SIGN IN THE DALLAS COWBOYS' LOCKER ROOM

[My early movie producers] didn't want it good. They wanted it Thursday.
—RONALD REAGAN, 40TH PRESIDENT

Jesus stood silently before His accusers during His trial. Like a sheep led to the slaughter, He went along. He had been through a mock trial by the religious leaders and then sent to Pontius Pilate, Herod Agrippa, and back to Pontius Pilate.

Of all those who could plead for Jesus' release, it seems odd that a Roman governor would be the sole voice. The bloodthirsty crowd cried for Jesus' death. "Crucify Him!" they bellowed in one voice.

The second time Jesus stood with Pilate, this time facing the crowd, Pilate noted Jesus' silence, and His presence. Pilate may have lacked the religious training of those who accused Jesus, but he did recognize perfection when he saw it, and he made it a point to acknowledge it. He told the crowd, "I have examined Him in your presence and have found no basis for your charges against Him. I find no fault in Him. Neither has Herod, for he sent Him back to us. As you can see, He has done nothing deserving of the death you cry out for."

The crowd mindlessly persisted, and Pilate signed the death warrant for Jesus. But Pilate went to his own grave knowing that he had seen perfection personified once in his life. He had a vision of excellence engraved in his memory. His words are a written testimony to Jesus' perfection.

—LUKE 23:4, 13–15

Jesus never did anything halfheartedly. He eschewed mediocrity. He despised it. If Jesus were head of a business today, He would run it as He did His ministry, with perfection as the aim and excellence as the hallmark of daily operation. He knew that to flirt with mediocrity meant to be engaged to compromise, and this is a lesson we must learn today. Mediocrity equals compromise. "An excellent plumber is infinitely more admirable than an incompetent philosopher. The society which scorns excellence in plumbing because plumbing is a humble activity and tolerates shoddiness in philosophy because it is an exalted activity will have neither good plumbing nor good philosophy. Neither its pipes nor its theories will hold water."[1]

We have tolerated mediocrity for too long in this country, and we are paying the price for it. In a 1987 Roper survey reported in *Harper's* magazine, only 6 percent of West Germans felt that the words "Made in America" equaled quality. We have been surpassed on nearly every front in terms of quality and excellence, and it is time to take back lost ground.

The Japanese established themselves as front runners in the automotive industry, not because they create the slickest ads (in my opinion they still have a long way to go to lie as well as our ad agencies), but because they produce some of the finest quality products on the market. Car doors fit snugly, their paint jobs outlast the competition's, and their materials are among the best money can buy. Because of their commitment to quality, Japanese cars have no need for lengthy warranties and guarantees. Their product is reliable. They may lack the bells and whistles of American cars, but they beat us in longevity every time. Frankly, I would prefer ordinary excellence over extraordinary mediocrity any day. So would your customers.

Achieving excellence in your business, church, club, or personal life means a change in priorities. It means saying farewell to tradition. It means the end of looking out for number one and focusing in on numbers two and three. It means sacrificing money for other things that on the surface seem less important.

Excellence is a value statement. You will adhere to the things you value most. Tenure, seniority, and tradition are as dead as the man's withered hand in Jesus' day. What you value will be the catalyst that drives you. If you value excellence, you will live for it. It will wake you in the middle of the night with ideas. It will be the modus operandi of your business, and it will tell those who spot it that you value it more than anything else. As a leader, you will demand excellence and will not settle for less. Sam Walton's right-hand man said that Sam arose every day determined to improve something. What a great value statement! Your employees will perform better if they feel you truly expect them to. Once word gets out that you value excellence, employees and suppliers will rise to meet the challenge.

The Three Faces of the Big E

As I observe businesses, ministries, service bureaus, and government agencies, I find three common, glaring problem areas that require a mental shift toward excellence.

1. Excellence in performance. Name the last time a company went out of its way for your benefit with no regard for self-interest on its part other than to satisfy you, the customer. Tough one? It shouldn't be, but the fact that it is only highlights the critical need for improvement in this area. Businesses that are self-serving will find themselves suffering from the customer revolution taking place in this country. As Tom Peters points out a number of times in his books, there are a number of companies offering incredible service out there, but they are few, they are the exception, and (a point Tom seems to avoid) they make you pay through the nose for the privilege. As consumers we expect to receive incredible service with a smile and with promptness from our local hot dog vendor, and we don't want to pay eleven dollars per dog to get it.

2. *Excellence in quality.* If quality is first, it should be number one on every agenda at every meeting. If quality is number one, then every step should be taken in your organization to eliminate this business of reworking something to death. In book publishing I am constantly under the gun to get my editors to loosen their grip from a project and let it go. Find the areas in your business that are being reworked and manifestly determine to stop the insanity, and do it right the first time.

Caterpillar Tractor Company is so sure its products are superior that it guarantees customers forty-eight-hour delivery time, anywhere in the world. If not delivered on time, the part (regardless of the size, shape, weight, or price) is free. They are that confident. Maytag offers ten years of problem-free operation on all their washers and dryers. Even the gigantic Ford corporation has opted to exchange the desire for position with the desire to produce a quality product, and they are bold enough to say so in their latest tag line that at Ford "quality is job one."

3. *Excellence in relationships.* Let's assume your company manages to drastically improve in the areas of performance (turnaround time, delivery time, etc.) and quality (products that last beyond their warranty dates). Without step 3 in the triad of excellence, yours will become a two-thirds company. The world has less patience with a two-thirds company. They will pity the one-third guys by saying, "Well, at least they're trying." They will laud the three-thirds guys for "making the grade." But the two-thirds companies receive a cold-shouldered "Come on, get with it." So if you intend on working toward the goal of excellence, remember that the leap

between one and three is a precarious one and needs to be bridged quickly.

This third area tends to be the last of the three areas of consideration because it is the most difficult. Relationships in business means more than just customers; it means building relationships with employees and vendors as well. If you spend too much time building relationships with your employees without also building relationships with your customers, the ones laying down money for you may resent it. But there is also a problem when a company favors the customer over the employee. Workers develop a wait-a-minute, I-deserve-better-than-this attitude and begin to walk for fear of being considered the company stepchild.

You will need to work on building relationships with both groups simultaneously.

Build faith in your customers, employees, and vendors by listening to them. Often those people know better than you do how to run the company; they just don't know how to facilitate the changes necessary. Whether a vendor, customer, or employee, begin establishing a mental attitude of "I have faith in you." Sam Walton was famous for traveling from Wal-Mart to Wal-Mart and chatting with clerks, stock boys, and customers. He awoke at 2:30 A.M., stopped at a local baker to buy four dozen donuts, and took them to an all-night distribution center to find out what was happening in their department. Walton seemed to have an innate sense of what produced excellence, part of which included listening skills.

SIX CHARACTERISTICS OF EXCELLENCE

If excellence is the dream you wish to achieve, either professionally or personally, you should know the six characteristics of excellence.

1. Excellence is attainable. Few businesses are running an excellent race. Those numbers discourage the average manager or CEO into thinking he or she could never build an excellent company. Size is no respector when it comes to excellence, either. True, companies like Hewlett-Packard, Dana, Wal-Mart, and Nordstroms come to the top when compared to most others, but there are a great many businesses of three to twenty employees working toward, and achieving, excellence.

Excellence is attainable if you burn it into your mind, heart, and soul. It must become you, not just a part of you. It is corporate; one or two doubters in your organization will become the cancer that stifles progress. You, as leader, must cultivate excellence in every capacity, in every job description, in every task. You'll know you have arrived the day you hear a frontliner ask in a meeting, "Yeah, but is this as perfect as it can be?" Yet, while excellence is attainable, it is ongoing. Rest on your laurels more than a day, and your excellent crown will quickly shift its position.

2. Excellence is painful. In many cases, achieving excellence is a laborious, treacherous road that most would rather not travel. More often than not, it means layoffs. When the Dana Corporation voted to head down this path, they went from five hundred down to one hundred corporate staff. Many of those were good people who had given their lives to Dana. Hewlett-Packard weathered the 1980s recession by asking their employees to work a four-day workweek for a time, and to take a cut in pay. Those who did bubbled to the top when the company rose again in the nineties. Executives in the Wal-Mart corporate headquarters must endure the "empty-headquarters" rule, which tells bosses to get out of their offices and into their stores. Expenditures may be cut. Benefits may change. Staff may quit, but nearly every major surgery involves removing something to make the body work better. Before true revival can come to a church, it often means losing as many bodies as are added. In the final analysis, the church may not have grown in numbers but in spirit. And spirit is what excellence is all about.

3. Excellence is a measure of success. True, you may double your income in ten years by playing lowball with your vendors or salespeople, and you might even gain a reputation for superior service through slick advertising gimmicks, but none of that can endure for long before the wary eye of the public sifts out the truth. Once that happens, no force on earth can save a drowning company from the death it probably deserves.

Look back. Once you, your staff, your organization, and/or your customers declare you a success in one way or another, reflect on the road to success. If your measuring stick comes up short with regard to excellence, your success is short lived and in vain. Measure your successes by steps of excellence. If you can honestly sit back and say, "Yes, I gave them the best possible product through the best possible service at the best possible price," then your success is worthy.

4. Excellence is a motivator. Excellence demands that we think beyond our dreams—it demands that we take action. It tells us to line our ducks up in the right order, evaluate them, and possibly shoot a few in the process. It tells us that staying up at night is OK, and arriving before the sun rises is the norm. It speaks volumes about inconsistency, incompetence, and incompatibility. It measures every thing against every other thing and asks for scrutiny of the remainder. It never stops. It never falters. It never gives up, gives in, or gives a rip what the rest of the world says. Excellence says you can when the world screams, "Impossible!" It challenges the heart, encourages the soul, and excites the mind. But excellence is never, never boring.

Once the seed of excellence hits your blood, you will stop at nothing to continually achieve excellence. You'll go the extra mile, even if to the extreme.

Striving for excellence is the motivator that makes a difference.

5. Excellence is a process. Author Leo Buscalia has the same philosophy I do about life: Never say, "I have learned something,' but say, "I am learning something." If you asked me about my spiritual walk, I'd say I'm a pilgrim in a time warp on an excellent adventure. I am growing and learning. Life is a process. Enjoy the process, and don't get bogged down on the details without growing through them.

Excellence can be attained, but it takes a long time to get there, and once there you will find more places that need an excellence overhaul. Hang on and enjoy the ride. You'll find that traveling this path of excellence is like a roller coaster: lots of turns, twists, hills, and breathtaking plunges; and once you get to the finish, the car only slows down enough to let the weak ones depart before you're off for another wild ride. The search for excellence never stops.

6. Excellence is a standard. Jesus told His followers, "Be ye perfect, even as I am perfect." Pretty tough standard by which to measure your success. Without some standard, you will have no gauge to measure progress, let alone achievement. In order for there to be excellence, there must be something we consider less than the best. I contend that Jesus and His business standards are the best. They are the standards by which we can measure success. You may compare yourself to other contemporaries, but what happens when you've surpassed Wal-Mart or Nordstroms? You then become the standard by which others measure themselves. Are you willing to become an icon? For how long? At what risk? To whose detriment? Rather, why not measure your successes by an unchanging standard that has endured two thousand years of scrutiny? Why not strive to be like the One who is a shining example of perfection for us in our personal and business lives?

So, let's get down to the nitty-gritty. If you plant some of the following seeds of excellence in your work, you will begin cultivating an excellent spirit among those around you. Insist others do the same, and watch the garden of excellence produce in abundance. Like a seed packet, I am going to give you the whole packet and let you separate and plant them one at a time.

SEEDS OF EXCELLENCE

- Remember names and people.
- Be a comfortable company.
- Avoid egotism.
- Develop interest in others.
- Continually refine and polish.
- Heal misunderstandings.
- Award achievement.
- Regret disappointment.
- Give before getting.
- Feed your staff needs.
- List objectives.
- Plaster excellence everywhere.
- Smile realistically.
- Look people in the eye.
- Shake hands vigorously.
- Listen intently to everyone.
- Get excited about your work.
- Work toward perfection.
- Read inspirational material.
- Train your people.
- Be flexible.
- Practice generosity.
- Isolate problems and deal with them.
- Celebrate more often.

Let me close with this thought. Wouldn't it be great to be able to stand at death's door and, like Jesus, declare to the world that your purpose for being here was finished, was perfected, and excellent?

PRACTICAL TIPS

1. Determine to raise the quality of your product noticeably by next year.

2. Treat everyone you pass better than you do now.

3. Set a goal for excellence and the date you plan to achieve it.

4. Visit at least five excellent businesses, and evaluate why they are.

5. Read two books this year on excellence.

CHAPTER 14

HIRING: HOW TO HANDLE HIRING AND FIRING

If you aren't fired with enthusiasm, you'll be fired . . . with enthusiasm.
—VINCE LOMBARDI, PROFESSIONAL FOOTBALL COACH

Here lies a man who knew how to enlist into his service people better than himself.
—ANDREW CARNEGIE'S EPITAPH

"Peter," a hushed voice spoke. "Peter, did He come back yet?"

"Umm?" Peter grunted as he rolled over on the dewy grass. The rising sun struck his eyes, and he rolled back.

"Peter, He's been gone all night. He's going to choose. How can you sleep?" Andrew asked.

"With you around, it isn't easy," Peter complained. He heard the murmuring of the awakening crowd; hundreds of men, women, and children rose with expectation as Jesus descended from the hill where He'd been praying all night. Many of them had followed Jesus for weeks. This morning, He would choose twelve to be His apostles.

As the crowd popcorned to its feet, Jesus approached. They formed a complete circle around Him.

Jesus spoke. "I have been with My Father. We are in agreement of the twelve I must choose. I know many of you," Jesus said as He touched the face of a child. "I know the sacrifice you would make to follow Me, but you do not. The ones I now choose will sacrifice everything to follow Me." He broke through the crowd and reached out His hand to Simon Peter and his brother Andrew who joined Jesus in the center of the circle. Jesus turned again and reached for James, John, and Philip. Bartholomew and Matthew were next, followed by Thomas, James, son of Alphaeus, Simon the Zealot, and Judas, son of James. Lastly He chose Judas Iscariot.

These did not know that they had been chosen to change the world; they only knew they would follow the one called Jesus around a dusty, noisy community. They had no dreams, no aspirations but one: to please the One who chose them. As the crowd dispersed, comments came from those not chosen.

"They were just lucky, that's all."

"John's been sticking next to Him like flies to honey. No wonder he got chosen."

"I don't know what He sees in that fisherman Peter. At least I went to school."

"Three weeks I followed Him around. And for what?"

"I'm going home to bed."

"Mommy, I want to be big and important like them too."

Jesus and His twelve apostles turned and walked in the other direction; they never looked back.

—LUKE 6:12–16

Jesus understood the primary dynamic in business. He knew that a fantastic business plan was not the way to success, nor plenty of capital in the bank, or powerful friends in high places. Jesus knew that people were His greatest asset. He hired well. He'd been well into His ministry and spent a great deal of time with a number of candidates besides the Twelve. He knew many others as well as He knew the final twelve He chose. He did not select complete strangers, as some suppose. No, He knew these men well. He spent enough time with them to know their weaknesses as well as their potential. They had already been with Jesus; He was merely moving them up. In today's lingo, Jesus promoted from within.

HAVE I GOT AN EMPLOYEE FOR YOU

In today's business world it is much harder to get an employee off the payroll than it is to get one on. Radical surgery is much more difficult than preventive medicine, as any doctor will tell you, so it pays to do the work up front to avoid painful consequences later. Even while operating under all the legal ramifications, hiring can often be an easy process. It must be done right. There are guidelines your organization and the government have set down regarding hiring and firing procedures. Abide by them. Yet there are still some considerations when it comes to hiring often not mentioned in manuals.

Look for loyalty, not ambition. You do want employees with a sense of energy and excitement. You want someone who wants to work for you and wants to make the organization prosper. What you don't want is someone who is out for themselves. I have actually had someone say to me that the reason I should hire him for a particular job was because he needed money. Even worse is the applicant who aspires to be president of the company before he even has a chance to work in the mail room. We had a young lady whom we hired from overseas. When she inquired of the salary figure, we faxed it to her. She admitted later that when she saw the number, she was disheartened; but she believed so much in our mission that in spite of our low salary, she agreed to come. When she arrived at our office to fill out the necessary papers, she then discovered much to her surprise that the number we had given her was not her monthly salary as they pay overseas, but her weekly amount. The dear lady was loyal from the beginning and remains loyal to this day. Loyalty is a rare quality. Jesus understood that. He knew that His men would give their lives for Him. When you find loyalty in someone, do all you can to get and keep that person.

Look for a trainable spirit. The day before I left college, I stood before the want ads posted in the school lobby wondering what I would do for a living. I graduated from college with high hopes but with little future. One older visionary offered me a position as a schoolteacher in a private school. Coming out of the midwest to Fort Lauderdale seemed like a great idea to a twenty-two-year-old, so I accepted. When asked whether I felt qualified to teach in his school, I remember telling him, "No, sir, I don't. But if you will teach me what I need to know, I'll learn it and do it your way." I got the job, and carried that spirit with me my entire career. None of us know a bazillionth of what we ought to know. You should hire people who know their limitations and are willing to work on improving themselves for the good of the business.

Determine the skills your hires need to do their jobs well and contribute to your company. When you scan the list of men Jesus selected, the question always arises: How on earth did He choose that motley crew? From every possible angle, these were the wrong guys to choose to lead and spread a newfound faith. Hindsight is always better than foresight. Yet Jesus saw something in each of them that He knew He needed to further His cause and to propagate His message. Know what you need and hire to meet the immediate need as well as future possibilities.

Don't hire on instinct or gut reactions. You're halfway through the second interviewee. She's got the same ideas about the president, baseball cards, and the Rams as you do. She makes you laugh, and her outgoing personality would be a great asset to your company. You decide to cancel the day's other five interviewees because you know in your heart this is the one for your company. Beware! Gut reactions like that can cause real damage to both you and your organization. If instinct were so right all the time, then more people would be making a living telling fortunes. Unfortunately, it doesn't work in either the darkened gypsy tent nor in the executive hiring room. Gut reactions will fail you. Common sense business practices will not. If Jesus had hired on reaction, Peter might have been eliminated.

Consider potential for the future more than past records. The biggest weakness we have when it comes to hiring in this country is our overglorification of past accomplishments. I am not saying you shouldn't review and consider them; just don't make them more than they are. I have had conversations with individuals who graduated from respected schools who'd bore the socks off a dead man. I've met industrious, bright young people who only went to community colleges. One U.S. president self-educated himself in a country cabin and failed dozens of times before becoming president; another held presidential offices of every major club and group and even held claim to being a Rhodes scholar. Past record is no indicator of future greatness. I've read resumes that looked as if these people should be working for the U.S. Embassy. One cartoon put things into perspective for me. It showed a boss talking across the desk to an applicant and saying, "Well, the fact that you even want to work here is a strike against you already."

Beware of safe, influential, or powerful candidates. "John Cone down at Oxide Metals said he was going to call you about my application." Maybe you have heard, "I do know the councilman personally, and I think I can help you with your building code problem." How about, "I have a clean record. Call my previous employer." Watch out. People who are squeaky clean, overly influential, or powerful are destined to cause you problems. Don't run out and hire immoral scoundrels, but look at Jesus' example when hiring. None of His chosen staff were safe, influential, or powerful. Jesus knew those people in His community, but He avoided them.

Never hire anyone till everyone's so overworked they'll welcome the new person gladly. I know it sounds selfish, but it works. I have seen companies grow explosively, then have to cut back because of overstaffing. The way to hire well is to wait till the people are ready to walk out, pull their hair out, or stand on tables in protest. Then hire someone and watch how much the employees appreciate them.

Listen, don't talk. Hiring is 90 percent listening and 10 percent talking by you. Interviewers have a tendency to talk all the time. They feel that if they're not asking question after question, then the interview hasn't gone well. Try silence. It works wonders. The candidate's true character may come out by what they don't say as well as by what they do say. Listen to the words and listen for the meaning between the words. When you ask candidates what kind of boss they like, their saying that they prefer a hands-off, uninvolved type may be the opposite of your style. In that case, what they are saying is that they are a poor fit for you.

Use the rule of 50: If someone has 50 percent of what you need, he or she is a viable candidate. Don't spend forever looking for the perfect candidate. Jesus didn't. The candidates you need are ones who show great potential and have at least 50 percent of the skills and talents you need. It gives them goals to reach. It gives them a chance to improve and a chance to prove themselves.

Ask questions. Here is a list of questions you should consider asking. Under the guidelines of your company and the government there are a number of questions about sex, religion, age, or health you may not ask. Consult them and your attorney before endeavoring to interview someone. As a help to the interview process, though, over the years I have kept a list of questions to use when interviewing a candidate and am providing it for you here.

Questions to Consider Asking an Applicant

- Tell me a little bit about your childhood and your family.
- What was your first job? How old were you?
- Tell me about high school. What were your favorite subjects? Least favorite?
- Tell me about your two favorite teachers.

- If you went to college, tell me your favorite subjects and teachers there.
- Did you hold any jobs in college?
- Why did you take the major you did?
- If you could manage your career all over, how would you do it differently?
- What kind of bosses do you like and dislike?
- How far do you expect to go in this company?
- Are you available to work overtime?
- Tell me about some people you didn't get along with at your last job.
- What is your one greatest strength and weakness?
- Specifically, what did you do in your last job?
- Were you promoted? Why or why not?
- Why do you want to leave your current position?
- Why do you want to work for me? For our organization?
- What type of work interests you most?
- How much money do you want to be earning in five years?
- Do you have any hobbies or interests?
- What type of training do you think you'll need for this position?
- Why should I hire you?
- What do you consider your three greatest achievements in life?
- What was the worst mistake you ever made at your last job?

Consider candidates from within the organization first. It boosts company morale, eliminates the need to check references, and reduces orientation and training time. The benefits far outweigh the drawbacks. Only if no internal candidate is qualified should you go outside the organization.

Establish and maintain a ninety-day probationary period for all new employees and transfers. This little policy can be your lifesaver in the event you royally blow it and need an escape clause.

YOU'RE FIRED!

In the unlikely event that the candidate snowed you during the interview process, passed the ninety-day probationary period, and now needs to be terminated for whatever reason, bear in mind that the task of firing an employee can, and often does, go smoothly. Job security has become the great American myth. No one is guaranteed a position. Layoffs and terminations are part of the work scene now, so you might as well get used to it.

When it comes to firing, however, there is a right way to do it and a wrong way. Do it the right way. Don't let the courts decide whether you did it right or not. Jury Verdict Research, Inc., a company that monitors jury decisions, reports that employees who sue their companies for wrongful dismissal have an 86 percent chance of winning the case.[1] Again, consult your company and government manuals regarding termination policies, but feel free to use some of these ideas if and when the time comes to let someone go.

Don't be cruel. Instead of saying, "Terri, you're fired!" use softer words like dismiss, terminate, or let go. There's no need to make an unpleasant scenario worse than it already is.

Don't postpone. Not firing a nonperformer causes as much morale problem as firing him. We've seen it more often than not. A manager delays and postpones the inevitable. Meanwhile, the rest of the staff decide that either the manager is a bowl of Jell-O, or he and the bum have some deal going on. Perhaps they reason that if Joe Shmoe can get away with nonperformance, they can too. Or worse, they may be exceptional employees who feel no need to remain so. After all, they too can join the ranks of employed nonperformers.

Always set an end date for volunteers. You can't fire them. They don't officially work for you. They aren't on payroll. They are wonderful when they're wonderful, and they are an unbelievable problem when they don't work out. We call them volunteers. Other people simply don't call them. The easiest way to avoid unforeseeable problems is to build into the volunteer job description some sort of ending date. At that time you can determine whether you want to assign another project for another specified period of time or continue the current one. Whichever you choose, set the end date in writing and evaluate it then.

Know the major valid legal reasons for termination. They are: disruptive behavior, poor performance, excessive tardiness, ethics problems, excessive absences, or theft. Those are the biggies under which most terminations fall. If you have a case outside those boundaries, you will need to be extra careful when proceeding with a dismissal.

Document reasons that may lead to termination. The steps that must be maintained are simple but time consuming.

List specific areas of measurable nonperformance. You cannot approach an employee and say that he's not working up to snuff and he has to go. See you in court. The dismissal must be measurable against a standard, and it must be measurable in terms of improvement.

Give examples of how to improve. Some organizations consider this counseling. However you view it, you owe it to the individual to help him or her improve. After all, no one wants to be a failure. Set standards of expected improvement, goals if you will, and keep written records for both you and the employee to refer back to if necessary.

Put everything in writing, especially all reprimands. Be sure that both manager and employee sign anything in writing. If the employee refuses to sign, call in another manager as a witness of what was discussed. At this point, the employee ought to get the message that you are serious.

Meet again on the established and agreed-upon deadline improvement date and reevaluate performance. This is the employee's chance to appeal. If performance hasn't improved, begin termination procedures. Issue another memo telling him that this is his final warning. If he doesn't show immediate improvement, termination will come.

Always work from a prepared script and don't deviate from it. Slick talkers will use every maneuver at their disposal to dissuade you from your final decision. Hold fast.

Don't argue; stay calm. Employee reactions will vary from denial, crying, shock, anger, and accusation to physical threats. On every point you must remain a professional and you must remain in control. You just pulled the cliff out from under their feet, and they're falling fast. They are, shall we say, temporarily out of their mind and justifiably so. You must take charge of the moment.

Don't chitchat. Get to the point. If you have done your homework, this moment will not come as a surprise to your employee. Get it done and over with.

Always terminate in the morning early in the week. This allows the employee and peers time to process it. Professionals disagree on this point. Some will tell you to do it Friday afternoon. In my view, that only serves to allow the employee to gain employee sympathy; it makes the other employees fear any meeting you might call on a Friday afternoon; it gives the employee time to mull the scenario over two empty days and worsen the shock; it also gives the person thinking and commiserating time. He or she will talk to friends who may counsel him or her to seek legal counsel. Weekend firings are, in my opinion, ripe for trouble.

Firings by themselves are trouble enough. Jesus was fortunate enough to never have fired one staff member. The reason is obvious: He hired well. Most of us inherit our problems. That's all right. They can be dealt with too. Yet Jesus' strategies in the area of hiring probably avoided the need to fire in the long run. He used a probationary period to get to know the disciples and for them to get to know Him. The interview didn't end with one brief meeting; He interviewed in depth during the probationary period. Those He kept on were loyal to Him, they were trainable, and they had humble spirits. They stayed with Him for the rest of their lives. Can you imagine saying to your board that other than for growth purposes you didn't have to add or subtract any employees? It is said that a man is judged by the company he keeps. I would say that a company is judged by the men and women it keeps.

PRACTICAL TIPS

1. Keep loyalty and teachability as the two needed characteristics when hiring.
2. Never hire someone based on a gut reaction.
3. When interviewing a candidate, ask briefly, then shut up and listen.
4. Establish a permanent policy to promote from within whenever possible.
5. Keep detailed records when proceeding with a termination.

CHAPTER 15

INSIDER INFORMATION: COMPETITION

A competitive world has two possibilities for you. You can lose. Or, if you want to win, you can change.

—LESTER C. THUROW, DEAN,
SLOAN SCHOOL OF MANAGEMENT, MIT

The way to conquer the foreign artisan is not to kill him, but to beat his work.

—RALPH WALDO EMERSON, AMERICAN POET

The final confrontation. The beginning of the end.

One of the largest crowds ever assembled to hear Jesus sat around on a hillside. Here and there stood clusters of Pharisees and high priests, opposing Jesus at every turn, trying to trick Him with their crafty words. Like a dazed and angry fighter in a boxing ring, Jesus had endured three solid blows to His purpose, and when He mentally arose from the canvas He verbally came up swinging.

"Woe to you, scribes and Pharisees, hypocrites! For you travel sea and land to make one convert, and when he is made, you make him twofold more the child of hell than yourselves."

Five more times Jesus belted the words, "Woe to you, scribes and Pharisees, hypocrites!" These seven deadly blows had never before been uttered. No man dared speak to the Pharisees as Jesus did, nor did any man after Him speak so. But Jesus had heard and seen enough. The people had been blinded, and the only way to reveal the Pharisees' true nature was by ripping them apart and exposing their foul odor. The blind leading the blind had met a man of vision.

What crime had He committed? He only said what the crowd already thought, but for this the red-faced, elegantly robed religious leaders would have Jesus crucified.

Jesus turned to them. "You serpents, you generation of vipers, how can you escape the damnation of hell?"

Jesus' disciples sat open mouthed, listening as He passed, cursed, and condemned the religious leaders. The crowd listened, but none dared stop Him. They knew the power and corruption of the Pharisees. Now this One whom they had followed so faithfully for three years had jumped a chasm, and no one could save Him. No stone under which the scorpion lay remained unturned.

The religious asps eyed their victim, and they readied their venom. When Jesus finished, they returned to their nests to plot His demise.

In two days, Jesus would be dead. They would kill their chief competition. The Light of the world would be extinguished, and the dark robes of legalism would again rule the earth. Or would they?
—MATTHEW 16:11–12; 23:13–29

Pretty bleak picture, isn't it? If you didn't know the outcome of the story, it would be quite defeating. Yet businesses and organizations in no worse circumstances than the one Jesus found Himself in completely give up hope and surrender to the inevitable. Some, like Jesus, arise victorious. Others, like the Pharisees, continue in their stodgy ways until time washes them away. In the world of business as in the world of religion, if you stand still long enough you will soon be passed and surpassed. Change is the only thing that keeps both alive.

HOW ABOUT A LITTLE FIRE, SCARECROW?

Many businesses and the individuals within them fear competition. Why? Competition is good for companies and for

customers. Organizations with no competition lose the motivation to improve, to shake things up, and to drop the dead
wood. When competition is alive, the consumer benefits from
the improvements. Don't fear competition. Remember that
kites rise against the wind, not with it. The stronger the wind,
the higher the rise. The tougher the competition, the better
you become. You have to, unless you want to be eaten for
lunch.

I love the stories of the little guys who took on the giants.
David and Goliath. Wal-Mart and K-Mart. Saturn and Toy-
ota. In these cases, the underdogs competed even when they
thought they couldn't and when the opposition seemed overwhelming. We can think of every excuse in the universe not to
compete. How about these:

- "We're too small." (Since when did size matter? Rome
  conquered the world.)

- "We don't have money." (Why not try brains and determination for a change?)

- "They have powerful lawyers." (Einstein's law: For every
  high-powered lawyer, there is an equal and opposite
  high-powered lawyer. Apologies to Albert.)

- "We're happy the way we are." (You're lying. You'd die
  for the chance at number one and you know it.)

- "They've been doing it longer." (Sure they have. That is
  to your distinct advantage.)

- "They hired the best and brightest." (So, you hired
  idiots? There are herds of mavericks who'd love to take
  on the big guys with you.)

There's a royal catch to this competition thing. To be able
to do something as well as others isn't enough. You must be
better. "In the land of the blind, the one-eyed man is king,"
said Machiavelli. Did you get that? There can be no tying for
second. Someone must be first, or what are second and third
for? If you plan to compete, then plan to win. The company
with a second-best competitive attitude will only be second

best. Like it or not, you're in competition. No matter what product or service you offer, you are in competition. Somewhere out there is someone who can do it a little better and a little smarter than you're doing it. All it takes for them to beat you out is time and tenacity. You are both armed with the same weapons. Speed, training, and agility will win the day.

CHECK OUT THE COMPETITION

The only way to know what the competition is doing is to find out yourself. Don't leave it up to a competitor analysis firm. Those guys, if you can afford them, are great at taking a bunch of information and presenting it all nicely on paper, but they don't have a passion and an understanding for your business like you do. You and your staff must investigate and analyze what your competitors are doing, and you must do it on several levels: locally, nationally, and globally.

"Wait a minute," you might say, "we're just a mom-and-pop operation." All right, then what are you going to do when another mom-and-pop operation opens up three blocks from you? What if a nationally recognized conglomerate opens up by you? What if some brave entrepreneur from overseas plans to bring his ideas next door? In the world we live in, none of these possibilities are too unbelievable. They happen every day to every kind of business imaginable.

That's why you must see what the others are doing. You must know where they are going and why. When you personally see a similar product on a competitor's shelf, your eyes will light up. You will formulate a competitive plan, not because the numbers say so, but because your heart drives you to do so. That drives competition better than a spreadsheet.

You'll have to focus on new competitors as well as old ones. The problem with the big three automakers is that they continually looked at the other two. They realized too late that international import sales were climbing. They had to resort to legislation to keep their market share, a move that cannot last long. They shouted "protectionism at all costs," and the consumers were not willing to pay that price. "Yeah, Zabloski, but I'm just making pizzas, not cars," you might argue again. The same rule applies. If you blindly believe that you are the only pizza man around, think again. Some bright kid who doesn't have a cent's worth of business savvy but a barrel full of zeal will steal your pizza business away from you if you're not careful.

When you watch the competition (you will, won't you?), don't look for the bad they're doing. Look at what they're doing right. Who cares what they do wrong? What they do right is selling a product and is bringing home their paycheck. What they do right is costing you a customer. What they do right is something you ought to be doing that you're not. So investigate your competition's successes. Forget their weaknesses. They're trying to.

HEY, CAN I BORROW THAT?

Go in to your competitor's place of business and shamelessly borrow (not steal—that wouldn't be ethical) their best ideas. Every good idea you come out with is one you didn't go in with. Don't come out unless and until you have a good idea you can bring back to your organization.

Someone may say, "But, Zabloski, don't you really think it's stealing someone else's idea?" I'd have to say no, it isn't. It's business. It is applying the Bible's understanding that there is nothing new under the sun. Those guys didn't come up with their ideas out of the blue sky. I guarantee you that their best ideas are a compilation of other ideas. When authors write a book, often they take ideas from other books, rearrange them, and add their own thoughts. That's called research.

To blatantly steal and exactly duplicate your competitor's ideas is plagiarism. For that you can pay a stiff penalty. I would never recommend attempting such an underhanded tactic, but I *would* recommend that you implement and adapt your competitor's best ideas to suit your needs. Massage, manipulate, mold, and make the idea yours. Their idea will never work for you because you are not them. You and your organization are unique. Your strategy is unique. Your business plans, goals, and objectives are unique. If you don't adapt them, they will become a mockery and only remind the consumer of your competitor; thus, it will produce the opposite effect you planned.

Let me give you an example. One major discount retailer discovered that one of their stores had set up door greeters who met and welcomed customers as they entered the store. The head of the corporation thought it was such a grand idea (borrowed from the high-end retail chains) that they adopted the plan as a standard for every store in the chain. People loved the idea. Consumers embraced it. The practice became a calling card of the company, among other things. Then this discount chain's competitors got the idea that if it worked for the other company, it would work for them. It backfired, however, for every time a customer walks into the competitor's store and is greeted by someone, they are reminded of the company that started the practice.

Another example is found in advertising. This first chain of stores decided to stop posing stiff, expensive, professional models in their sales ads and started using company employees for a fraction of the cost. Great concept! But the unimaginative competitor started doing the same thing. Every time I see one of their ads I think, "Come on. Come up with an original idea already." You know what I would have done? I would have taken the idea of using company employees and expanded upon it. I would have contacted actual people who *bought* those products, ordinary everyday Joe's and Mary's, and asked them to pose for my sales ad. Think about it. Those folks whose pictures are found in the Sunday sales ad are going to call every relative on the planet and tell them to read the sales flyer. Feel free to borrow winning ideas from competitors, but for good business' sake adapt them to your own needs and be creative about it.

Memorize your competitors product line and pricing structure, if possible. At least you ought to know what their best products are. It goes back to knowing what they do well. Sometimes that's not easy information to get. Perhaps they don't have a local retail store you can observe; maybe they're a national carpet cleaning service. Then to find out where they are and where they're going, you might want to buy a share of stock in their company, which would permit you to get a stockholder's report. There are many ways to find out what's going on behind the competition's closed doors.

One practice not done much these days, but one that works is called "reverse engineering." Essentially it means taking their product apart to see how it works. If some engineer hadn't done that, we'd all be using the same brand ink pen, the same sticky note pads, the same refrigerators, and the same telephones. Find out what makes their product so good by finding out what the ingredients were that went into it. Then borrow and build upon it.

In a recent international strategy meeting I attended, we were trying to determine what makes a company number one. Someone suggested that if a consumer buys your product instead of someone else's, it means you're the best. I disagreed. I believe that the best automobile on the road today is the Rolls Royce. Unfortunately, I cannot afford a Rolls, so we drive a little four-door compact car. It is not the best car available. Millions of people are not driving the best cars available; they are driving the most affordable ones. My point here is that you must keep your retail price as low as possible if you hope to compete. It may be your only advantage, and you must consider it.

The religious leaders of Jesus' day were well known. As you study Jesus' strategy for dealing with His religious competitors, you notice that He did not talk often in general terms, but in specifics. He didn't say, "Well, they don't know what they're doing." No, He warned their followers that they were tying burdens on the backs of people and never lifting a finger to help. In our opening illustration, Jesus listed seven specific things the Pharisees were doing, seven things for which He had a clear and better alternative. Get out of the habit of talking about your competitors in glittering generalities; that's nothing but complaining. List specifics and deal with them individually. Do it publicly when appropriate, but certainly do it with your staff. Whenever you hold meetings, mention the competition. Your people need to realize and remember that someone out there wants their job, and they will get it if the competition wins.

Talk to your competitors to find out as much as you can. Don't aggravate them unnecessarily. In fact, I'd try to befriend the competition. They might just share some ideas with you. You catch a lot more flies with honey than with vinegar. For all of Jesus' animosity towards the Pharisees, the Scriptures reveal at least one time when He accepted a dinner invitation from a Pharisee and dined with him. Your competitors are a river to be crossed, not a city to be crushed.

Remember that competition means lots of frequent changes. The reason the Japanese auto industry swept away barrels full of American dollars is because they could turn their designs around on a dime, and the cumbersome American automakers were like an ocean liner that took forever to regroup. You are in a race. When you see the competition sneaking up, you must change course. When they sneak up again, time to change again. Only those who can change often, change willingly, and change quickly can survive in a competitive world. That strategy in itself can be your winning edge. Keep the competition guessing. Be unpredictable. Nothing should please you more than to know your competitors are sitting around saying, "What on earth are they doing now? Why are they doing that? What are they up to?" While they're trying to figure out what you're doing, you're already doing it and heading on into another idea.

When I was a child, we boys would gather around a large hill at the end of our street and play King of the Hill. We'd fight like mad to be the one who got to stand at the top, at least for a few seconds. Why'd we get to the top? So others could try to push us off! It was my first lesson in competition. I learned that you must keep looking back over your shoulder for the little guy behind you as well as the big guy in front. The only way to stay on top of the hill as king was to use your agility and quick movements. The big guys had a harder time. They couldn't turn around fast enough. I was a pip-squeak who could duck and turn and jump and dodge. I knew Mike would try to get me in a half nelson, and I knew John would try to kick my feet out from under me. From those days I learned how to compete—fairly, honestly, and spiritedly. Now as I study the principles of Jesus Christ, I see that He lived by those same principles. He took the kings of the hill, learned their weaknesses, then confronted them. He showed us that competition is not only healthy, it is required to survive.

PRACTICAL TIPS

1. Make a list of every possible competitor you might have.
2. Make it a point to visit your competitor personally to see what they're doing right.
3. Consider "reverse engineering" your competitor's product or service.
4. Talk about the competition with your staff every chance you get.
5. Write down every excuse you can think of not to compete, then refute it.

CHAPTER 16

LEADERSHIP: HOW TO INCREASE YOUR SELF-CONFIDENCE

Use what talents you possess; the woods would be very silent if no birds sang there except those that sang best.

—HENRY VAN DYKE, AUTHOR

I'm really a timid person—I was beaten up by Quakers.

—WOODY ALLEN, ACTOR, DIRECTOR, WRITER

The caravan trudged on for a day's journey. Children played stone-kicking games alongside the plodding donkeys. As the caravan slowed to a stop, Joseph reached to grapple with a tower of goods toppling from the donkey's back. "Jesus! Come quick! I need Your help!" But the wares fell into the dust, and an angered Joseph went from family to family in search of his twelve-year-old son. His search came up empty. His heart raced as his anger shifted to panic. He ran back and grabbed Mary's shoulders. "He's missing. No one has seen Him since we left Jerusalem. We must go back." They ran. They walked. They wept. They prayed.

At sunset they arrived at the city gates, and the gatekeeper, seeing their anxiety, bid them entrance. They wandered from house to house, business to business for two full days. "Jerusalem is not such a big city," Joseph warned. "We should have found Him by now." Mary remained silent and fell into a weary sleep in his arms as they rested in a doorway.

When they awakened in the morning, the thought came to her that they had not looked in the temple, and Joseph scoffed, saying that children were not permitted to play in the temple. But for her sake, they would go.

What did they see? Surrounded by the wisest teachers, the richest politicians, and the most pious priests—Jesus. Their son.

Mary covered her mouth and whimpered as she ran to embrace the boy. "My son!" Then her anxiousness turned to anger. "Your father and I have been looking everywhere for You. Why have You done this to us?"

And with a sense of purpose they would not understand for many years, He replied that destiny compelled Him to be in the temple.

—JOHN 8:58; LUKE 2:43–49

Jesus is the embodiment of perfected confidence. No fear. No uncertainty. Only pure, unstained, tamed confidence. Unlike Jesus, most of us must go through grueling years of self-searching to find out who we are, why we are, where we are, and that we are. None of us is born with confidence—it is developed over time. If you are without it, or are running low on supply, take heart. Confidence is attainable, and not at the price some will tell you must be paid.

The PMA (Positive Mental Attitude) gurus travel from town to town telling people to "smile, cheer up; things could be worse!" And sure enough, things get worse. I love what Charlie Tremendous Jones said to his wife in a fit of rage in his best-selling book, *Life Is Tremendous:* "I can't wait to get successful so I can move to a plush office downtown where I can fail in style."[1] It is spoken tongue-in-cheek, but compare it with other best-sellers such as *Think and Grow Rich and You Can Become the Person You Were Meant to Be*. Think confidently, they say, and you will be confident. That's all there is to it. You and I know, however, that if it were so easy, we would all be confident, happy, and successful.

OVERCOMING CONFIDENCE KILLERS

I will assume you are missing one or all of those traits of confidence, happiness, and success, or you would have skipped over this chapter. You want to exude confidence when you walk into a room or speak in public. You want people to say, "Wow, who is that person?" You want and need a model to follow or a formula to embrace.

Looking for someone as a model of confidence is as simple as reading the words of Jesus. From age twelve when He respectfully stood up to His parents, He knew who He was. Throughout His recorded three-year ministry, He described Himself by telling people, "I am the bread of life; I am the messiah; I am the eternal one; I am the light of the world; I am the Son of God; I am the door; I am the resurrection and the life; I am the true vine; I am the alpha and omega; I am the first and the last; I am the way, the truth, and the life." Make no mistake—Jesus knew who He was and what He was about. So what are some confidence killers?

Fear is the number one killer of confidence. Entire governments have been built upon fear. Though fear is a powerful motivator, Communists learned that it lasts only as long as you can keep people scared. As Communism fell, it waved a white flag of surrender that was soon replaced by colorful national flags waving in victory. Once people lose their fear, they regain their confidence. Walls are replaced with roads; tollbooths replace guard gates; lines for bread are replaced with lines for Big Macs. Like a sinking steamship, it is not the letting out of air that sinks it, but the letting in of water. Once traces of confidence begin hacking away at fear, the laws of nature take over. The way to successfully eradicate fear is to hit it in different places with forceful, stratigically planned action.

The Navy learned years ago that curing a sailor of his fear of water didn't come with weeks of counseling or by teaching classes on the effects of water molecules on lung tissue. The cure came by throwing the sailor in a pool of water crammed with able-bodied lifeguards. Victims of airplane accidents are encouraged to immediately get on another plane and fly somewhere to help them kill the seed of fear. Some people are afraid of flying. Some are afraid of dying. Others fear lightning, dogs, bridges, spiders, snakes, or enclosed spaces.

I have two fears: spiders and heights. To the best of my knowledge, I have never fallen from a high place, and I have never been bitten by a spider. But I can remember clearly the seed that planted those fears. At age six, a girl in my first-grade class named Roberta went to Arizona on vacation and returned with her arm bandaged. When I asked her the source of her injuries, she said she'd been sleeping in a tent when a tarantula bit her arm and laid eggs in it; she was waiting for the eggs to hatch so the millions of baby spiders could emerge. Ridiculous story . . . but I kept my eye on her for the rest of the year just waiting for a spidery eruption to occur. At age seven I recall my brother Johnny holding me by my feet upside down over the front porch banister directly above a patch of thorny rose bushes, threatening to end my life unless I revealed the whereabouts of my cache of chocolate candy. The fall would've been little more than a foot or so, but in the mind of a terrified child, those were heights. Who knows why I never developed a fear of rose bushes, banisters, or my brother Johnny? But I feared heights and spiders until my late twenties when something snapped, and I knew I could never become a confident leader until I first conquered those fears.

I conquered my fear of heights by climbing to the top of Saint Paul's Cathedral in London. To get there requires climbing story after story of slatted steps (the kind with no backs that let you see to the ground floor). I climbed. I shook. I froze. I moved one step at a time. I forced myself to look down. I reached the pinnacle in an exhausting two-and-a-half hours, after which I surveyed the entire city of London and said, "I won." Last weekend I stood on the roof of my house without tethers, cutting overhanging branches and sweeping off the leaves.

And lest you're thinking I conquered my fear of spiders by jumping in a pit of tarantulas, think again. I'm not an idiot. I overcame that fear by exposure. I read everything I could get my hands on and watched every video and TV program discussing spiders. The more I understood these fascinating creatures, and the more facts I had, the less I feared a worldwide conspiracy among spiders to lay eggs in peoples' arms. In this case, it was a lack of information that fed my fear.

I do not know what your fear may be, but I do know that the solution is conquering it. A step stool, ladder, and even my rooftop pale in comparison to standing over London. The rodeo rider doesn't recover his fear of being thrown by starting again on his child's rocking horse. The diver doesn't lose his fear of the deep by wading in the bathtub, and you won't lose your fear by playing it safe. You lack confidence because of fear. Find your fear. Face up to it. Say, "This is what I'm really afraid of." Eleanor Roosevelt said, "You gain strength, courage, and confidence by every experience in which you really stop to look fear in the face. You are able to say to yourself, 'I have lived through this horror. I can take the next thing that comes along.' You must do the thing you think you cannot do." On that point she and I agree. Search for the original source of your fears as I did. Then determine when and how you can overcome that fear, and do it big.

A lack of purpose is confidence killer number two. From early in His childhood, Jesus knew what He was about—His Father's business. Jesus did not come to earth to make a living, and neither did you. You have a higher purpose for being here. You must find it by asking yourself, "What is my mission?" If you answer, "Well, to be the best manager I possibly can be," then you're in trouble. What happens when you retire? What happens if you are laid off and can no longer manage? You see, your purpose must be larger than life; it must transcend life. Your purpose for being here must supersede you when you are gone.

Before you lay your head on the pillow tonight, write down what you believe to be your purpose for being. The value of this exercise is not to frustrate you into some metaphysical frenzy, but to give you a reason to go on. Confidence is destroyed when an individual has no reason to get out of bed in the morning. In my opinion that is the major cause of death for retirees. They spend thirty-five years managing a corporation, then suddenly find themselves looking through the paper each evening for the best early-bird dinner special. Give that same group the responsibility of cleaning up the Everglades, and watch them thrive into their nineties and beyond. The person with a purpose is humankind's greatest asset. Without a purpose we become Carl Sagan's billions of chaotic molecules temporarily shaped into the current form to validate the Big Bang theory. Find your purpose, and you will see confidence increase.

The third critical blow to building confidence is the need for constant justification. Managers and corporate bosses love to play schizophrenic mind games with their employees just to keep them on their toes. One day the boss walks into the office and declares that all wastebaskets ought to go under desks because visitors don't want to see garbage at every turn. The next day the boss denies ever saying it and threatens to fire the rumor monger who started such a ridiculous policy. In a quandary, the employee mascot goes into the boss's office to see where he placed his basket, only to find that he has one under his desk and one next to his desk. The office explodes into such chaos over the issue that the boss finally resorts to issuing a memo stating that all wastebaskets are to be placed three inches to the left of every desk. All wise employees file said memo for future reference. A year later when asked by the employee replacing Sally Secretary why she ever kept such a silly memo, she simply states that "you need to keep a paper trail to justify why you do things should the boss call you on the carpet."

I trust you can see what constant justification does—it destroys confidence. It forces employees to walk on eggshells, to withdraw from creativity, to avoid taking risks, and to build a repertoire of reports and papers "just in case."

There are three classes into which you can be divided: (1) you are a leader who forces people under you to constantly cover themselves due to your poor administrative abilities, (2) you are a subordiante, constantly covering yourself for fear of getting called on the carpet, or (3) you are not in either category, in which case life is grand.

I have been in meetings where those attending come literally with stacks of papers several inches thick because somewhere in them lies their salvation when the boss points in their direction. That is no way to run an organization, nor is it a way to build self-confidence. There is little you can do if you are in an organization that perpetuates the mentality of constant justification. I have been through it for a number of years, and the only way to kill the snake is to cut off the head. You may not be in a position to facilitate that little task, and there are some legalities involved in such a move. But you do have it within your power not to perpetuate the problem whether you are a lineman, secretary, worker, manager, or the big muck-a-muck. If you are the muck, find ways to raise the integrity level in your company. Begin by apologizing to the entire crew and make amends. If you are the muckee, you are down to two choices if you want to build your self-confidence. Neither one is pleasant. Here they are:

(a) Quit.

(b) The next time the boss calls you on the carpet and you feel the urge to pull a piece of paper to defend yourself, stiffen your back and ask him politely, "Are you calling me a liar?" No self-respecting leader would challenge you on it, especially if you are right. If he does, refer to option number one.

KEYS TO CONFIDENCE

For every negative, there is a positive. For every confidence killer, there is a way to overcome it.

Giving is the beginning of confidence. Specifically, I am talking about the giving of yourself, not of your money. Healthy self-sacrifice ultimately leads to healthy self-confidence, but beware. Sacrifice quickly can mutate into a martyr complex, and that destroys confidence. This confidence builder must be kept in constant check, and it requires a lot of practice.

No one gains anything from the individual who is selfish with himself or herself. Look at your life. You are a conglomeration of your total years' input. You are made of your past, present, and future dreams and aspirations. You are a representation of failures and successes. You are a bundle of intertwined relationships. You are a mass of formed opinions and ideas, prejudices, and impartialities. You laugh at certain times and are moved at others. To not share some of yourself with other people is to deny them the opportunity of knowing your uniqueness. To hold yourself back is to deny the world your greatness. You are tremendous, and only you can give us what you have. How is that for building your self-confidence? Learn to share. We won't know how wonderful you are until you reveal yourself to us and give yourself to us; and as is true with most people, you won't know it until we tell you. Charlie Ward is a great example of what can happen when a person gives and receives because of it.

Charlie came into the world on the worst side of town. As a young boy, he sold newspapers to help pay his family debts. Then he shined shoes and as a teen found himself serving others as a cabin boy on a freighter. He tired of life in Seattle and tired of serving others. He did what every young man daydreams of—he hit the rails and traveled with bums on passing trains. Charlie saw the States and made his living by stealing and petty thievery. His railroad journeys satisfied him for several years, until Mexico enticed him. He drank. He fought. He won, but more often he lost. He discovered gambling, which allowed him to win bigger and lose bigger. Finally, U.S. authorities caught Charlie and tried him for trafficking in narcotics. Bitter and angry, Charlie claimed the authorities framed him even as he passed through the gates of Leavenworth prison.

At age thirty-four, Charlie Ward hung on to the end of his emotional rope. He had lived for himself for sixteen years. He had given to no one and taken from all. But his life turned around when Charlie read the only material then available to prisoners: the Bible. By reading and rereading it, Charlie's life transformed into something he never thought possible. He burned into his mind to forgive those who wronged him. He decided to become Leavenworth's model prisoner.

He wanted to improve himself, and his opportunity came when he heard from a prison guard whom he had befriended that there would be an opening for a trustee in the prison electric plant in three months. Charlie knew railroads, not electricity. He read every book on electricity in the prison library. He prayed and asked God to give him that job, and in return he would learn to give. He studied, and at the end of three months, he not only passed the test, but due to his vibrant personality he won the hearts of the prison officials.

In a short time, Charlie became superintendent of the prison power plant with one hundred fifty men working for him. Charlie became everyone's friend, including the newest white-collar prisoner named Herbert Bigelow who entered because of tax evasion. Because Charlie gave of himself to help Herbert Bigelow adjust to his situation, his new friend responded in kind by telling Charlie that when he got out of prison to look him up in Saint Paul. Bigelow's sentence ended, with Charlie's several months behind.

When Charlie knocked on Bigelow's door, he received a handshake and a job offer as a laborer. A bit disappointed, Charlie overcame his situation by giving again. His reward came in leaps—within the year Bigelow promoted him to superintendent. From there Charlie rose to the rank of general manager and then vice-president. His triumph came when Bigelow made Charlie Ward, exbum and excon, president of Brown and Bigelow Industries. Charlie remained as president, taking the three-million-dollar company to the stature of a fifty-million-dollar company until his death at age seventy-three.

Charlie learned one principle in prison, which he read again and again: Give and it will be given to you, pressed down, shaken together, and running over.

Preparation lays the foundation for confidence. Charlie Ward's story would have ended quite differently had he not studied for the exam on electricity. That goes for every lauded celebrity, athlete, businessperson, politician, and religious leader as well. It takes a great deal of preparation before the confidence comes. When world-famous cellist Pablo Casals granted an interview with a reporter, his wit and charm stuttered the writer's pen. Casals told the reporter how long he'd been playing and how much practice it required. He told the reporter that every day he practiced six hours a day. The astounded reporter, wanting to double-check his facts, asked, "Mr. Casals, you're ninety-five and the greatest cellist who ever lived. Why do you still practice six hours a day?" To which Casals replied, "Because I think I'm making progress."

Practice = ability = performance = confidence. It does not matter whether you want to become a better manager, organizer, public speaker, or even a better spouse. The formula is still the same. You might retort, "Yes, but what if I practice and practice and still never get any better at the thing. Will that build my confidence?" The answer is a resounding yes! You will have discovered one of the billions of things you are incapable of doing, and you will have the assurance that you will never be able to conquer the thing, so you can set your sights to improve upon the things you can do.

For example, I am an avowed nonathlete. Part of that comes from my stature (I'm a five-foot-seven ectomorph). Another part comes from my lack of interest. I am just one of those guys who can find 147 things to do around the house other than watch a basketball game on TV. I will watch an occasional Monday night football game if the Dolphins are playing, but only after the kids are in bed and my work is done. The other third part comes from genuine inability. I am a four-footed tennis player, I can't punt, pass, kick, or throw anything besides a fit. Rattling off sports statistics is beyond my mental capabilities. You get the idea. The point is that I know my limitations, and because I do I have all the confidence in the world that I cannot do certain things, which gives me more time to improve on the things I can do.

Objectivity builds confidence. Nothing can break your confidence streak faster than having someone tell you bad news about your abilities. When Lucille Ball attended the John Murray Anderson Drama School in 1927 as a would-be actress, her instructor told her to try any other profession besides acting. A young, talented singer received some unheeded advice from Grand Ole Opry manager Jimmy Denny back in 1954. The advice? "You ain't goin' nowhere, son. You ought to go back to drivin' a truck." The singer? Elvis Presley.

The Bible tells us that wisdom comes from a multitude of counselors. It means that confidence is gained from a second opinion. But be careful not to overdo. The Danish have a saying: He who builds according to every man's advice will have a crooked house. Find corroboration among the counselors, and follow the path of common sense.

While traveling on a transatlantic ocean voyage, actress Billie Burke (Glinda, the good witch of the north from the Wizard of Oz) took pity on a man suffering from a severe head cold. She sat at his table and asked if he felt uncomfortable. He blew his nose and nodded.

She told him, "I'll tell you what you should do. Go back to your stateroom and drink lots of orange juice. Take a couple of aspirins. Then cover yourself with all the blankets you can find and sweat out the cold. I know what I'm talking about. I'm Billie Burke from Hollywood."

The grateful man smiled, rose to leave and said, "Thanks. I'm Dr. Mayo from the Mayo Clinic."

Freedom and empowerment send confidence soaring. These two are grouped together as the fourth key to confidence, not because they would not work separately to build confidence but because they work so well together.

I know there are those who disagree with me on this point, but it is possible to empower people without giving them freedom, just as it is possible to give people freedom without empowering them. Until you can reach level four in the Hierarchy of Delegation, as I call it, or until you have empowered your employees to that level, confidence is less than a sure bet. The four levels in the Hierarchy of Delegation are as follows:

1. Bring me the facts. I'll decide.

2. Offer a recommended decision and let me know what it is. I'll agree or disagree.

3. Do something. Tell me about it and report the results whether good or bad.

4. Do something. I don't want to know the results.

Jesus entrusted His followers with tasks. He quickly took them to level four. He trained them, warned them, and empowered them. He rested easy when He gave them tasks because He knew that they would succeed. He didn't assign tasks beyond their ability level, but in order to build their confidence He assigned tasks geared to their current level, and which would propel them to the next level.

Until you (or your employees) reach the point of empowerment found at level four, your organization will never reach its fullest potential and neither will the people involved in it. I am passionate about this. I have watched dozens of phenomenal workers squished under the thumb of management because workers were kept at level two or three. And I have seen as many companies sit in the red because they refused to let the employees soar; they clipped their people's wings rather than cut them free. I don't know whether you'll get this revelation or not, but here goes. You don't run the company.

The employees do. Want proof? Go to work tomorrow by yourself. Run the business all by yourself for the next year. I'll see you in bankruptcy court.

Now that you've been made aware of a fact that your staff has known for years, what are you going to do about it? At the very least, be strong enough to admit it . . . to yourself and to them. Then set about finding ways to promote as many of them to level four as you can. And if you are an employee somewhere between levels one through four, give your boss a copy of this book and place a bookmark in this chapter.

Confidence. Jesus had it. You can have it too. In fact, you already do. All you need to do is call it up from your depths, unleash it, and let it become what it was meant to be. You.

PRACTICAL TIPS

1. Find your fear and face it.
2. Give more of yourself every day.
3. Study, prepare, and train for something you always wanted to do.
4. Seek counsel from wise individuals and go with the consensus.
5. Empower everyone around you, and include yourself.

CHAPTER 17

LEADERSHIP: CHOOSING A LEADERSHIP STYLE

Jesus alone founded his empire upon love; and to this very day millions would die for him.
—NAPOLEON, FRENCH COMMANDER

In order to be a leader a man must have followers. And to have followers, a man must have their confidence.
—DWIGHT D. EISENHOWER, 34TH PRESIDENT

Dusty sandals hiked through the Israeli countryside. Their owner, dressed in weather-worn clothes traveled from place to place, eking out a living by doing carpentry jobs here and there. His olive skin was darkened even further from time spent in the sun. Like the wealthy merchants who passed this way every day, He walked the road along the sea to catch an occasional breeze. He had no jewelry, no camels, no entourage of servants. As He planted His feet on the roadside, a cloud of dust swirled around Him and blew past several men repairing their fishing nets on the shore. Peter coughed, turned to face the Passerby, and before he could say anything his eyes caught the stare of Jesus. A long, wordless pause was broken by two words that forever changed the life of this fisherman.

"Follow Me."

It was not a request. The strength of the language was an imperative with a meaning beyond simply following. It implied walking in One's shadow, step for step, to get behind, to take on the characteristics of the One casting the shadow. Peter handed his torn net to his friends, stepped beside the stranger, and continued along the path shoulder to shoulder with Jesus.

—MATTHEW 4:19; 8:22; 9:9

On the surface, Jesus had none of the characteristics we would require of a leader. He wasn't rich. He wasn't highly educated. He hadn't earned degrees, written books, or created companies. How was it possible for a lone preacher from Galilee to forever change the world?

NAPOLEON AND JESUS

Colin Powell said in a September 1995 interview with Barbara Walters on *20/20* that "leadership is the ability to motivate people to achieve objectives." By that definition, every manager is a leader who can get his employees to clock in on time. Every mother who can get her toddler to eat his broccoli is a leader. For that matter, every toddler who can get his father to bring him a drink at two in the morning is a leader. In reality, it isn't all that difficult to lead because people want to be led. Most people won't cry out for a leader as long as things are running smoothly. But let the road get rocky, and despite all the hoopla about freedom and rights, people will seek out a leader to tell them what to do, how to do it, and when. So, I take exception with Powell's definition of leadership. What he describes is management, not leadership.

We already have managers barking orders to employees, mothers yelling no to their children, and children shouting yes in return. We have a plethora of leadership books on the market with an opening statement that "Leadership is . . . ." The more I study leadership, the more convinced I am that leadership cannot be boxed in. Authors design leadership definitions to make readers feel good, to get them to say, "Yep, that's me all right. I'm a leader." The problem is that the old model doesn't fit us as well as we think. Like the python swallowing the pig, we can cover up our inadequacies with a pat definition, but the swine outline still shows through.

What we need is a new model of leadership, not a new definition. Employees are tired of the leadership style espousing anger, division, and greed. They seek a leader who brings peace, unity, and caring; they will follow one who enhances the body, mind, and spirit as well as the bottom line. Find a man or woman who has been in business for thirty or more years, and they will be able to rattle off a dozen or more leadership books that have come and gone during the course of their career; perhaps they even embraced a few different leadership styles. But there is one Man whose style is worth taking another look at because it has endured two thousand years of testing.

Napoleon had a leadership style. Jesus of Nazareth did too. Napoleon: What a leader! He leaped the Mediterranean Sea, dashed across the desert, and smote slothful Europe. He made laws, built bridges, and conquered kingdoms. He became ruler of Italy at twenty-six, Egypt at twenty-eight, France at thirty, and Europe at thirty-two. His subjects feared him. Yet for all his leadership ability Napolean spent the end of his young days banished to St. Helena's Island, cursed and rejected.

Jesus: What a leader! He walked on the Galilean Sea, stopped to talk with beggars, and healed blind Bartimaeus. He made but two commandments, built no monuments, and conquered only human hearts. His followers loved Him. He spent the end of His young days dying on a Roman cross, cursed and rejected.

Today, no one follows Napoleon. Millions follow Jesus. Why?

NO FEAR

The answer is simple. Jesus knew and understood that getting people to obey was not enough; He knew they needed to be won. He knew that it is better to get people to follow you out of love, not fear. He knew that if He was to succeed as a leader, He had to somehow get His followers to think, act, and strive to become like Him. He had to eliminate fear of retribution with desire for success. Do you want to build a leadership style that people will follow for years? Then lose the Fear Factor. It's true that people will respond out of fear. They will obey because they are supposed to, but not because they want to. They will respect your superiority, but not your significance. Fear is never a long-term motivator. Managers may get away with using it, but a leader never will.

After graduating from college I joined an organization with a Fear Factor leader. His style was to walk the halls and make his presence known. He required attendance at every after-hours gathering. He ruled with a fist of iron and paid with a handful of copper. I had youth and ambition behind me; he had experience and power. After six years of towing the line, I stood in the shower one April morning and said, "I don't care if I don't get a check next week. I don't care if it costs me my career. I cannot go on like this." With that, I threw in the towel and handed in my letter of resignation that same day. I didn't quit . . . I learned. I learned that leadership isn't power; it is respect. I went on to a different company and career.

Fear Factor's successor called me two years after I'd left and offered his hand in reconciliation. He didn't pick up his boss's leadership style—he learned. He learned that replacing nearly three-quarters of an organization's staff is more painful than humbling oneself and apologizing. He learned that the king often dons the servant's clothes. He learned that the fallout from running a Fear Factor leadership style can trickle on for years, but a style based on love and compassion will win over hearts and build loyalty.

He also learned that the servant-leader will flourish while the Fear Factor leader will not. To be a servant-leader requires character and a willingness to get down into the trenches with your people. Jesus demonstrated that point by washing His followers' feet. He acted out in His own lifestyle what He wanted His followers to do. He knew that leadership did not exist for the leaders but for the benefit of the followers. He knew from watching the Roman guards around Him at the time that even in battle the officers ate last. This is a lesson to be learned by managers and leaders today. We often try to prod and administrate our people rather than lead them. We often treat them as personnel, and, to our shame, at times as numbers.

The most classic example of a modern servant-leader was Sam Walton. He despised corporate fat cats. He could (and would) handle the cash register as well as stock the shelves in any of his Wal-Mart stores. He drove an old, rusty, dented pickup not to prove a point but because it still had plenty of good mileage left in it. He told his staff on more than one occasion that "if American management is going to say to their workers that we're all in this together, they're going to have to stop this foolishness of paying themselves $3 million and $4 million bonuses every year and riding around everywhere in limos and corporate jets like they're so much better than everybody else."[1]

The only way you'll get your people to follow you is to become a servant-leader. It means typing a letter for your secretary when she's overwhelmed trying to decipher your handwriting. It means handling the front desk for the receptionist so she can call the school to check on her sick child. It means staying late to help the new employee get familiar with the facilities. It means doing things for your employees that they would do for each other. It means becoming one of them so they can become one of you.

FIVE LEADERSHIP CHARACTERISTICS

Various leadership programs will tell you that there are anywhere from three to twelve dominant characteristics of a leader, including things like a desire for purpose, self-knowledge, persistence, daring, and life itself. After studying the life of Jesus for twenty years, I have narrowed His leadership style down to five characteristics.

1. BE AN AUTHORITY FIGURE

One of the things that stands out in Jesus' lectures is the frequent use of imperatives. He never said, "Gee, if you'd like to do this, then . . ." or "If you're up to it, why don't you . . ." or "If you can find the time . . ." No, His words were demanding. No matter which translation of the Bible you read, you find Jesus speaking with authority. When He went head to head with those in authority, He usurped them by answering their question with a question. He knew that the one asking the question always is above the one answering it. He made it even tougher on them by asking questions He knew they could not (or would not) answer. He did not become defensive in their presence. He had full authority, and He intended to exercise it when necessary. He did the same with His followers. He told them to follow Him. He told them to seek not the things of this world. He told them to love their enemies and to do good to those who hated them. He didn't suggest it. He spoke the truth without apology.

Jesus used His authority in a positive way. Every time He one-upped the ruling leaders, He became effective in the eyes of His followers. Validation of your authority only comes when you exercise it wisely. When His followers saw Him take control over a situation and exercise authority, they said to themselves, "Hey, He's one of us and look what He does." Little did they know that in a short while He would tell them that whatever things they saw Him do, they would also do, and even greater things would they do once He was gone. He said do it . . . because He did it.

2. BE AN EXAMPLE

You have heard the old adage, "Don't do as I do, do as I say." Jesus went a step further by telling His staff what to be as well as what to do. He encouraged them to be perfect. Among other things He told them to love, to obey, to pray, to walk, to listen, to hear, and to follow. Yet He did it without a hint of pride or a sarcastic smirk.

Imagine walking into your office Monday morning, gathering your staff together, and gazing into their weekend-worn eyes, asking them to follow you and become like you. Your reaction is just about what theirs would be. But be encouraged, because like it or not, many of your staff *will* become like you. They will see your ways and will emulate them. The good? Yes, perhaps. The bad? Yes, probably. You see, it isn't important for you to ask your followers to imitate you—they will. That is a given.

Charles Barkley, basketball star, said on national television that he was not a role model for young African-American youth and he didn't want to be one. When I heard that announcement, I said out loud to no one listening, "Too bad, Charles. You are one. Now what?" Ditto for you. People will imitate you. Whom will you imitate? Napoleon? Caesar? Trump? Jesus? Be ever mindful that what you say and do and how you say and do it will be repeated somewhere, sometime, by someone else. The choice is yours.

3. BE A DECISION MAKER

Someone once said that it is easy to be decisive because nearly everyone else is indecisive. If only it were that easy. There are a number of things that play into making good decisions: an innate gut reaction, emotions, logic, history, experience, responsibility, accountability, and knowledge. You shouldn't make decisions because of emotions, whether yours or others. Leadership decisions must often be made on the basis of common sense and management principles. Business decisions are best made in light of what is good for the business. This may or may not include the feelings and emotions of others; but you cannot make rational, wise decisions if you overemphasize the feelings of others. Being decisive and earning respect often mean bypassing the committee appointed to do such things and doing it yourself. It may mean standing up to the one in charge of you and holding your ground. It may mean humbling yourself and offering an apology later if the thing goes awry. It may mean taking risks. George C. Marshall said, "Don't be afraid to take a big step when one is indicated. You can't cross a chasm in two small jumps." Make decisions and move on. As my father used to say, "Fish, or cut bait!" Sometimes we make wrong decisions, but that's the risk we take.

A man named Fred inherited $10 million, but the will provided that he had to accept it either in Chile or Brazil. He chose Brazil. Unhappily it turned out that in Chile he would have received his inheritance in land on which uranium, gold, and silver had just been discovered. Once in Brazil he had to choose between receiving his inheritance in coffee or nuts. He chose the nuts. Too bad! The bottom fell out of the nut market, and coffee went up to $1.30 a pound wholesale, unroasted. Poor Fred lost everything he had. He went out and sold his solid gold watch for the money he needed to fly home. It seems that he had enough for a ticket to either New York or Boston. He chose Boston. When the plane for New York taxied up, he noticed it was a brand-new super 747 jet with red carpets and chic people and wine-popping hostesses. The plane for Boston then arrived. It was a 1928 Ford trimotor with a sway back, and it took a full day to get off the ground. It was filled with crying children and tethered goats. Over the Andes, one of the engines fell off. Our man Fred made his way up to the captain and said, "I'm a jinx on this plane. Let me out if you want to save your lives. Give me a parachute." The pilot agreed, but added, "On this plane, anybody who bails out must wear two chutes." So Fred jumped out of the plane, and as he fell dizzily through the air he tried to make up his mind which ripcord to pull. Finally he chose the one on the left. It was rusty and the wire pulled loose. So he pulled the other handle. This chute opened, but its shroud lines snapped. In desperation, the poor fellow cried out, "Saint Francis, save me!" A great hand from heaven reached down and seized the poor fellow by the wrist and let him dangle in midair. Then the gentle but inquisitive voice asked, "Saint Francis Xavier or Saint Francis of Assisi?"[2]

4. BE A FRIEND

Can you honestly say that you are genuinely friendly with your employees? We all pass by people and ask how they're doing without waiting for an answer. But I'm talking about the genuine I-care-and-I'll-do-whatever-I-can-to-help kind of interest. Do you identify with your people? Do you know their likes and dislikes? Do you know your subordinate's favorite color? Do you know their favorite food? How many kids do they have, and what are their names? A friend would know.

It was not part of Jesus' leadership style to be aloof. He touched the shoulders (and feet) of all of His staff members. There were no unimportant people in His life. One well-known businessman said he started out his life with that mentality. He said he learned early on that the secret to being a leader on campus was to speak to people coming down the sidewalk. More than that, he spoke before they did. He continued that philosophy through life. He determined to always speak to people and not divert his eyes away as most people do. He called them by name if he happened to remember it. Soon he says he knew more people on campus than anyone else, and they knew him. That recognition and simple act did more to build friendships than anything else. It is just that attitude that made the man into a billionaire. How many leaders can you name who would pass people on the street or in a store and genuinely greet them with warmth and sincerity? How many people do you greet with the same attitude?

5. BE AN INSPIRATION

The last in the combination of Jesus' leadership traits is the one most often written about: motivation. In all of Jesus' teachings, there are no rah-rah rallies. There are no pep talks. He motivated and motivates people without the expected tape series, seminars, or best-selling books. Well, OK, *one* best-selling

Book. He had something that no promo gimmick can outsell or overpromote. He had integrity. Want to motivate your people to greatness? Be a woman or a man of integrity. Abraham Lincoln said that "nearly all men can stand adversity, but if you want to test a man's character, give him power."

I have worked for men with zero integrity, and because of it I saw ethics, morale, and motivation crumble. I have seen that same organization resurrected to unbelievable heights because a man of integrity rose from the ashes to take the helm. Nothing—no seminars, motivational programs, or video series—will motivate your people greater than the knowledge that their leader is a man or woman with integrity, one who cannot and will not be bought, who will die before compromising his or her convictions.

So, do you still want to pattern your leadership style after Jesus'? It may take some soul-searching, but it is not an impossible task. Remember, good leaders know their strengths and weaknesses and are willing to make changes where necessary to become better role models. If you are going to follow a role model, why not go for perfection?

PRACTICAL TIPS

1. Perform a self-analysis and eliminate Fear Factor tactics you may be using.
2. Live as though all employees were going to pattern their lives after yours.
3. Evaluate your strengths and weaknesses when it comes to decision making.
4. Develop genuine interests in the lives of your people.
5. Become a servant-leader in everything you do.

CHAPTER 18

MARKETING: ADVERTISING YOUR COMPANY NAME, PRODUCTS, OR SERVICES

Doing business without advertising is like winking at a girl in the dark: You may know what you are doing but nobody else does.

—ED HOWE, AMERICAN JOURNALIST AND EDITOR

When business is good, it pays to advertise; when business is bad, you've got to advertise.

—AMERICAN BUSINESS MAXIM

Drawing thousands of people, the freakish beast of a man stood in the Israeli desert. He called himself John the Baptist. He was unshaven, dirty, and overbearing. He had no class, no finesse, and no manners. He yelled at those who opposed him, and many came long distances only to have this spectacle call them snakes and vipers. He ate locusts and honey.

What could draw so many to such an oddity? Between him and the crowd bubbled the river. It, like the baptizer, was unclear. As John lifted the hair from his eyes, he viewed the crowd for the One whom he had announced for months. Day after day he told the weary wanderers that One was coming whose sandals he was not worthy to remove. The crowd came now less to hear John and more to see this wonder he proclaimed.

Still holding up his bangs, John stopped. He stared, frozen. His eyes met another pair, and he began wading into the waist-deep Jordan River. The crowd's eyes turned to follow,

and they spotted another man approaching from across the
river.

"Is it Him?" "Could it be?" "He's not at all what I thought
I'd see." The crowd mumbled among themselves as John
silenced them with a raised hand dripping water.

"Behold! The One of whom I have spoken these many
months."

With this declaration, the public ministry of Jesus began.

—MATTHEW 6:1–4; 9:29–31; 8:4; MARK 1:44–45

Jesus had the most unique advertising/marketing staff
known to man. His name was John. This man had been drawing crowds in the desert, telling people that someone great
would show up soon. His voice echoed from one mountain to
the next, and with each return came more people. He captured
people's interest on a grand scale. Then Jesus showed up.

John announced Jesus' arrival in decibels even a deaf man
could hear. He called everyone's attention to Jesus and what
He was about to do. Follow that up with the miracles Jesus
performed publicly: men, lame from birth, rose from their
beds and walked; blind beggars received their eyesight; scores
suffering from leprosy had their youthful skin returned to
them. Jesus added fuel to the flame with His words and His
speeches. Jesus understood the principle of advertising, and
waged one of the most brilliant ad campaigns in history. He
managed to get His name before the public with an explosion,
and He has kept it in the public eye for two thousand years.

GIVE ME AN *A*, GIVE ME A *D*

What is the purpose of advertising and marketing? Can't a
product sell itself? Sure it can. Eve was the only woman in the
garden. It was a sure bet Adam would bite. But if you have any
competition at all, you are going to need to advertise the dif-
ferences and benefits of your company, ministry, or business.
Jesus did.

Advertising reduces the amount of effort you need to put into sales, because a sale starts long before the salesperson calls on the customer. Suppose you decide not to advertise. What is the customer likely to respond when you approach him or her to buy your product or service? Undoubtedly you will hear, "Who are you?" "What is your company record?" "Anyone I know ever buy your product?" "Never heard of you." "What are you selling again?"

You might argue that you have a great location. People know you are there. No need to advertise. Location is just an address, and unless you are selling real estate, it means very little in terms of acquiring customers.

Others will reason that they spend 10 percent of all they earn getting the word out through radio, television, and print media. I cannot recommend the shotgun method of advertising. We easily develop a fetish for complexity, and common sense in advertising demonstrates that simplicity is the better avenue. This was Jesus' pattern. If you are going to spend money to advertise, ask yourself what the best methods are (i.e., the simplest methods) to achieve maximum results.

JESUS' AD CAMPAIGN

Jesus had a marketing strategy that bears some investigation, and perhaps repetition, for your business. The first part of Jesus' advertising plan involved several factors.

PREPRODUCT ADVERTISING

Though we are not given specifics about the timetable, we do know that John the Baptist spent time announcing Jesus' coming. When Jesus finally appeared on the scene, all that remained was for John to tell the crowd that this was the One he'd been speaking of.

One of the most successful strategists in this area today is Disney. Buy any Disney video, and you are bound to be hit with whatever new product is in the works, to be released at a theater near you within the next few months. Movies will occasionally try it through billboards announcing the coming of another film. Look at your product line. What are you offering that you could capitalize on in this manner? Isolate one product or service that you think the public may not readily recognize but should. Formulate a plan to preadvertise it for a period of six months (yes, six months!). It must pick people's curiosity, grow in intensity, define a deadline, and direct them to a place. It must also be big.

The trouble with many small businesses is their failure to dream big dreams. So they place an ad in a little corner of the phone book or newspaper and hope someone will notice. They apologize for taking up space in someone's newspaper by printing the ad in black and white instead of color. Or worse yet, they print a full-page ad, then mess it up with line after line of ad copy no one will ever read. The oldest campaign strategy in the world is still true today: SIBKIS (See It Big and Keep It Simple).

HUGE BLITZ USING ONE MEDIA (NOT SHOTGUN)

The second strategy to success is to hit the marketplace using one media. Unless you happen to have a bazillion dollars to spend in advertising, you must make your dollars work expeditiously and economically. It is a waste to shotgun valuable advertising dollars all over the place. Jesus' strategy suggests that you concentrate your efforts. If you are worried about what magazine the ad will hit, what radio station it will play on and when, what bus system will carry the poster, etc., you will spread yourself too thin and lose your effectiveness. You can lay a nail down flat and pound with all your might till the thing goes into the board, or you can stand it up and hit it on the head. Both ways will get the nail into the board, but which is the better use of the hammer? Stay focused, and your audience is likely to also.

FOLLOW-UP IN THE FIELD

Once the deadline passes and the mystery is over, you must saturate the field with people and events to keep the item in people's minds. They must see your name, the company name, and the product every time they turn around. Jesus amassed huge publicity by traveling from town to town, often announced ahead of time. While there, He stayed in the public eye and withdrew only to refresh Himself. People knew He was there even when they couldn't find Him. It compares to having your company name sponsor little league baseball teams, walk-a-thons, and the like. Your name is visible, even if you aren't.

Follow through on this idea by performing community service. Work the soup lines for a day. Help those less fortunate. Sponsor a kid's club, community event, or public forum. The more you become involved in community affairs, the more respect and familiarity you will gain.

GOOD PRODUCT TO SUPPORT THE CLAIMS

The most obvious key to any prepublicity campaign is to have something worth advertising. Of course, the best marketing tool is a great product or service. You can advertise Edsels till you are blue, but without the goods to back it up you might as well forget being in business.

FROM MY MOUTH TO YOUR EAR

The second part of Jesus' marketing strategy has nearly been forgotten today, yet it is undoubtedly the best-selling method going. Let's say you want to buy a piece of complicated equipment, such as a laptop computer. Where are you most likely to go for advice? You could read all the ads in trade journals, or watch the ads on television, but after a while the thought will strike you that you may be getting sold a bill of goods. After all, they have to make a living at getting you to buy their brand. More likely than not, you will end up getting advice from a friend or relative who just bought a laptop and did the research for you.

As a business owner, you must seriously consider this scenario. As a seller of a service or product, how much influence do you think word-of-mouth advertising has on your new sales? My guess is that you will underestimate its value. The truth is that most new sales come from word-of-mouth recommendations, not from ad placement. As a seller, you do not have to sit by and hope it happens. The point is that you can put as much stock into a word-of-mouth advertising campaign as you do into a magazine or television ad. You must plan. You must be organized. The program must be thought through.

You've heard it touted since you began your business: "Word-of-mouth advertising is the best kind of advertising." Have you ever wondered why so few companies have learned how to harness it? You've heard the excuses: "It's not something you do, it's something they do, the customer." "It is beyond your control." "You can't make people talk about you." I disagree. People have to talk about something. It may be the weather, someone's marriage, some tragedy, a favorite song, Aunt Lulu's phlebitis. Why not get them to talk about your company, service, or product? The problem with all the arguments is that they are not arguments; they are excuses.

You can wage a complete word-of-mouth advertising campaign; it simply takes much more time than preparing a print or radio ad. Consider putting a word-of-mouth communications section in your next set of marketing plans. The results are greater, lasting sometimes for years, but the returns are slower in terms of sales response. Most businesses need a quick return on their investment, which is why few invest the effort. Jesus' only form of advertising was word of mouth, and the world is reaping the benefits some twenty centuries later. Name another ad campaign with those kinds of returns.

Once the message is established ("Garmonds' fravostats are quality," or "If you need a hemmulator, go to Garmonds"), the boss must decide whom to target. The point is this: the message is only as widely spread in direct proportion to the degree of secrecy it is supposed to hold. Jesus used reverse psychology. He performed a great deed, then told the people

He helped not to tell anyone. Jesus knew human nature. Tell someone not to tell, and they'll blow it every time. He did this repeatedly. You may want to target the industry you represent ("They have WHAT! How'd you find out?"). You may wish to zero in on financial institutions ("I never knew they had that much capital"). It may be directed to customers ("Do they really give you two if the first one breaks?"). You may want to reach the community using the press ("They closed the office to raise funds for a little girl's operation?").

After the initial phase is set in motion, and the secret has been released, you must closely monitor the results. The obvious is a market survey asking customers how they heard about you or your product. Track the increase in boxes marked "friend." You can increase effectiveness of the campaign by staging events in which satisfied customers rub shoulders with noncustomers. Circulate testimonials in newsletters, or print ads and mail them to noncustomers as well as customers.

Word-of-mouth advertising cannot build your business reputation alone. It works in conjunction with other advertising and community service. If you are doing no advertising at all (word of mouth, print, radio, TV, park benches, or whatever), you can be certain that you are not practicing the oldest and most fundamental tenets of business. And your business is the loser.

PRACTICAL TIPS

1. Avoid shotgun advertising and focus in on one major media campaign.
2. Preadvertise a product six months before it hits the market.
3. Fire most of your ad copy writers unless they learn to SIBKIS (See It Big and Keep It Simple).
4. Formulate and strategize a complete word-of-mouth advertising campaign.
5. Never invest in an ad campaign unless it can produce tangible, verifiable results.

CHAPTER 19

MOTIVES: VALUES AND INTEGRITY

I am proud of the fact that I never invented weapons to kill.

—THOMAS ALVA EDISON, INVENTOR

A verbal contract isn't worth the paper it's written on.

—SAM GOLDWYN, AMERICAN MOVIE MOGUL

As Jesus sat on the side of a mountain, He taught many things. He preached about love, hate, divorce, revenge, and giving. He sat with hundreds around Him. He saw the abuses of those in authority. He knew and felt the pain of the religious leaders who did not live up to their own laws, but who used them to their own advantage. He knew many by name, and He knew their weaknesses as a people.

The Romans had influenced this unique culture. From generation to generation, they passed down lessons, stories, and dreams. This was a verbal society for the most part. A man's word sufficed for an agreement. The days of proclamations, edicts, and written laws had come, but they meant very little. Man had added laws to the Law, and laws to the government, and he changed and broke them at will. The people saw it. So Jesus addressed it.

"You have heard it said from long ago," He began, "that you should not break your word. But I tell you," He continued as He walked through the crowd, "don't swear by heaven, or earth, or even by Jerusalem. Don't commit to have your head removed should you fail in keeping a promise. That is worthless. Rather, simply let your 'yes' be 'yes' and let your 'no' be 'no,' and let it go at that."

—MATTHEW 5:33–37

The problem of integrity extends well beyond our borders. The problem of integrity and value is worldwide. In my business, I deal with nations from around the world, and for the most part the people with whom I deal personally are upstanding and forthright in their business practices. But each of those clients can list a myriad of cases where their value system is unique from most of their culture.

A NATION OF HONOR

In the September 14, 1995, Fort Lauderdale *Sun-Sentinel* newspaper, an article by columnist Ann Landers reported a number of outrageous judgments passed down by government officials. In one such case, a man from Hollywood, California, faced misdemeanor charges for beating and choking his girlfriend and for strangling her pet rabbit. The courts charged him with both crimes. For beating and strangling his girlfriend the possible maximum sentence would be a year in jail and a $1,000 fine. For strangling the rabbit as an act of cruelty to animals: one year in jail and $20,000. If the courts place more value upon the well-being of a bunny than upon the welfare of a woman, how can we hope to do better?

Society hands us a set of values they believe we should embrace. Seldom have we ever seriously questioned the validity of those values, and we suffer because of it. Integrity in business is not an option anymore. Many people could not tell you what integrity is. Some will say integrity is being nice to your fellow man. They might tell you it is being honest. They might simply stare at you dumbfounded. I believe the best definition for integrity is this: Integrity is doing what is right and what is expected whether anyone else thinks it's right or expected.

Listening to customers and employees seems to be the business hot button these days. "Gather your staff about you," writers may say, "and hear what they have to tell you. Listen to their concerns. Listen to the customer and watch how your business prospers. Do it to increase profits. Help out the poor in your community to get your company recognized." Hogwash. Listening to customers and employees is useless without integrity as the reason and basis for doing it. You might succeed. Your company might prosper, but time will flush out your real motive if it is anything but honorable. We must learn to do business right because it is right, not because it will make our profit margins look good at the end of the quarter.

Hard work will get a company to the top. Integrity will keep it there. Billy Graham said, "Everybody had a little bit of Watergate in him," back in the days of that political debacle. He knew, as we all do, that it is against our natural bent to do right regardless of the outcome, to do right as the orator once said, "even if the stars fall." Perhaps you are one of the rare business partners who has no problem with integrity. Fantastic! Then would you read through this chapter and pass it on to someone who needs a little help in this area? Most people, I am convinced, do not want to do wrong. Most want to improve their people skills and want to become better people themselves. To do it, there must be internal changes. The beginning is to do the external things, yes, but to do them with the right internal motive. We must do business honestly and with integrity. We have some problems. How do we fix them?

I Meant What I Said

Human beings have an incredible capability of spotting a liar. Unfortunately, we seem to lose this ability as we grow older, which explains why the scammers take advantage of and prey upon the elderly first. Jesus set the example every day by being a man of His word. He did what He said He would do. He used an example in His teaching to illustrate the point when He asked the crowd about two sons. One said he would do what his father asked, but then didn't do it. The other son argued and said he would not do the task, but then went and did it. "Which of these two did as his father asked?" Jesus asked. The answer, of course, lies with the second son who obeyed and did what was right.

According to the best of our records, Jesus never signed a contract. He was a man of His word. When He said He would come, He did. When He vowed to heal someone, He followed through. There were no "to-from" memos by Jesus to cover His tracks, no reason to put things in writing or on paper, and no formal documents witnessed by a semicircle of people as we have today. Jesus was His word. The Bible speaks of Jesus in these terms: "In the beginning was the Word; and the Word was with God, and the Word was God." It does not say in the beginning was a contract or in the beginning there was a memo. The ridiculousness of it makes us laugh. Just the thought of a man of such value and integrity as Jesus needing to write things down seems ludicrous. Why can't we as businessmen and businesswomen operate under such integrity? I believe we can.

The first question you should ask yourself as an internal warning system is, "Why am I doing this, really?" By doing so, you will keep at bay impure motives; you will guard yourself from becoming one of the crowd; you will be a better person. It isn't easy to do self-evaluation for every policy in the works or for every contract about to be signed, but it will become a habit if practiced often enough. There are a number of areas you can question.

- Do you have integrity and value for your distributors, customers, products, systems, and services?

- Have you asked enough questions?

- Are your distributors treated equally?

- Do you prefer one over the others? If so, why?
- How do you think the other distributors feel about this? Do they know? (Who are you kidding? They know.)
- What about your customers?
- Which class of customer do you treat the best? Why?
- Why is the large-volume buyer treated differently than the single-unit buyer? Aren't they of equal value in your eyes? Why or why not?
- What can you do to raise the value level of the single-unit buyer?
- Do you deal honestly with your customers? Do you value them all equally?
- Are you giving them the best possible product money can buy?
- Is your product constantly quality checked? Against what standard?
- Are you checking it against itself or against a better product on the market?
- Would you use your own product? Why or why not?
- Is there any way to give the customer a better product than you are now producing?
- Can you do it without raising the sales price?
- Are you making an unreasonable profit margin?
- What about your internal operating systems? Do you have one set of standards for some people and another for the rest?
- Whom on your staff do you look forward to seeing each day and whom do you avoid?
- Are policies built around the ones you avoid?
- Is the discount system for your staff fair? Can it be improved?

- Is there a level of trust demonstrated among all employees, or just the "important" ones?

- To whom would you give the company key and from whom would you withhold it? Why?

- Have your employees been told to prefer one operating standard above others?

- Are your services the best you can provide? Are you cutting service to cut cost? Where and why?

- Is someone beating you in the area of service? How are they doing it? Can it be done and still maintain a level of integrity?

Introspection can be painful. Customers may not see the pain on your face, but they will notice it in other ways and they will recognize you for your valiant effort. You will be rewarded. We are judged more by our honesty and consistency than by our successes. I don't care how good your service or product is; if your customers, employees, suppliers, or distributors believe that you are ripping them off, you are destined to fail. It is a cosmic contract. Honesty pays. Good guys may finish last, but they can rest easier at night.

Whatever values or motives you operate by, in the end you must learn to live with yourself. Several years ago financial wizard and multimillionaire Donald Trump sold Paradise Island and all its assets to TV wizard and one-time entertainer Merv Griffin. Both held tight on the negotiations, and in the end it seemed that Griffin had gotten the better deal. Several months after the contracts were dry, Trump confessed to having taken Griffin for a ride. He prided himself on having won the deal to his benefit with a smirk. After watching an interview, I asked myself why anyone would be foolish enough to do business with such a character after that. Would you? Probably not. No one wants to be taken advantage of. No one wants to be dealt an unethical blow. We all want to be able to lay our head on our pillow at night with a clean conscience. It can be done. Just remember, they can take your possessions, job, and life, but not your honor.

VALUE STATEMENTS

Valuing people and operating with integrity are not options. These principles can be found throughout the words and actions of Jesus. There are a number of ways you can raise the value level of your employees. I am sure you can think of many more ways than these (and you ought to), but perhaps adopting these ten value statements will encourage you to do more in this area.

Value Statement 1: Employees are associates, not workers. More and more companies are seeing the value in making employees partners in the business. Sam Walton made the concept famous, and associate fever is spreading around the country. The difference between workers and associates is clear. Workers clock in and out; associates work until the job is done. Workers have no stake in the outcome; associates take pride in it. Workers do a job; associates have a career. Workers have no loyalty; associates own the company.

The owner of the Malden Mills company, makers of Polartec, understood this value statement. As the facilities went up in flames before Christmas 1995, the owner kept his word to the employees that no matter what, he would keep them on the payroll and rebuild the mill. He valued them as much as himself, and he backed his value up with a paycheck. That story is a true demonstration of making employees associates. You must find ways to make your employees associates in the business because employees are the business.

Value Statement 2: Employees are people, not personnel. This value statement seems silly to mention in a mom-and-pop operation. Five or six associates all reporting for work, living in a family-like atmosphere. But once the business grows to thirty or more people, this "we-they" attitude begins to infiltrate the organization. Soon the company hires a "personnel director." You may say out loud, "Come on, Zabloski, what do you expect me to call them—people directors?" The issue is not the title. Call them cattle prodders for all I care, but beware of depersonalizing your staff and associates. The issue isn't one of titles or positions but of how we value our people.

Value Statement 3: Recognition is the universal motivator, not money or perks, so we will do all we can to recognize integrity, quality, and achievement. Our company works on an incredibly lean budget. We don't have the funds for lush banquets or give-away cruises. We motivate ourselves into a frenzy at times, and management does nothing to stop it. Why would they? Most of our managers are masters at giving recognition for superior service or for employees who go the extra mile. Our advertising manager virtually cut her advertising budget in half just by taking the initiative and by having a what-have-I-got-to-lose attitude. She called her clients and, in her sweetest, nicest, most sincere Bambi voice, asked if they couldn't please reduce the cost of placing an ad for us. It worked! We recognized her for it publicly. The industry standard to produce book covers ranges anywhere from $3000 to $7000 per cover. Our art department produces a book cover for $350 to $750, and the quality is equal to those high-priced guys. Our editorial department receives dozens of letters about the quality of our books over the industry standard, yet our books sell for one-fourth the price of most titles. Our people work hard, and their compensation is minimal in terms of perks. But I do all I can to recognize these people and show them how much I appreciate them and their attitude.

Value Statement 4: Where there is trust, there will be risk. Where there is risk, there will be growth. We trust our people. We are still in a learning curve, though. I recently had a conversation with the man in charge of maintenance in our facility who complained a bit when my new assistant asked for a building key so she could come in on Saturday to catch up. He commented that so many people had keys to the building that it was out of control. I asked him to draw up a list of people we don't trust with company keys and give it to me so we could distribute it. I told him I thought everyone in the building ought to have a key. If people want to come to work and not get paid for it, who am I to say they can't? Even our president admitted to learning some new things when he changed the policy of turning on the air-conditioning for these wayward adventurers on Saturday. Sure it increases electricity bills. So what? If you trust people, they will not fail you. If they fail you, again so what? At least you will know you tried to do the right thing.

Value Statement 5: The loading-dock associate is as important as the vice president. Everybody has a job to do. Everybody has a job description. Some people make sure boxes are loaded and unloaded properly, and others make sure corporate accounts are serviced properly. The philosophy that the box handler is of less value than the contract handler is passé. Everyone in your organization has equal value. They may not get paid the same due to varying responsibilities, but all are equal. Beware of the attitude of the Pharisees who looked down with contempt on the lepers and prostitutes of their day. Jesus demonstrated our example. There is no room for a prima donna in today's workplace. Incidentally, to prove this point, when was the last time your vice president had lunch with the warehouse guys? Better yet, when was the last time he actually donned coveralls and worked side by side with them?

Value Statement 6: The warehouse washrooms are as clean as the office washrooms. This is not to say that the warehouse bathroom won't get dirtier than the office bathroom. By the very nature of the work involved, it probably will, but it ought to be as clean the next morning when everyone arrives for work. The cleaning crew (if you have one) ought to consider that room as valuable as others when tidying it up. We went the extra step in our facility. We gave our warehouse guys a carpeted, air-conditioned place to eat their lunches instead of having to sit on the dock bay dangling their feet in the heat. If they want to, they can come up to the company cafeteria and join the president for lunch. We strive to have a classless society in our business, and so should you.

Value Statement 7: We will give bonuses for associates as well as bonuses for management. How on earth can a corporation ask their people to be a team and still treat associates like second-class citizens? Are managers better because they wear suits and ties or heels and dresses? Do they deserve a bonus because they have a masters degree? How does one justify giving bonuses to one group and not the other? I'd love to hear it, because if we are to follow the teachings of Jesus and to follow His business strategies, we must treat everyone equally.

Value Statement 8: Managers are responsible too. I am constantly getting into trouble for stirring things up. Here comes this little bald guy digging around, looking under rocks for corporate creatures. I can't help it; it's my nature to strive for excellence and improve things. It should be yours too.

Recently I offered to help a coworker with a project. He needed to copy some information on large floppies down to the three-inch diskettes. He didn't have six diskettes or the time to go through the ropes to get them.

"What ropes?" I asked, hoping I'd just found another rock to overturn.

"Well, we're all computerized here. Everyone has a computer on his desk, but when you need one lousy diskette you have to fill out a form and hunt down the computer man in information services to get a diskette. It's like these things are the Holy Grail around here. I'm a manager, for crying out loud." On that note, he left. I had just discovered another roach under a rock, and with my roach-ridder hat and my best smile I headed down to computer services.

When I arrived, in the office sat the computer services guy and his manager, and the finance director as well. (Yes!) I popped in casually.

"Uh, excuse me. I have a question? Maybe you can help me. Can anyone tell me who the keeper of the diskettes is around here?"

"Yes, I am."

"Well," I smiled, "I've got a guy in charge of a million-dollar editorial budget who wants to know why he can't have access to a seventy-five cent diskette? Any answers?"

At this point the manager piped in, "People go through those things like water around here. They disappear if you just hand them out."

My smile turned upside down instinctively. Regrettably, I cannot put in print the rest of the discussion. Suffice it to say that everyone now has access to as many diskettes as they need because we worked through the problem and discovered that this regulation had been set many years ago due to ex-employees abusing the privilege. This poor guy only inherited the problem. Which leads us into value statement 9.

Value Statement 9: We will have no humiliating regulations. Ask employees what is the most demoralizing regulation they must tolerate. As with my diskette saga, you will find many areas of your organizational bloodstream that need to be tied off or rerouted. Until you dig, though, you will not find them. Until you ask, few people will volunteer. Everyone in computer services admitted that they really hadn't had time to investigate all the policies that developed over the years. You know how it is. One guy fifteen years ago did one stupid thing, and the company developed a policy about it. All those policies add up and soon become traditions, and traditions die hard deaths. Seek to rid your place of anything that demeans people. Eliminate all but the most crucial regulations and policies. Challenge everything; leave no stone unturned. The first time someone says, "We've always done it that way," send up flares and pull the fire alarm (not literally, of course). But use that as a signal and a warning that change is due.

Value Statement 10: We will live by our company bill of rights. Our company is still in the process of refining a bill of rights after fifty years in business. Some companies call them shared values. Others call them commitments. Whatever their title, your people must understand the values under which the entire organization will operate, and it needs to be in writing. I cannot give you a list here, because a bill of rights for a yacht building company may be different from a caterer or a church. However, the purpose of this book is to encourage you to develop your business around the infallible teachings of Jesus. I suggest you begin there. It is a two-thousand-year-old bedrock upon which you can safely build.

Why do you do what you do as a company? What are your motives? What are your values? Do you operate with integrity? Do you value everyone equally? Will you continually strive to do so? Jesus' teachings and example are not impossible to follow. The path of integrity is a bumpy and often difficult one. Often it will be easier to take the smooth route and cut corners or cheat here and there. Don't do it. Keep your motives pure. Raise your standards higher than the competition. Remember, the higher you raise your flag, the more likely people are to see it from a distance and be drawn toward it.

PRACTICAL TIPS

1. Vow to keep your word no matter what the consequences from this day forward.

2. Develop a recognition plan for large and small accomplishments for your staff.

3. Trust everyone in your organization or fire the ones you don't.

4. Find three ways to link up management with frontline associates.

5. Look at every single policy in place and evaluate its usefulness.

CHAPTER 20

NEGOTIATING: HOW TO NEGOTIATE PROPERLY

I'll make him an offer he can't refuse.
> —DON CORLEONE, *THE GODFATHER*

Let us never negotiate out of fear. But let us never fear to negotiate.
> —JOHN F. KENNEDY, 35TH PRESIDENT

As Jesus stood teaching in the temple, the crowd asked Him many questions about the law and life and God and man. The ever-present Pharisees stood in the shadows, waiting like black widow spiders to make their move. Question after question Jesus answered.

"He is one for answering questions, isn't He?" asked one leader to another.

"Umm, perhaps we should take advantage of this man's answers to embarrass Him in front of the people. Gather around," said another priest as the other priests formed a web around him. When they finished their huddle formation, the chief priest approached Jesus.

"Teacher," he said, "I have a question for You."

Jesus turned toward the leader. They stood inches from each other, and yet in spirit they were miles apart.

The priest continued, "Tell me, by what authority do You teach the things You teach? Who gave You this authority?" The other priests beamed with delight at the trap. They, the authorities, had asked a question. They, the leaders, demanded an answer.

"I will answer your question and tell you by what authority I act if you will answer Mine," Jesus responded. "Tell Me if you can: John the Baptist's baptism—was it from God or from man?"

At this the Pharisees regrouped into the shadows. They battled among themselves with various reasonings.

"If we say it came from God, the people will ask us why we didn't follow Him."

"Yes, and if we say it wasn't from God, then the people will hate us all the more."

"Indeed, they followed the Baptist and his teaching."

"Less than they follow this one."

"What do you say, great one? How will you answer him?"

They approached Jesus.

"We . . . we don't know," the priest said as he lowered his eyes.

"Then," Jesus retorted, "neither will I tell you by what authority I do these things."

—MATTHEW 21:23–27; 7:12; JOHN 19:8–12

Negotiating is a way of life for those in the Near East. It always has been. The art of haggling is not as well-loved here in Western culture. The value of negotiating is tremendous, though. Think about this example. When you negotiate the price of a new car, if you spent five minutes getting the dealer to drop $100, that amounts to making $1200 an hour. Pretty good hourly rates, I'd say. Yet we often back away from negotiating in business or in nonbusiness situations because we don't understand the dynamics of negotiating.

HOW TO WIN THE NEGOTIATING WAR

Jesus often answered questions with questions. A question demands an answer and puts the asker in a superior position. It assumes the one asking has a right to know. When the leaders asked Jesus questions, they felt they were in a superior position. Apparently, no one had ever used the question-for-question technique before because time and time again Jesus used it and time and time again they fell for it. One of the standard principals to starting negotiations is by asking the other party to name their best offer. Once they do, immediately follow up with, "Is that the best you can do?" Never accept their first offer as their final offer.

Jesus used another strategy in several situations: remaining silent. Again, this gave Him a superior position. In his mock trial, Pilate asked Him questions. Pilate was the civic leader. No one in government stood higher at the local level. When Jesus refused to answer, apparently the usage of silence so stunned Pilate that he is quoted in John 19:10 as having said, "Do you refuse to speak to me? Don't you realize I have the power either to free you or to crucify you?" Silence can be used to great advantage. It often makes the other party uncomfortable enough to add more information or to regroup and reconsider the offer.

I have been negotiating business contracts for ten years. I consider myself pretty good at it; so does my company or they wouldn't have kept me on. One idea I read repeatedly in manuals, training materials, and best-selling books is that negotiation is an attempted equal win-win. That, I believe, is a fallacy if not an impossibility. The bottom line to successful negotiation is reciprocity, not equality. Jesus' golden rule says to do unto others as you would have them do unto you. There is no follow-up to the statement indicating that all deals must be equal before they come to closure. You and the other party may strive to give each other the best possible deal, but experience has shown that someone usually gets a better deal than the other.

How do you do that? Make other people want to do it by giving them what they want and telling them how they can get it. Here's a true example. Every teenager wants to drive a car, and not just any car, but the finest car the road can display.

One father used that knowledge to his benefit. The father knew the value of reading and knew that his son needed to read more. So, he negotiated with his son and told him that he had created a recommended reading list for the fourteen-year-old. For every book the boy read and did a report on, his dad would put $10 into a car fund. If the boy read in style, he'd ride in style. The boy developed an insatiable urge to read! The dad got what he wanted by giving his son what he really wanted, and the dad told him how to get it.

STRATEGIES TO WIN

One negotiating idea I am learning is to *avoid letting the other party think they have something you want.* Approach them with the attitude of "Oh, well, I can see not much good is going to come from this, but let's go ahead with the formalities anyway." Don't look like you enjoy negotiating. There's nothing a good negotiator enjoys more than a wrestling match that takes forever to end. The more they see you liking it, the more they'll dig in their heels to resist.

Learn to see through the other person's eyes. Sympathy works wonders when negotiating. Saying "I know how you feel. I don't know how those guys can ask you to come to the table with those kinds of figures" often helps win them over to your side.

Stay strong. Jesus did not back down to the political and religious leaders. When Jesus stood before Pilate, He never backed down from His position of authority. This tactic made Pilate reconsider his position, and in fact, turned Pilate to Jesus' side. Pilate, who at first felt no sympathy for Jesus, later pleaded for Jesus' release. There are many ways to concede without looking like a weakling. Don't toss up your hands in retreat or surrender.

Stay calm. Not once in the four Gospels is Jesus ever shown as being anxious or afraid. In His day, there was much to fear: Roman soldiers, religious leaders, family position, incurable diseases, and abject poverty. Yet the one character trait people mention when they think of Jesus is peace. Jesus held His peace. While those chickens around Him had a lot of ruffled feathers, Jesus managed to keep His composure. This is critical to successful negotiating.

Be patient. He who masters time in negotiations can often use it wisely. Pauses can be used during conversation. It may make the other party nervous when there is a lull in the conversation. Pauses can be used during lengthy negotiation time in terms of days. Taking several days to get back to someone who needs the deal can be intimidating. Not advertising your deadline can be good, especially if they have one too. Push the negotiations to the edge if necessary, and watch for signs that they are approaching their deadline. They may bring others into the negotiations to hasten them, or they may add new suggestions or stipulations. Their eagerness to beat the deadline is a critical advantage you may consider playing.

Use your eyes and body language. Sitting with one arm over the back of the chair indicates an open position. Arms and legs crossed reveal just the opposite. Your partner may not know the signals, but intuitively the mind receives and processes them. Use your physical body to win negotiations through signals.

WHAT TO SAY AND HOW TO SAY IT

Most negotiation is verbal. As a result, you must develop a knack for saying the right thing at the right time, and this only comes with practice. I have been in negotiations where I could just kick myself for having said something that caused my partner to rear up and attack. Never try to back the other party into a corner. Doing so forces the situation into a stalemated win-lose situation, and the talks will end.

Help the other party save face personally and professionally. Remember that negotiations are seldom a one-time deal. Often you will renegotiate the same deal, or will open up a completely new one with that same person. You don't want to eat crow by having to apologize next time you deal with that person. Be kind to them. This isn't war; it's business. Negotiating isn't like opening one door and closing it behind you once the deal is done. It is more like opening one door and walking through it to another and another until you've created one long corridor that represents relationships you created over the years. You may want to return through those open doors some day, and the trail you blaze may lead some of the others in that corridor to negotiate with each other. They will have you to thank for that, and they will be indebted to you, which is not a negotiating strategy you plan for, but it is nice if it happens.

Let's take this idea a bit further. When things get tough, consider bartering something in the negotiations. Be perceptive and keep an open ear to the other person's needs. For example: one of our affiliates took the opportunity of offering a five-thousand-dollar printing job to someone in exchange for five thousand dollars worth of TV advertising time. He could afford the printing as it cost him much less than the bartered amount due to his other relationships and discounts. When it came time, he asked for a favor in return. If there arises a sticky point that seems to have no resolution, consider bartering a supply or service. Picture it as two people in a wrestling embrace offering to scratch each other's back.

Always try to give your negotiating partner more than one option. If you come to the table with only one way to do something or with only one solution or decision, then you fail at negotiating. The story is told of a man who fell off a cliff. As he hung from a branch that protruded from the side of the cliff, he called out, "Help! Help! Is anybody up there?" Suddenly he heard a deep, heavenly voice thunder out, "I am here my son. I will help you, but you must trust in me first." The man answered, "OK, OK, I trust you! Just tell me what to do." Then the voice said, "Let go of the branch." After a long, thoughtful pause the man called out, "Is anyone else up there?"

You know the old saying, "You can lead a horse to water but you can't make him drink." Well, one of the oldest negotiating strategies is to add salt to their oats to make them thirsty before you lead them to the water. When I know I have some serious and possibly long-term negotiations to handle, I will present something before the negotiations begin, something I know will interest them and that will probably be brought up later. Negotiating takes planning and replanning. Any soldier who walks into battle without sharpening his weapon first is just asking for a whipping. Think out your strategy long before the official negotiations begin and set things in place that will work to your advantage. Above all, *remain ethical*. Remember that the goal is reciprocity, not equality. Striving for equality takes too much time and is seldom, if ever, attained.

Don't hold out for the perfect deal. There is no such thing. Go for the best possible scenario for both parties. As I often tell my four-year-old son, Ross, "No one ever gets what they want in this world, and no one ever gets their way all the time." There are no ideal negotiations, just really satisfying ones. Do your best to make both parties happy, then move on. Here's what I've discovered about this principle. There is a law in business called the Law of Diminishing Return. Essentially, it says that no matter how fantastic the deal is, the service, product, or deal will begin to lose its luster in about ten days, after which the party begins to question its value.

The last point to consider when negotiating is to make the other side reveal their strategy before you do. Shakespeare wrote in *King Lear*, "Have more than thou showest; speak less than thou knowest." Jesus knew what strategic moves His opposition would make and knew how to surpass them. The Pharisees made accusations against Jesus, and Jesus answered the accusations with questions. (Bishop to Queen.) Pilate asked Jesus questions, and Jesus responded in silence. (Queen to King, check.) Pilate at the demand of the Pharisees proclaimed a death sentence on Jesus, and in response Jesus rose from the dead. (Checkmate.)

For humankind and for God, the first true win-win situation occurred, and everyone in heaven and earth benefited equally.

PRACTICAL TIPS

1. Set as your goal for each negotiation reciprocity, not equality.
2. In order to get what you want, try to give the other party what he or she wants.
3. Use time as a negotiating maneuver.
4. Answer questions with questions to gain the superior position.
5. Try finding ways to barter a service or supply as a part of the negotiation.

CHAPTER 21

PROMOTIONS: TRANSITION TIPS FOR NEW MANAGERS

It is easier to apologize than to ask permission.
—GRACE MURRAY HOPPER, U.S. NAVY ADMIRAL

As a manager the important thing is not what happens when you are there, but what happens when you are not there.
—KENNETH BLANCHARD, CHAIRMAN,
BLANCHARD TRAINING & DEVELOPMENT

The fame of Jesus' resurrection had begun to spread. He had appeared twice, and now on this third visit Jesus roasted fish with His disciples on the shore. The fire crackled as the fish were scaled revealing the true flesh underneath. Jesus spoke with all the men and then focused in on Peter.

"Peter," Jesus asked, "do you love Me?"

Jesus had asked the question twice before during the same meal, and now this third time Peter answered with a strength he had not shown before. Yet there was a sense of bewilderment in his answer. "Lord, You know everything. So You know that I love You."

Jesus said, "Then feed My sheep."

Peter grabbed a stick and inserted it into the fire. Sparks flew into the night air along with smoke. The smell of fish surrounded the men. Jesus, perhaps sensing the hurt in Peter's expression, put His arm around Peter to comfort him.

Jesus whispered to Peter, "I tell you the truth, when you were younger you dressed yourself and went where you wanted; but when you are old you will stretch out your hands"—with these words Jesus stretched out His hands in the same fashion He had done when He suffered crucifixion—"and someone else will dress you and lead you where you do not want to go."

Then Jesus stood and told Peter to follow Him. He had many other things to teach him to prepare him for his new position as a church leader. As Jesus and Peter walked, John rose to follow them.

Peter asked as he nodded his head back toward John, "And what about him?"

Jesus answered, "Don't worry about him. You must follow Me."

—JOHN 21:15–22

Few people saw much potential in Peter. His parents perhaps. His wife, maybe. Yet of all the people of that day, Jesus saw, believed in, and demonstrated what I call the Peter Potential. He had the uncanny ability to see beyond the obvious and to look at the potential of an individual. Because of what He saw, more is written later in the Book of Acts about the adventures of Peter than of any of the other men in that group. The Peter Potential took effect, and Peter lived up to Jesus' expectations. Peter moved from a subservient position to one who would later help lead the embryonic church. Jesus warned him, trained him, cared for him, encouraged him, rebuked him, and embraced him.

Many people have Peter Potential. They, too, have been warned, trained, cared for, encouraged, rebuked, and embraced. They may have been promoted to a new position as supervisor, manager, or even president. Yet, like Peter, perhaps they need some last-minute encouraging words to catch their attention before they head down the road of management.

You are reading this chapter for one of three reasons: (1) It follows the one you just read. (2) You are considering promoting someone into management and are looking for help.

(3) You recently became a manager and desperately need help. In any case, the following tips will help anyone get through the bumpy early stages of management and beyond.

Use your honeymoon period wisely. The law of promotions tells us that everyone has an opportunity to shine. Whether we are promoted to head cook and bottle washer or to president of the United States, every newly appointed manager has ninety days in which to prove himself or herself. Ninety days is just long enough for you to shake up the world before it settles back down. It is just long enough for your people to learn your idiosyncrasies and habits, and to learn how to circumvent them. Ninety days is also the end of your probationary period in most companies. If you blow it, there are no second honeymoons. This is peak excitement time for you and those under you.

Learn the traditions of the people you will work over and participate in them. Like Dorothy in the Land of Oz, you were dumped into a group of people who already have developed their own subculture. They have their ways of doing things, and they have their own traditions. Some are worth keeping. They probably celebrate birthdays as a group a certain way. Find out why and celebrate with them. That does not mean as a leader you become pals; it means you immediately take an interest in how they live their lives day to day enough to participate in it.

Change something—anything—right up front. People expect change from new management. In fact, they are disappointed if it doesn't come. It offers a new opportunity for life. Your group longs for a breath of fresh air. It matters not whether you change the way they address envelopes, the positions of their desks, the coffee-break schedule, or the use of the company vehicle; you must find something immediately to show that you are in charge as a recognizable leader.

Take the president's place in attitude and value. The president of your organization cannot be omnipresent. Jesus eventually left the earth, but He commanded His people to represent

Him and His work in His absence. You must take the president's place in both values and vision. You will have your own set of values and vision for your department, but you must be able to make decisions as if they were made by the head. To do that, you must first find out what those shared values are.

You are taking on a new role for which you have not been trained. Managers are the least trained-for positions in any company. We expect leadership to be intuitive and innate. It isn't. You must insist on getting some training in dealing with employee emotions, fights, schedules, and the like. In the absence of a formal training session, read everything you can get your hands on. Strain out the pulp and keep what you like, but subject yourself to as much help as you can get. You'll need it.

Now they're talking about you around the coffee pot. Remember when you were one of the gang, sitting around, talking about what an idiot the boss was? Well, now you're that boss, and now you're that idiot. If that hurts, then perhaps you are too thin-skinned for management. It is a near guarantee that soon you will pass several people huddled in a whisper who will either cease whispering or break up and go along their merry way when you approach. Chances are pretty good that they were talking about you. Rather than say to yourself, "Haven't they got anything else better to talk about?" you should consider yourself flattered that they have taken time out of their busy schedules to invite you to lunch, even if you happen to be the main course.

Staff must establish their positions. They have spent a long time snuggling up to the previous manager and settling in to a comfortable pecking order. Now here you come along and upset things, so they have to start all over again. There may be a tinge of resentment about having to go through this process by your staff. Just understand why they barrage you with needs. They are seeking their place in your eyes.

You will encounter criticism, loneliness, weariness, timelessness, loss of identity, unpleasant decisions, and worst of all, power. You will need an antidote for each of them. For criticism, develop a rhinoceros skin. For loneliness, draw intimate with your spouse and friends. For weariness, take some needed vacation time and leave town with no forwarding number. For timelessness, learn to prioritize and practice saying, "In a minute," "Later," "I'll be right with you," or "I'll get back to you." You might also try saying "no" and "not now" once in a while for good measure. For loss of identity, take up a hobby outside of the organization to which you can nail a plaque that has your name on it. You ceased becoming a person when you became a manager. Find something entirely you. To handle unpleasant decisions, seek out a friend to talk to, including God. To handle power, read how others handled it.

Your new job came because you did your old job so well. No one had any idea whether you could manage or not. You did a bang-up job at handling gizmos, so logic prevailed and someone suggested you must be management potential. Take heart. Like Peter, someone saw potential in you. Though you probably feel woefully inadequate to handle the task before you, remember that someone thought enough of you to give you a chance. Make the most of it.

Your loyalties must change. The times of loyalty to your friends in the gang are now passed. You are not the gang. You are management. Your loyalty must be to everyone on the management team, and to those above you in rank. Understandably, this change in mental affection will take time, but don't take too long. Your staff will likely challenge your loyalty right from the start by making critical comments about your boss or another management member, and you must defend them now or risk being seen as one on whom they can feed.

You can't afford to see them the same way. By the same token, you cannot see your staff as you used to. These are now people you have files on in your personnel drawer. These people have lost the rights of secrecy to you. Their salaries, goals, failures, family information, and work records are all open to your scrutiny. Because of that view, you will never look at them the same.

Remember that subordinates have needs. As much as you need to get a product out on time using cost effective methods, you must remember that people are your tool to accomplish that. People, specifically your staff, have feelings and families, disasters and triumphs. And they will bring all of that with them when they come to work. Be sympathetic and remember that this is not their life; it is their livelihood. When you find a staff member sitting at his or her desk crying, you will have to deal with those needs. When they ask for time off early during a critical project to take care of a feverish child, you may have to put their needs before yours. At least be open to emergencies.

Beware of people using you. Nothing will embitter you faster than finding out you had trusted one of your staff only to discover that he or she was using you. I trust it doesn't happen to you. Most people are honest and sincere. Always begin with that premise, but beware of a staff member who cozies up to you or who suddenly invites you over for dinner. You must learn to be part fox, dove, owl, and snake. Watch out for someone pitting you against another manager or the president. Don't get dragged into someone else's fight.

Empower your people. Do it immediately. Find things that they can do for themselves that they used to have the previous manager do. Let them make decisions after clearly explaining the boundaries. At first, you may have to let them fly tethered to see how they adjust to the power. But I believe if you give them the opportunity to soar, they will.

The first day I became a manager I told my staff that I believed strongly in empowerment. I did not want to, nor did I intend to, make every decision for them. Later that day, a staff member brought a purchase order to me. I told her to fill it out herself and don't bother me with trivial stuff. When it was later filled out, she returned it to me for my signature. I again told her to sign it herself. She hadn't been given that authority, she argued. "You just have," I replied. Without using the exact words, I told her that I trusted her enough to make decisions.

Beware of jealousy of other managers. It is sad to have to mention this, but it may be a pitfall in your organization. There may be someone in management who is jealous of your promotion. Worse yet, there may be jealousy on your part of another manager whom the boss seems to favor. For the first scene, I can offer little advice except to be patient. If you are the one dealing with jealousy, try to focus on the job you have to do and don't worry about the relationships. Jealousy will get you nowhere, and it will not spoil a favored relationship anyway. It only serves to make the jealous party look immature. Be mature and rid yourself of it.

Develop a favorable attitude toward those in charge. We all go through ups and downs in attitudes. There have been things you may not have agreed with. Decisions your boss made may have been poor in your estimation. You may have had a reprimand from someone in command and that is still eating at you. It is understandable. But you will not last long in a management position, nor will you be effective for those under you if you harbor a bad attitude about those in charge. It is for your benefit that you deal with your attitude and get on with a happier life.

Be willing to rule. Even under the team concept that I espouse, there comes a time when a leader must rule and a decision must be made. Someone has to split the vote and cast the deciding ballot. Someone has to tell the team to work an hour overtime this week to get a project done. While you should strive to be a leader, do not be afraid on occasion to be the boss. Don't apologize for it either. After all, that's really what you're being paid for.

Stand out from the crowd in attitude. You may have to fake this one, but you should spend as much time as is necessary working yourself into a positive, optimistic outlook on life and on the business at hand. There's not a manager who doesn't struggle with this, so you are in good company. The only difference between you and them is that they have mastered the art of developing a great attitude, and you have yet to learn the secret: when you've got one, you've got one; when you don't, you fake it.

Remain calm. This may come as a complete shock to you but you cannot do everything at once, on time, and to perfection. If you try, you will fluster yourself into a frothy panic. Do the important things, do them well, and then move on. My father used to tell me as a child to do my best. He expected no more of me than I could possibly do, and he expected no less of me than I could possibly do. Why should your standards be any higher? Do your best, but be like the duck on the water. Look completely calm on the outside, but paddle like mad underneath.

Don't be intimidated or ridiculed by past pals. Chances are, if you were promoted from within, 80 percent of the people around you were happy about it and 20 percent were ticked. They felt they deserved as much of a chance as you did. They may ridicule you or tell you that they really know you and all your problems. They may tell you that you're doomed to fail. Ward it off and see it for what it is: jealousy, envy, and a tad of disappointment. Your best course of action is not to address it, but to be such a phenomenal manager that they'll end up wondering why you didn't get the well-deserved promotion sooner.

Strive for success for your staff. Very early in your new position you should inventory your staff. Find out their individual strengths and weaknesses, and think of ways to make them successful by not only using the talents they have now, but using the additional training you intend to give them. Good management is not a demonstration of how successful you are, but how successful your staff is.

Find ways to make your staff's job easier. Ask them once a week formally or informally this question, "What is the dumbest/ most irritating thing you have to do in your job that you'd like to change." Evaluate it, and then change it if it has merit. The following week ask your staff individually, "If you could change one thing about how we do things around here, what would it be?" Then change it if you can after appraising it. Every time your people tell you something that bothers them, they are in essence highlighting areas that need improvement. Your job as a manager is to make improvements and to make things run smoother and more economically. Eventually this exercise, if followed through every week, will become more and more difficult as things get fixed. When that happens, you'll know you have made significant progress.

Show appreciation. I am a big one for praising people. I learned it well during my early days as an elementary school teacher. Praise works. Flattery doesn't work. Some managers operate under the assumption that praise is like a diamond; its value is due to its rarity. Hogwash! People need to be told that they are terrific and they need to be told it often. Praise costs you nothing and means everything. I used a number of phrases on homework papers, and they are still valid when I write them on complex business proposals. Don't overdo it. Always use an exclamation point. Feel free to copy them: Great Job! Thanks for the good work! I knew you could do it! Thanks for your help! Super! Good news! Thanks for the follow through! I knew I could count on you! Terrific! Wow! Perfect!

Remember birthdays and anniversaries. Either have someone do this for you or do it yourself. Write down on a yearly calendar the birthdays and anniversaries of everyone on your staff. Then buy a box of cards and fill them out one weekend with generic greetings if you're swamped with work. Sign it, seal it, and put the recipient's name on it. When the event rolls around, you'll have the card done and won't have to feel guilty for missing it.

Hit the ground running. Every new manager knows he or she is in line for the position. There is preparation time, research time, and meditation time. Whether the amount of time granted is long or not, you need to let people know you have arrived, and you need to make them glad you did. On promotion day or the day after, present your plan to the entire group, and begin a program of some sort that day that is uniquely yours. Most people take this advice as theory, but I also mean virtually hit the ground running. Give the impression that important things are happening with you in the office, so pick up your walking pace to a near run.

Fix small things right away (twenty-four hours or less). You need to learn quickly the difference between the big and the small things in your staff's eyes, and then solve the small problems quickly. This gesture makes you appear to be an authority with the answers, and it allows you to spend time adequately solving the big dilemmas.

Challenge everything, including all traditional ways of doing things. Be a maverick. Scrutinize, investigate, dissect, question, study, and challenge every detail of your operation. Hold nothing sacred because nothing in business is. Everything that exists in business can be improved. Make it your mission to improve what you can.

During the recent acquisition of our company by another, I spent time going over as many things in my job that I thought could and should be changed immediately, from the company letterhead to the locks on the building. Most of the things I recommended I had nothing to do with, and no one was offended that I know of. Let your creative juices flow. Don't take the attitude that if it isn't broken, don't fix it. Rather look at it more deeply, and you will probably find something that can be fixed.

The more you do for your staff, the less you supervise. Many managers find themselves picking up the pieces that their staff dropped behind, or feeling sympathy for the staff's workload and doing some of their work for them. You cannot afford the luxury of coddling people. You should help them do their tasks more efficiently, yes, but you should not do those tasks for them. If you have to do it for them, then you don't need them. Your job as a manager is to be certain they do their jobs. That's how you do yours.

Attend to the details. Business books emphasize that the job of manager or supervisor is to see the big picture and to leave the little details to others. I disagree. There are a number of things that as manager you cannot afford to let slip through the cracks. Take work hours for example. No one but you will be monitoring the salaried workers' office hours. It is a detail that, if not scrutinized, will quickly blow out of proportion. Before you know it, you'll find half your staff coming in late and leaving early every day. Watch the fine points as well as the big picture.

Keep flexible plans. Managers are off the clock because disasters often come at ten minutes before closing time. I try daily to set goals, and I work my best to achieve those daily goals. Some days I go home frustrated at seemingly not having accomplished a thing on the list. So I take the list, write down the things I did accomplish that day, and cross them off. Unless you find meaningfulness in the tasks you manage to perform, you will live in a constant state of frustration. Computers break down, clients show up unexpectedly, and people have emergencies.

Live by a daily planning sheet. I designed a personal daily planning sheet that works for me because none of the daily planners provided by other companies sufficed. I found my day filled with things to do, calls and faxes to make, and occasional appointments. You must plan—daily. If a commercial planner doesn't work for you, then create a custom-made one.

Spend early morning minutes planning. Once you have a planner you can use, then spend the first fifteen to thirty minutes of your day planning. Eyes usually widen when I say that, but twenty years of experience in this area bears me out. Early morning planning beats midday crises and late day boredom every time. Some items on your list will be a transfer from what you didn't accomplish the day before. Plan, prioritize, and prepare. Then get to work.

Give up some tasks you used to do. Along with your promotion trailed a few tasks from your previous job. It almost always happens. You find yourself doing everything in your current job description in addition to a few from before. Maybe you could not give up the sacred tasks that you loved so much. Perhaps you feel limited in your training ability or in your current staff workload. Forget it. You cannot keep doing what you did before while doing what you must do now and be effective. Take some time to ferret out the weakest, most mundane jobs you do (clerical tasks should be first on your hit list), and delegate them to someone else.

Know your limitations. He who tries to be all things to all people at all times cannot. She who thinks she stands the tallest is destined for the longest fall. Get ready for some difficult news: you cannot do it all. Stop trying to do the impossible. You are human. You need sleep. You need breaks. Golda Meir once said to another head of state, "Don't be humble. You're not that great." Meditate on that.

Management no-no's. There are five things you must avoid if you wish to be an effective and long-term manager: (1) Losing your cool in front of the group. Maintain your composure at all costs. You do not have the luxury of blowing off steam. You must be above such petty temper tantrums. (2) Inconsistency in moods. This applies to men as well as women. Ladies often bear the brunt of accusations of moodiness, but I have worked with men who were among the moodiest people around. Whatever your excuse, work on being levelheaded and sure-footed when it comes to your emotions. (3) Exclusive personal relationships with staff. I believe it is possible to have relationships with *everyone* on staff. Jesus did. Despite the writer of the Book of John stating that Jesus favored him, there is no real evidence that Jesus preferred one staff member over another. If He favored Peter, He certainly didn't show it by His words or actions. Beware of selecting out one or two persons and befriending only them. It breeds contempt and disruption. (4) Breaking a trust. This is a death threat to any manager's effectiveness. Your staff will trust you a little at a time. You are not free to share anything they tell you with any other staff member unless you have their permission. If you do, they will lose trust not only in your confidence as a friend, but as a leader as well. No one wants to work for a gossip, and, incidentally, things they may have told you before you received your promotion must also be buried. (5) Treating with inequality. If you appear to favor one employee over another, you will breed dissension. You cannot allow one employee to take time off to see his or her child's kindergarten program without allowing others. The situations may not be parallel. For example, Tony may ask why he cannot go to his sister's wedding, since you let Theresa go to her son's school play. Be aware that inequality opens up a Pandora's box of troubles.

So, there are my transition tips for you. Peter was not that lucky. All Jesus told him was to prepare for a horrible death and to love his staff until that day. Not much to go on really, but perhaps it was enough. Since Jesus told Peter the ending, anything else was unnecessary. You, on the other hand, do not know the ending, so you must be as prepared as possible for the trip in-between.

PRACTICAL TIPS

1. Develop a personal daily planning sheet and use it every morning.
2. Write down the birthdays and anniversaries of all your staff members.
3. Praise every staff member once a day.
4. List three new ways you can empower your people.
5. Review your tasks and take steps to eliminate several of them.

CHAPTER 22

SECRETARIES: PROFESSIONALISM AT THE FRONT DESK

We can lick gravity, but sometimes the paperwork is overwhelming.
— WERNER VON BRAUN, ROCKET SCIENTIST

Complicated equals ineffective.
— ANONYMOUS

On several occasions, people blocked the passage of those who needed to reach Jesus. As He traveled toward Jerusalem, parents, friends, and relatives—we are not told who—formed a band, gathered all the children in the crowd, and approached Jesus. They decided to ask Jesus to lay His hands on the children and pray for them. But as they approached Jesus, His disciples blocked their path. Jesus turned to the disciples and rebuked them, saying, "Let the little children come to Me. Do not stop them, for the kingdom of heaven belongs to ones who have hearts like these." Then Jesus heeded the request, and He laid hands on them and continued His journey to Jerusalem.

While on the way, the crowd swelled to enormous proportions. There was joy in the air. Shouts from hundreds of people declared the approach of Jesus as He neared Jerusalem. Those shouts were heard by two blind men who had no sight but had great voices. When they recognized the approach of Jesus, they shouted together above the din of the crowd,

"Jesus, have mercy on us!" Believing this was a time for celebration and not healing, the crowd tried to anticipate Jesus'
thoughts. They tried to hush the sightless ones. But the blind
men had nothing to lose, and they didn't care what the crowd
wanted. They wanted to see, so they shouted all the more,
"Jesus, have mercy on us!"

Jesus—the center of attention, the most important One in
the crowd—stopped to hear the cry of the beggars. Knowing
what they wanted, He still asked them, "What do you want
Me to do for you?" Those who blocked Jesus' way quieted
down to hear and learn.

"Lord," they pleaded, "we want to see."

Jesus granted their request, and they received their sight.
Then they joined the crowd that followed Jesus, a crowd
who, like the blind men, now saw things in a very different
light.

—MATTHEW 19:13–15; 20:29–34

At first, it seems a stretch to say that Jesus had receptionists
or secretaries in the same sense as we think of them today. Yet,
there are a number of ways in which the actions of Jesus' disciples and followers do compare to the job descriptions of
today's modern secretaries or receptionists. Much as in Jesus'
day, your receptionist is the client's first impression with the
outside world. Those children and blind men who came to
Jesus had to go through Jesus' entourage first. These men
handled Jesus' personal affairs such as lodging and food when
they were traveling, they intercepted visitors, and they handled the money for purchases. On most occasions, Jesus
trained them and then let them do their thing, but as in our
illustrations, Jesus sometimes had to call them into account.
He had to teach them a new way of thinking. So it is with our
secretaries, assistants, and receptionists.

Like Jesus, who understood the pain of the blind men,
sometimes we must put ourselves in the shoes of those who
seek us out. When you are away from your office, you should

call in occasionally to see how the receptionist or secretary answers. Ask your customers and clients how they are treated when they call in. Check your defense system. If you are too hard to reach, you might want to consider changing things to keep more in line with Jesus' style of operating.

IF YOU'D LIKE TO SPEAK WITH GOD, PRESS 1

According to that style, there should be no unapproachable employees or clients. That very sort of defense caused a young man to film a scathing documentary on one-time GM president, Roger Smith. *Roger and Me* formed a cult following of individuals who tired of the corporate bigwigs and their icon-like mentality. One cannot watch the film without being repulsed by the corporate mentality that classes are more important than customers. Jesus remained approachable to everyone, from Pharisees who hated Him and plotted His murder to little children who loved Him and played on His knee. Be careful not to give the impression that you are unapproachable, especially if you use your secretary or receptionist to give that impression.

Not everyone approached Jesus spontaneously. One elderly priest scheduled a midnight rendezvous with Jesus for fear of being seen by his fellow priests. Scheduling is certainly appropriate, but do it with some class. Remember that your secretary or administrative assistant is human and needs training. Not everyone is cut out for the task. I heard one businessman declare that secretaries have no ambition to become managers. That may or may not be true, but is that such a bad thing? Do you honestly want someone working for you who, you know, is out for your job? There are a number of qualities you ought to look for when considering an assistant, regardless of whether the position is for receptionist, secretary, or administrative assistant.

QUALITIES OF A REALLY GREAT
SECRETARY/RECEPTIONIST

They must be talented and capable. The Broadway play and movie version of *How to Succeed in Business without Really Trying* contains a song titled "A Secretary Is Not a Toy." I should say not! He or she may be the most important asset in the development and success of your career. Hire one wisely, and hire the one with the best skills available.

They must be detail oriented. You don't want to retell every major step a task needs. You need someone to whom you can give an assignment and know that every detail will be followed through regardless of whether you listed them all or not. They will think through and see through the entire assignment.

The best kind of secretary is a devoted one. I don't mean in the puppy-toward-its-master kind of devotion. I mean that your secretary ought to defend you in time of need to and in front of others. He or she ought to recognize your moods and deal with them accordingly. You need a secretary who will sense the stress you are under and will sympathize. If you have such a devoted person on your staff, treat him or her like royalty because they are hard to find. Show your devotion in return as a boss.

The most helpful secretaries have a good memory. Just days before the blind men incident, Jesus rebuked His disciples for blockading Him. So you'd think the disciples would have remembered the lesson and then jumped to the aid of the blinded and ushered them to Jesus. Not so. They had short memories. Good assistants should have good memories. Occasionally, you need assistants who remember that they have an address from several years ago that you're looking for. They know exactly where to find it too.

Organizational skills are a must. You cannot afford to have an administrative assistant who can't find an important document. That person is wasting two people's time. Look for and develop skills that help with scheduling, correspondence, and filing. Good secretaries know that filing is not for storage; it is for retrieval. They know that the papers they file have the potential of being pulled in the future, perhaps in the far future, and will need to be able to be found quickly.

But a secretary also knows that the more you file, the more that can be used against you. With that in mind, this person knows the value of not filing as well as the value of filing. I'm not advocating covering up illegal activities. That option is completely out if you plan to follow the teachings of Jesus. I am saying that some things simply need to be gotten rid of immediately. Some inappropriate comment to a peer about an employee could land you in discrimination court if written down and filed. File business papers. Keep the rest to yourself.

Eighty percent of the paper we file is never used again. Train your secretary to think in terms of one-fifth. All you need is one-fifth of what you have. Clean out your file cabinets and whittle the saved documents down to one-fifth their size. Then have your secretary do the same thing to her personal files. Get rid of your paper glut. You'll drown in it. When I took over my first management office, I found files about previous correspondence dating back thirty years! I cleaned house, pleaded ignorance, threw away four-fifths of the files, and never looked back. Want to know something? I have yet to have any need for what I disposed of.

In this age of wild computer capabilities and storage, I am still amazed at the amount of paperwork we generate. The paperwork for a Boeing 747 weighs more than the plane itself. As a tactile society, we need paper. We're addicted to it. We need to feel what we see lest our eyes deceive us. Though we must deal with paper, I say the less of it, the better.

The secretary or receptionist you need must be emotionally mature. There is nothing wrong with hiring a young adult. Many of them are mature for their age, but those are the exceptions. Of course you can't discriminate because of age.

That's not only unwise, it's just plain stupid. Many young people have as much to offer as older employees. What you must look for has nothing at all to do with age; it has to do with internal attitude. Look for an assistant who demonstrates responsibility and follow-through, and perhaps shows some class. Those things are a bit undefinable, but you'll know them when you see them.

Finally, your assistant must have a trainable spirit. I have seen bosses bossed around by their secretaries as if they were children being nagged by their mommies. They probably deserved it, but I wouldn't recommend a steady diet of that. You need someone who will come around to your way of thinking. You are, after all, the boss. When you need to add another skill, you need someone to jump on board and go along. I suppose that was the most difficult thing Jesus had to deal with in His disciples. They were slow to learn. Jesus often repeated Himself to get through to them. It does get tiring.

PHONE ETIQUETTE 101

OK. Jesus never used the phone, but He certainly was a master communicator; as such, He set the example for us. You also want someone, male or female, who has good phone etiquette. I am appalled how many businesses never train their employees, especially the frontliners such as receptionists and secretaries, on how to use the phone. Every staff member should be trained in some basic ought-to-do's and ought-not-to-do's that I believe are plain old business common sense. Train everyone (not just those we're discussing here) on these basic phone rules, and I believe you will see a dramatic rise in customer satisfaction.

The phone should never ring more than three times. Never. Something ought to pick up, even if it's voice mail. Four rings tell a caller that you're not serious about business.

Compose yourself before answering. Maybe you just got out of a heated discussion and the phone rang. How will you answer? "HELLO! WHAT DO YOU WANT?!" Even if you're working on a proposal, stop a second and take a breath. Then pick up the phone.

Smile. Yes, smile while on the phone. I know it sounds silly, but the voice at the other end can tell. Singers will tell you that smiling while delivering a song often affects the tone and delivery of the piece overall. Smiling will change your attitude about how you answer and how the rest of the conversation goes.

Say hello and introduce yourself. Don't you hate it when the party at the other end of the line picks up and says, "Luigi's"? Even worse is hearing a gruff "Hello." How about calling a department store and getting "Draperies"? Don't these people have names? Be sure that when people answer the phone, they introduce themselves. That suggests the other person do the same and generally makes them feel warmed into a conversation. Conversation leads to sale and sale leads to . . . well, you know the rest.

Concentrate on the use of voice quality, tone, and expression. Don't tell; train. Send the receptionist to drama school. Suggest the person take speech classes and music classes. There are entire companies dedicated to training your staff to properly speak on the phone. Use them. They're worth the money if it increases sales and builds relationships.

Rarely put anyone on hold, and always ask permission first. Never let a client sit in "hold purgatory" for more than thirty seconds. Pop back in and tell them they haven't been forgotten. If you must transfer them, then be sure to transfer right the first time and tell who you're transferring to. That way they won't get bounced around from person to person, and they'll know where they were supposed to go if they get cut off in the process. Give your receptionist and secretary (maybe all staff members) a guidebook of who does what in your company to reroute calls better.

The phone can be a help or a hindrance to business and to our lives. This is one area Jesus never had to worry about. But

He did have to deal with communication problems, organizational problems, and staffing problems. True, Jesus never actually hired a secretary, or had to deal with telephones, but He also never had many of the things we have today to help us manage our businesses. What He had, however, were timeless principles upon which we can base our operation. He had wonderful organizational skills, something the busy manager must have to succeed. If those skills are lacking, then he or she needs the second best thing—a secretary.

PRACTICAL TIPS

1. Think of three ways to improve your secretary's skills.
2. Encourage your secretary to enroll in speech or drama classes.
3. Provide phone etiquette training for the entire organization.
4. Follow the rule of one-fifth filing and clean out your files.
5. Teach your secretary when to run interference and when to let you be accessible.

CHAPTER 23

TEAMS: BUILDING PEOPLE AND SHARING INFORMATION

All for one, one for all.
—ALEXANDRE DUMAS, FRENCH NOVELIST AND PLAYWRIGHT

We're all in this alone.
—LILY TOMLIN, COMEDIENNE

The stone-walled room had one window, which allowed a beam of light to penetrate through and touch the dirt floor. Flickering dust particles jumped into the beam, then disappeared into the darkness. The shuffle of feet kicked up more dust. Someone ruffled his robe, and the dancing particles became a mob in the shaft of light. More than a dozen men and a handful of women sat still and stared at the beam of light. A slight whistling could be heard from the fat man across the room as he breathed through his nose. In the near quietness, they saw themselves in the beam.

They were in hiding. Some time had passed since they left the hillside where Jesus had disappeared, ascended into a cloud as witnesses reported it. The Roman government had had enough of Jewish rumors, Jewish insurrections, Jewish uprisings, Jewish disobedience, and Jewish intolerance. The prisons and dungeons were filling up with captured insurrectionists. The catacombs were filling up with hiding insurrectionists. This group now sat quietly awaiting their fate.

For three years they had followed Jesus. They listened as He spoke parables. They watched as He performed miracles. Some left families to follow Him, and some families joined them now in hiding. From different walks of life they came. From different philosophical teachings they melded into one. Next to Simon the Zealot sat his new brother, Matthew the tax collector. Three years before, Simon and Matthew would have been enemies; now Simon sat with his arm around Matthew's shoulder in a darkened room.

Who could have foreseen this? Was it fear that brought them all together into this one room? No, fear could only bind them for a while. Other groups bound by fear had long ago dispersed. This group stuck together because of Jesus. They stayed together because they held secrets that no one else held. They snuggled arm in arm in a darkened room because they had become what they never thought possible— a family. Though only a few of them were actually blood related, they knew they were brothers and sisters. They were friends, allies, compatriots, and kinfolk. That this diverse group became a knitted family was perhaps the greatest miracle of all.

They saw themselves in the dusty beam. Once in darkness, now in light. Once chaotic, now following one cause. Hiding in the shadows, but piercing the darkness like a sword. They awaited their fate, but they did not fear it, really. They were happy to be a family and a team. They had a purpose as individuals and as a group. They had a message to spread. Little did they know as they stared at the beam that the message of Jesus would penetrate the world and forever change it.

—ACTS 1:13–14; MATTHEW 10:26–27; 13:11–13

The idea of becoming a team player frightens most Americans. Ours is a culture of individuality. People are afraid that teamwork will make them invisible or anonymous. They fear they will lose their identity. They will lose their purpose if shared with others.

Other cultures, particularly the Japanese, have built a reputation and an empire upon the concept of teamwork. We have this idea that the Japanese have always operated by this principle, but that is not so. Actually, the teamwork concept in Japan began in the 1960s when Dr. Kaoru Ishikawa combined the theories of W. Edwards Deming and J. M. Juran to form what is known today as quality-control circles, the basis for team programs. He wanted to find a way to get the Japanese workers' hands on the transistor radios they were producing, and to recommend and adopt changes for their betterment. Those of us who were around then will recall that the label "Made in Japan" meant cheap price and poor quality. In less than thirty years, the team concept propelled Japanese industries from a bottom-line laughing stock to a major force in the world market. They went from twenty team circles in 1962 to more than one million teams comprised of more than ten million workers in the mid-nineties.

WE'RE NUMBER TWO!

Jesus long ago understood the concept of building and developing a team. He was a master at it. He knew how to take twelve incompatible personalities and make them think and feel as one. Teams accomplish more. Team companies perform better, generally produce better products than do their nonteam competitors, and individuals within the teams prosper and develop a sense of purpose more than do individual employees competing with each other.

Call them what you will—quality circles, employee involvement groups, quality teams, productivity teams, winners' circles, idea groups, or progress groups—the concept behind the group theory has worked for millennia. As with many of the teachings and concepts of Jesus and as the old saying goes, "What goes around comes around." Wisdom comes full circle.

Team concepts are innate. An ancient Israeli story tells of a man who went to heaven and discovered all the people had casts on their arms locked in a straight position. *How horrible!*

he thought. *All these people will starve to death if they cannot feed themselves.* Then God answered him saying, "In heaven, we do not feed ourselves. We feed each other." The Israeli kibbutz teaches this concept to their children as well. Boys live together in cottages where they learn to develop team spirit. Their required clothing has only buttons down the back, so each child is dependent upon the other to button his shirt for him. Children understand the meaningfulness behind teams. We, as adults, need not go to such extremes to teach teamwork. A good example comes from Oceanside, California.

Mr. Alter's fifth-grade class at Lake Elementary School made headlines when the boys in the class decided by themselves to shave their heads. They did so, without embarrassment, because one of their own, Ian O'Gorman, developed cancer and had undergone chemotherapy. His hair began to fall out. To make their friend feel at home, to feel one with the crowd, all his classmates agreed to shave their heads (with their parents' permission) so that upon his return, Ian would not stand out from the class. No one would know who the "cancer kid" was. The teacher, Mr. Alter, was so moved by the spirit of his class that he too shaved his head.

Mr. Alter's class leaped the chasm of friendship that day and became a family. The family unit is the strongest bonding agent known to man. It surpasses money, fame, or fortune. Tortured prisoners have survived decades of misery with only the hope of seeing their families again. Soldiers braved insurmountable odds to return to their loved ones. People will live and die for their families. It is no surprise, then, that Jesus strived to change His pack of misfits into a family team. Once He accomplished that task, He could leave the earth in the care of "the church" with the knowledge that neither the Roman empire nor the gates of hell could prevail against it.

BUILD A FAMILY TEAM

Therefore, as you build your organizational teams, bear in mind that your ultimate goal is to develop them into family units. Teach them using family ideals. Use family terms whenever possible. The more your team looks and acts like a family, the tighter the bond will be. Whatever name you choose to give your teams, perhaps the best one would be "family team."

Modern organizations are flattening out their corporate structure. Without knowing it, they are moving from huge pyramid layers to simpler rectangular structures. The family is essentially a flat, rectangular flow chart. Under biblical precepts, there is a president (the father), the vice president (the mother), and the staff (the kids). All the kids are equal and can answer directly to Mom or Dad, but on occasion final decisions may be deferred to Dad. Lest I be misunderstood, I am not saying that structure alone builds an organization, any more than structure alone makes a family. There are many homes with a father, mother, and kids who have no team spirit whatsoever. They need common goals.

Even common goals alone do not build a family. A family (or family team) might know they have goals, but until they internalize the goals and burn them into their soul, the unit will be weak. A family team may have two of the four requirements down (the goals themselves and the mutuality of the goal), but they will fail without two other conditions: (1) the family members must know that they have a contribution to make toward the outcome, and (2) they must know that if their family succeeds, they succeed too.

I laugh at corporations whose presidents and CEOs write books about what tremendous teams they have developed, then mention how they traveled in the company jet or on first class to some destination. Think of the family when building a team. True, Dad and Mom drive the car, but *everyone* rides in the same car. Multibillionaire Sam Walton of Wal-Mart fame was renowned for riding coach class when he traveled because he wanted to relate to his people. Unless every member of the team can ride in limousines or expensive luxury cars, management should ride in Buicks or Chevys or Toyotas. Even billionaire Ross Perot drives his own midrange Oldsmobile. Jesus walked everywhere with His staff, though several times they tried to crown Him king and would have willingly carried Him.

You cannot develop family teams as long as you have a bunch of have-nots, are-nots, and do-nots in your organization. What do I mean? Look around. Does your company have an executive dining room? How about executive bathrooms? Private phones in managers' offices? Are there closer parking spaces for management than for other employees? Worse yet, do the spaces have someone's name on them? Is there a spirit of elitism? Are there those who have and those who have not? What about degrees? Are those with masters or doctorates elevated above the high-school graduates? Is the boss's son more important than the other employees? What about friends of the president's family? Are there those in your organization who are important and those who are not? How about chain of command? Do some employees have the authority to overnight a package to a customer while others do not? Are some staff members empowered to find solutions while others do not have the authority? Do some people take hour-long lunch breaks while others do not? Do some members unabashedly make personal phone calls during office hours while others do not? These things must be conquered and eliminated before an organization can truly claim it has mastered the family team.

Family teams help decrease egomania and multiply brain power. Ten heads are better than one (except in government). Teams decrease the likelihood that one ego will rise above the others. At one point during His ministry, Jesus sent all His disciples out by twos. The underlying reason, I believe, was to prevent any single person from developing a proud spirit for the miracles they had the power to perform. It kept them humble. It also doubled their effectiveness, more than if they had gone out separately. Finally, it reinforced them to think in terms of teams. True, later each of the twelve did separate and work individually, but virtually the first thing they did once they reached a particular destination was to add to "the church."

There are at least seven ways to build a functioning family team. These concepts are at work in the home and can be implemented to build family teams at work.

1. The atmosphere must be warm, relaxed, and informal. Team members must be comfortable enough to figuratively kick off their shoes and feel at home around the others.

2. Everyone participates in the discussion, even the shy ones. Everyone has an opinion and every opinion is valid.

3. Disagreement is permitted and even encouraged. It has ground rules, but a difference of opinion or an objection to someone else's is freely expressed.

4. Personal attacks are not permitted.

5. Everyone listens.

6. Decisions, for the most part, are by consensus.

7. No group leader can dominate the group. He or she is merely a facilitator or a traffic officer whose job it is to keep things on track. He ensures that everyone has the information they need to work as a team.

THERE ARE NO SECRETS AROUND HERE

No one was more brilliant at sharing information than Jesus. He managed to speak to thousands in such a way that only a handful knew what He meant while the other bunch went away thinking they knew what He meant. He was a master at giving away inside information. He spoke in parables (stories with hidden meanings). At times He had to explain the meaning behind them to His staff, but no one could ever accuse Jesus of withholding information. He laid it all on the table, and anyone who had ears to hear, if they wanted to, could hear and understand.

This business of keeping things from staff members is not only archaic, it is reprehensible. It destroys the family team concept. When families were going through the Great Depression in the 1940s, everyone in the family knew they had twenty cents left to spend. They all pulled together to help the family survive. Secret office memos and clandestine meetings are the bane of teamwork. Nothing will deflate teamwork faster. In 1946, employees at General Electric held a crippling strike. Secret information had leaked to the employees. Rumors piled upon facts. Relations executive Lemuel Bouleware reported to upper management that "somewhere, somehow, the employees got the idea that they were in the driver's seat." He withheld information from employees and stockholders until the dam blew up and nearly toppled the corporation. He never learned, despite his years in business, that unless you share information with employees they will react. If you withhold information, they will make something up. And what is made up is always worse than the truth.

Secrecy is bad. I reiterate often in meetings I hold with my staff that there are no secrets. The people under you are not idiots. They deserve to know. What you fail to tell them will hurt more than what you do tell them. Secrecy implies three things to your staff. It either tells them that you think they are such fools that they cannot be trusted with information—that you are so much better than they when it comes to loyalty—or it warns them that the secrets you hold are so horrible, so unimaginably wicked, that you dare not tell them for fear of the outcome. In any case, noncommunication and secrecy breed contempt and disharmony. Communicate everything you can. The more they know, the more they will understand and care. Like a family, if you can get them to care, they will unite; nothing will be able to separate or stop them.

I admit it. I'm a maverick when it comes to this. It probably stems from my years as an underling, as one of those kept in the dark by management. If I shut off a light for every time I heard an employee say, "Why don't they just tell us?" the world would be groping in darkness. Be a risk taker. Go the extra mile. Put your private payroll on a list, and post it on the company bulletin board. (I heard you gasp!) The reason you did is because either you're getting paid too much and you would be embarrassed if others knew, or they're getting paid too little and that embarrasses you. Would it cease being an issue if everyone in the company made thirty-two thousand a year? It is something to think about.

Consider this also: Your organization has one fate. If it goes down, then everyone goes. When a major surgical supply company took a downswing and started laying off people, secrecy became the operating standard. No one but insiders knew what monster approached, until rumors spread and leaks occurred. One employee transferred in good faith from the headquarters office to south Florida. He sold his northern house and arrived at the new facility only a few weeks later to find a pink slip awaiting him telling him he'd been laid off. In story after story, secrecy surfaces as one of the major reasons companies go into turmoil. Of course, other factors complicate matters, but the escalation of the problems might be lessened if enough information is shared with enough people who could do something about it.

The family team concept works well if team members are willing to let others take the credit. Jesus taught this concept well in the city of Cana when He changed jars of water into wine at a wedding feast. He did the work. He performed the miracle, but when the guests approached the bridegroom to comment on the excellence of the drink, Jesus let the wine steward and bridegroom take all the credit. I have a plaque on my office wall that says, "There's no telling how much good a man can do if he doesn't care who gets the credit." People desire an occasional pat on the back, and even though a brilliant idea may have come from one of the team members, credit should go to the entire team. They must learn that they are making a contribution, not a monument.

How does one go about setting up effective family teams? It isn't easy. Management cannot demand that teams operate functionally any more than a judge can insist a jury come to a consensus. Nor can true family team spirit develop overnight. It takes time and a record of success before the idea catches on. Just remember these seven guidelines to forming teams, and your success rate will increase.

1. Membership should be voluntary. This is not the military. You are trying to build a family unit. Human beings gravitate toward success and relationships. Once the naysayers see the bond between members of the team, they will yearn to join in and be part of the group.

2. Teams must in some way develop the abilities of the individuals in them. Any team organized for the sole benefit of the organization (for example, to reduce the budget) will ultimately fail. Even team members will demonstrate an occasional what's-in-it-for-me attitude.

3. The team concept must be fully endorsed and supported by all management levels. It's impossible to create a thriving team if one or two managers are against the idea. Management must agree and be supportive through the entire process.

4. Creativity should be encouraged. No holds barred. Teams should hold regular brainstorming sessions using round-robin contributions. A round-robin session means that each team member spews out ideas in rotation. One idea per person is given, and if someone draws a blank, they merely defer to the next person in line. No idea is laughed at or rejected. The sky's the limit.

5. Team members are trained in the art of problem solving. Management will provide whatever tools are necessary to make the family team concept a success.

6. Teams will be comprised of no more than eight to twelve people per group. Group leaders are to act more as "error-traffic-controllers" than as bosses. They keep the team on target.

7. Teams are discouraged from becoming a bunch of yes-men, or from evolving into what the 1960s termed "group-think." They must learn to function as one without becoming clones. Work toward developing unity rather than uniformity.

After studying the team concept, I can tell you that while it is not easy, it can be done. The results speak for themselves. Teams reduce the error rate. They increase employee involvement and increase company cohesiveness. They build friendships and develop leadership ability. Teams encourage creativity and improve communication.

Is it any wonder why Jesus chose to build a family team instead of developing soloists for His church? He understood the dynamics of family teams and spent three years of His life developing them. Two thousand years later, every single day, somewhere around the globe another one of His family units—called the church—is birthed based upon the principles He taught.

PRACTICAL TIPS

1. Set the ground rules clearly when developing family teams.

2. Locate and eliminate the have-nots, am-nots, and do-nots in your company.

3. Establish a policy of information sharing that destroys secrecy.

4. Determine to get the job done regardless of who gets the credit.

5. Beware of and restructure teams showing signs of evolving into "group-thinkers."

CHAPTER 24

TIME: PRACTICAL RULES FOR TIME MANAGEMENT

I'm going to stop putting off things starting tomorrow.

—SAM LEVENSON, COMEDIAN

He slept beneath the moon; he basked beneath the sun; he lived a life of going-to-do; and died with nothing done.

—JAMES ALBERY, ENGLISH PLAYWRIGHT

Jesus told many stories to His disciples. Some they understood, some not. He met with them near the end of His life to tell them the parable of the ten virgins, or maidens. They were to wait for the announcement of a bridegroom. The disciples understood that when a Jewish young man wished to marry, he spent time building his house. When he had finished it, he would then dress and parade over to the house of his bride. The thrill of the wedding day rested in the notion that no one knew the hour or day when his house would be finished, and so the bride must always be prepared for his coming.

As Jesus taught, His disciples discovered that this particular parable contained great joy and great sadness. Five of the bride's maidens had planned. They bought enough oil to keep their lamps lit for as long as it took the groom to prepare his house. Five other maidens, however, did not supply enough oil. They thought they had all the time in the world, but as

Jesus continued His lesson, He emphasized the sad part of the parable.

The foolish attendants called out to the five who had oil, "Lend us some of yours. The groom comes and we are out of oil." But those who planned for this time, and who used their time wisely in preparation, declined. "No, there may not be enough for any of us if we share. Go out and buy some and come back before the groom comes." So the five who wasted their time and resources fled into the marketplace, but in the meantime the groom came for his bride, and he, the bride, and the attendants went in and celebrated, locking the door behind them.

When those foolish five returned with oil in their lamps, they found the bride's home deserted. So they went to the appointed place of the wedding feast but were turned away. This parable Jesus concludes by telling His disciples, "Therefore keep watch, because you do not know the day or the hour."

—MATTHEW 25:1–13

MY, HOW TIME FLIES!

Time is the enemy of all of us. It is the only gift that can't be returned. It must be used and spent, and once spent, it is gone. Every living human has the exact same amount to spend: 1,440 minutes per day, 168 hours per week. We spend 19 years of our lives working, 23 years sleeping, 7 years eating and drinking, and 10 years doing recreational activities. We spend 4 years battling illnesses (it may seem like 10 to a spouse!), and 2 years will be spent dressing and undressing.

Our world is learning to utilize time better. Books can be published in less than ten days. You can get eyeglasses and photos in an hour. A letter can be faxed across the globe in seconds. But commuting to work, now that's another matter altogether. The average American spends more than 157,000 hours on the road commuting to and from work in a lifetime. To put that into perspective, he could drive around the globe six times and still have some miles left over to pull into a few fast-food places.

Out of all the time allotted, essentially you can break it down into three kinds: higher, lower, and optional. By that I mean that someone above you, such as your boss or civil authorities, will demand your time. Those lower than you positionally (working subordinates, children) will demand your time and the rest is up to you (optional). There is very little you can do about the spending of higher time, so I will focus in on the time over which you do have control.

After studying the Bible for a number of years, I discovered that Jesus mastered time as no other. Not a minute seemed to be spent in idleness or confusion. He knew He had but three years to accomplish what He needed to. Like the dying cancer patient, Jesus knew that every moment mattered. Yet, you and I act as if we had all the time in the world. Think of your life as a three-act play. Examine it right now. You do not know this moment whether you are in the beginning of Act 1, Scene 2 or if you are now playing out the final scene of the play, do you? The key to life and managing time is knowing that managing time means managing yourself. It is less important to know what scene you're in than it is to know how well you played the scene. That is what time management is all about and why it is so important. Play it well and people will remember the grand finale, not the few missed lines.

TIME'S A' WASTING

The good news is that everybody everywhere wastes time, so you're not alone. The bad news is that the excuse "everybody's doing it" is as weak now as it was when you were in junior high school. Most people have no idea where their time goes, and as a result, have no idea how to snatch it back. People manage to waste time in the most incomprehensible ways, but these few suggestions will give you some idea of where your time is most likely wasted at work.

Waiting until every job is perfect. I work in a publishing house with people whose natural bent is to ensure that every *i* is dotted and every *t* is crossed. The world comes to an end when a book comes back from the printer and a quotation mark is missing. There is a line where excellence crosses over into perfectionism, and once crossed, time becomes a wasted resource. How many times have you found yourself waiting for something because the one you are waiting on wants it to be perfect? And while they perfect the thing, you wait.

Waiting for ideal conditions. Not only do you find yourself waiting for the ideal proposal, you may also find yourself waiting for the ideal condition. "I'll talk to Framholz when the time is right," you may say to yourself. "Let's wait until the market is just right to launch this improvement," someone else may offer. In comedy, timing is everything. In business, you take it when you get it and you use it when it is available. Pauses in comedy accentuate the punch line, but pauses in business can kill momentum.

Waiting for equipment. How many years of your life will have been spent waiting for the copier to be repaired, waiting for a telephone call to come through, or waiting for the fax machine? Technology is great, but it can hold you hostage if you let it. Count the number of times in a month when you go to use the copier and find someone else in line making seventy-two copies for another department. You crinkle your paper a bit and return to your desk, only to return a half-hour later to find yet another copier hog doing a job that could have been done before or after office hours.

Waiting for ASAPs instead of deadlining. You do this one to yourself. You send a memo or a note to someone and then ask them to act on it and get back to you as soon as possible. They interpret your ASAP to mean "Adjourn, Stall, and Procrastinate." It isn't nearly as important to them as it is to you. Since you obviously don't need it by a specified date or time, "as soon as possible" gives them liberty to take as much time as possible.

Procrastination. Put off till tomorrow what you might have done today. That's the maxim of a sluggard. Old Pa Kettle used to say, "I'll fix the fence, Ma, soon as Crowbar gets the time." Meaning never. We procrastinate because we anticipate the outcome to be worse than it usually is. Seldom do people procrastinate the easy things. We like doing the easy things. After all, if a thing can be put off indefinitely, it must not have been that important to begin with, right?

Meetings. The biggest, unavoidable time waster in the corporate world is meetings. The reason they waste so much time is because often they are not organized, structured, and punctuated with a beginning and ending. We approach meetings much like we do our ASAPs: we end them "as soon as possible," which is never very soon. Time is wasted going to meetings, waiting for meetings to start, the meeting itself, chitchat after the meeting, and walking back to real work after that.

Doing or redoing subordinate's work. If you have a parent's love for your staff, you will find yourself doing their science project for them instead of letting them struggle through it themselves. Many managers face this dilemma. Perhaps you wrestle with the knowledge that you can do the thing in half the time, and you won't have to redo it if you do it yourself. What a great boss. Freeing up all that time for your employees so they have nothing to do. Soon you find yourself swamped with your work and work others should be doing.

Failure to delegate. Managers who take everything on themselves fail to see what a waste of time that is. You must understand that you cannot do it all by yourself. Super Boss, you're not. Even Jesus delegated tasks to His twelve because He chose not be everywhere all the time. The more you give others to do, the more time you will have to do things you ought to do.

Rifling through clutter. One of my previous bosses had a sign on the wall that read "A clean, uncluttered desk is the sign of a sick mind." It was humorous and was used on more than one occasion for not getting things done. If you find yourself digging through piles of junk, books, and stuff on your desk to get the information you need while holding someone up at the other end of the phone, or if someone waits in your office while you open and close file cabinet drawers, then you are wasting two people's time. That is a double sin, and it is inexcusable. Managers, even the creative type, do not have the option of being disorganized.

Reading junk mail. There it sits. The offer of a lifetime. You just can't pass it up. So you open it and read through lie after lie hoping to hit paydirt but wasting valuable time all the while. The latest gimmick being used by catalog sales companies is to use loose-leaf flyers instead of bound catalogues. It takes twice as long to read through it and is more difficult to just chuck away in one fell swoop. The typical executive gets more than 225 pieces of junk mail every month! Who has time to read it all?

These are all bad habits that can be broken. Your time is the most valuable commodity and possession you own. You may have gotten into a habit of wasting time; you can get out of the habit with a bit more work. Philosopher William James said if you sow an action you'll reap a habit; sow a habit and you'll reap a character; sow a character and you'll reap your destiny. Is this wasting of time the destiny you would have chosen for yourself? Do you feel good about how you use your time? Would you change how you use it if you knew you were now at the end of act 3, scene 3? How do you know you aren't?

HOW DO I GET THE TIME BACK?

The hardest part of managing your time comes from learning where your time is spent. To be honest, I hated doing what I am about to tell you to do. I excused it away saying I didn't have time to do it. But unless you are willing to undergo a painful incision, you will never have the cancer of time wasting removed.

Create a time log so you know how, when, and why you're losing time. Some management consultants would recommend doing it for a month. I find that a bit extreme. I believe you will see a pattern begin to emerge after only one week. It need not be a complicated log. Don't waste valuable time designing it. That's the very thing you need to avoid.

The log I use is quite simple and is divided into two one-week steps. The first week, use a notebook to write down every activity you do during a workday, and I mean *everything*. Include the exact number of minutes that activity took from start to finish. Don't make it fancy; make it accurate. For example, try something like this.

6:00–6:10.   Awoke.

6:10–6:30.   Showered, shaved, dressed.

6:30–6:50.   Ate breakfast while watching the morning report on TV.

6:51–6:55.   Kissed sleeping wife (well, I'm embellishing it a bit).

6:56–7:30.   Drove to work.

7:30–7:45.   Read my mail from yesterday.

7:45–7:50.   Wrote in my to-do list.

7:50–8:15.   Interrupted by so-and-so, discussing computer problems.

You get the idea after that.

The second part of the log is taking the information and analyzing it. Take a piece of lined notebook paper and draw out six columns. The first column can be smaller than the others. At the top, title the log "My Personal Time Inventory." Down the first column list time in half-hour increments from 7:00 A.M. (or whenever you usually awaken) through 10:00 P.M. (or whenever you usually go to sleep). The next five columns represent Monday, Tuesday, Wednesday, Thursday, and Friday. Transfer the information from log 1 to log 2. When possible, simplify. All phone calls simply become "phone," and all meetings become "meeting." Now evaluate your log. Where are the time wasters in your day? Can they be eliminated? Are the things on your list related to your personal and professional goals? Which ones aren't? Which of the things on that list could have been delegated away? Who or what is taking up the majority of your time? How can you rearrange your schedule into better blocks? One manager told me after using this method that he had no idea he was spending so much time listening to his voice mail. Another felt guilty for his frequent trips to the coffee pot, but added that "getting coffee is like fueling a car; no organization can run effectively without it!"

Find pockets of wasted time in your schedule and use them. Listen to tapes while commuting to work. I spend forty minutes a day going to work and another forty coming home. Many commuters buy, rent, or borrow audio tapes from libraries to listen to during those hours. Some people double up and use a car phone to make last-minute decisions. Why not read during down time in airports?

Work at home in the morning. I don't do it as often as I would like, but the times I spend working in my home office from 6:30 to 8:30 have been among the most profitable in my career. Why? The world is asleep and can't disturb you. No interruptions, no calls, no faxes, no mail to look at, no problems, no questions. Just pure, unadulterated, profitable work. If your business allows flex time, consider using this as an alternative. Jesus set the example for us. Several times the Bible mentions that He sought a solitary place to pray before the sun rose. I'm not suggesting everyone do that (though it is a great way to start your day), but to note that prayer *was* His business and that He did it early in the morning when He could be alone and productive in it. The best part of your day may not always be the earliest. I am much more of a morning person than an evening person. Find your peak performance times and schedule important work around them first.

Kill the television. Pull the plug. Put the idiot box out of its misery. I will try not to get on a soapbox, because there are some human beings who still feel television has some redeeming value to humankind. But I would wager that none of them are successful, independent, productive managers, or business owners. Rather than downing an unpalatable diet of junk the TV producers want to hand you, why not digest a book you've been dying to read but never got around to? There must be dozens of how-to books that would do you a world of good. It is sad that good men and women who would otherwise never tolerate vulgar language and silly behavior in their offices will go home and allow the tube to insult their intelligence with brainless, purposeless situation comedies.

I'm not saying you should deny yourself the World Series or a great football game now and then. Honestly, now, wouldn't your life be richer if you actually went to a football game with your family or friends instead of sitting in an easy chair nodding off? If you are going to purposely waste time, at least do it wisely.

Kill the telephone—twice. I am convinced that if a group of world leaders chose your home to confer about how to solve world peace, and the phone rang as the decision came down to the wire, you'd probably get up and say, "Just a minute, let me get that." You would return to the conference with the news that "Suzie's at Cindy's and won't be home until she gets her homework done."

Perhaps I exaggerate, but not by much. I have been in counseling sessions, business meetings, family outings, you name it, and have been interrupted by the phone. I cannot recall once ever having returned saying, "Boy, I'm glad I took that call." It is bad enough that we allow the ringing of a bell to interrupt our lives so dramatically, but it is worse that we allow some telemarketer to rule and ruin our day trying to sell us on a product we neither want nor need. Even Alexander Graham Bell had the telephone removed from his home later on in life because he found his own invention to be a nuisance, and he didn't have to deal with sales calls. Put the answering machine on if you must let the phone ring. But don't waste time jumping up to answer it, and don't waste other people's time putting them on call waiting.

Speaking of time savers, if your company has installed voice mail, by all means utilize it. Beware of the message you leave, though. Don't promise to return calls if indeed you have no plans to. If you find yourself inundated with messages, delegate some of the simpler responses to someone else if possible. Most systems have a forwarding option that allows you to pass calls on to the appropriate person. Voice mail, when it works right, can save you hours of listening to unnecessary calls.

Prepare tonight for tomorrow. Most people spend a lot of time picking out their clothes in the morning, hunting through the couch cushions for toll money, looking for their car keys, making their lunch, finding pens that write, and so forth. Preparation is the better part of working smart and saving time. When you think about it, Jesus spent thirty years of His life preparing for the next three. Prepare the night before, and the next day will go smoother. My wife is fantastic at that. With two toddlers, she learned to be organized and to get ready hours before the scheduled event. To this day I know I could never manage to get done all that she does and still maintain an active social life. I believe preparation is the answer.

Live by a to-do list. Be sure to prioritize your to-do list. The mistake managers often make is not in neglecting to list their tasks but in failing to prioritize them. They assume that if they accomplish something, then they should feel productive. When a major project sneaks up on them, they wonder how it happened. The answer lies in lack of prioritization. The big project was number sixteen of their twenty things to do. Get in the habit of using a to-do list, but don't forget to prioritize it.

Decide whether to do a task, not when. Every task you list may not be one that requires your doing it. Look over your work schedule and see how much of it can be lateraled over to another employee.

Cease linear tasking. Most managers do task after task rather than trying to accomplish more than one task at the same time. The problem with assembly-line jobs is that no one can work on installing the dashboard until the guys up the line have finished hooking on the doors. In some circumstances, linear tasking is necessary, but many of your jobs do not depend on others, nor do they depend on a previous step being finished before it can move on. It is possible to type while talking to someone. It is feasible to brew coffee while warming up with vocal exercises. You can read a book while soaking in a bathtub. Find areas where you can double up on activities to cut time spent.

Eliminate piles. A pile, by definition, is more than twelve sheets of paper. I knew a manager who prioritized his piles. Rather than deal with them, he labeled stacks of papers as hot, lukewarm, and cold. By the time he even got to the hot stacks, they were really cold. He became a paper shifter rather than a doer. The safest way to deal with piles is to take the bottom third of a pile and trash it. You'll never get to it anyway. If that isn't feasible, then file it. If that won't work, then deal with it. Piles are embarrassing. If you are a piler, you probably walk into your office with papers on your chair or taped to your computer screen. Do you know why? Because people don't want to get stuck in a pile. They want help immediately, and the pile syndrome tells them that they will be forever lost unless they get your attention some other way.

Clean your desk at the end of every day. There's nothing like coming in to a fresh, clean desktop every morning. It isn't always possible, I know, but it does help. Even if you only put away the pencils, rulers, pads, and straighten everything up into organized little (dare I say it?) piles, at least it will be easier to manipulate in the morning.

Use form letters and paragraphs. Personalized letters are impossible for any business of size, and people are asking too much to expect them all the time. Use form letters when appropriate. If you do write a bang-up personal letter, save it.

There may be parts of it that can be used in another letter sometime.

Cancel low-priority appointments. This time saver is not popular, but it is worth mentioning. You may find yourself having to meet someone you'd really rather not spend time with. It happens to all of us, but life is too short to spend it with someone you'd rather not. Don't insult them by being bored in their presence. Schedule such meetings with another employee better suited, or cancel the thing altogether. I had an agent repeatedly attempt to set up an appointment with me, and I finally had to let him down gently by telling him that I don't do business with agents so there was no need for us to meet. We had nothing to discuss. Cold? Perhaps, but I could not afford to take half a day's work meeting to discuss a dead-end topic. I already knew the outcome. As a manager, sometimes you must simply cut the cord.

Learn to say no to requests. The reason most organizations don't want a bunch of yes-men or yes-women in charge is because they soon become overwhelmed doing everyone else's work but their own. Say yes often enough and people will come to you in droves ready to dump their work on you. Say no on occasion and people will respect you for your strength. Then when you do say yes, they will believe you really mean it and want to. Saying no gives greater value to the yeses.

Cluster outgoing calls during the day. The president of our corporation said to me that he hates voice mail because he knows when he calls that people are sitting there and don't respect him enough to pick up his call. If I knew it was him, I would pick it up. If managers are to rise above the phone's mercy, then one way to do it is to group your calls to be returned once or twice a day.

Set meeting principles. Pass out agendas one or two days before the meeting. If possible, list members who need to bring information or who are responsible for related agenda items. List the approximate time given for each agenda item, as well as a beginning and ending time for the entire meeting.

Then stick to it like a sergeant. That will keep the topic of bonus plans from straying too far into vending machine items.

Request readable, understandable, and useable reports. I am a self-admitted numskull when it comes to reading financial reports. No two are alike, and they are generally next to impossible to decipher as far as I'm concerned. Why should you be held hostage to fumbling around with an 11x17 green-striped smudgy report when you'd rather have it on 8 1/2 x 11 paper? Why waste hours of valuable time searching for information that might be at your fingertips if only you could find it? Ask those generating such reports to make them the way you want. Don't be held hostage. Are you a boss or not? If you can't use the thing, change it. If it can't be changed, get better equipment. If those generating it won't change it when they can, consider dismissing them.

Time is precious. Something so important should be given its due respect. Some time ago, an unknown author wrote these words of wisdom regarding the importance of time.

> Take time to work—it is the price of success.
> Take time to think—it is the source of power.
> Take time to play—it is the secret of perpetual youth.
> Take time to read—it is the fountain of wisdom.
> Take time to be friendly—it is a road to happiness.
> Take time to dream—it is hitching your wagon to a star.
> Take time to love and be loved—it is the privilege of redeemed
> people.
> Take time to look around—it is too short a day to be selfish.
> Take time to laugh—it is the music of the soul.
> Take time for God—it is life's only lasting investment.

Jesus knew the value of time. In that regard, there is much we can learn from Him. Time is life's greatest treasure. Once the treasure is dug up and used, it cannot be buried again. Perhaps of all the business principles we can learn from Jesus, this one is the most poignant. We must reflect on those five piercing words of Jesus and apply them as best we can. The words? "The time is at hand."

PRACTICAL TIPS

1. Eliminate or change any piece of technology that causes you to waste time.

2. Find ways to schedule meetings to use the time wisely.

3. Delegate as many tasks as you can to free up time for yourself.

4. Commit to logging your time next week to ferret out the time wasters.

5. Prepare tomorrow's work tonight. Continue the habit.

CHAPTER 25

TRAINING: DEVELOPING PEOPLE

If I had eight hours to chop down a tree, I'd spend six hours sharpening my ax.

—ABRAHAM LINCOLN, 16TH PRESIDENT

I never let my schooling interfere with my education.

—MARK TWAIN, AUTHOR AND HUMORIST

The crowd of twelve hundred pushed and shoved their way toward Jesus, each wanting to touch Him more than the next. Hands clutched and yanked His robe; voices pleaded with Him. Day and night the crowd pressed and demanded and took. Even for Jesus, it was overbearing. His twelve faithful saw the strain on His face. One man noticed a large boat on the shore, and, dashing from the crowd, all thirteen entered it and pushed away from land. Several men found oars and paddled the boat into the deepest part of the lake.

Bartholomew, seeing his Teacher lying in the bottom of the boat asleep, gently covered Him with a fishing canvas. All were silent. "How peaceful," one whispered.

"The sea?"

"No, Him."

"He has barely slept for two days now. Let Him sleep. He has earned His rest. No matter what, let's allow Him to sleep. Agreed?" They agreed. No matter what.

Into the deepest part of the sea they drifted. The water grew darker, as did the sky. Black, rolling, rumbling clouds threatened the would-be sailors. Jesus heard none of the thunder. He felt none of the rain they shielded from His face. The tossing of the five-foot waves did not awaken Him. The tempest raged into a monster storm. Waves crashed on the tiny vessel. The men felt fear as never before. Fear was cold, and dark, and wet. It was here.

One yelled, "How can He sleep through all this?"

Another, "Perhaps we should wake Him!"

Yet another, "No, our vow. Remember. If He sleeps, then let Him sl—" He was silenced as a wave slapped his face and filled his mouth with water, choking him. Over his own coughing he heard, "Thomas! Give me your hand!" and saw the young man reaching up from the water as two men pulled him back into the boat.

"All right, all right!" shouted Bartholomew. "Let's wake Him."

"Jesus!" one yells but inches from His ear. "Jesus! JESUS! Don't You care if we drown?" A wave knocked the shouter to his knees. Jesus flung the tarp off His shoulders and stood. He looked at His men and held both hands into the stinging rain.

"BE STILL!"

The wind subsided, and there was dead calm. The storm had stopped by two words from one Man. He said one more thing before settling down again.

"Why were you afraid? Do you still not have enough faith?"

—MARK 4:35–41; MATTHEW 23:4

Jesus' twelve disciples (or staff if you will) were in training. Every moment of every day, for three or so years, they learned. As we all do, they learned by listening, watching, and, at times, by doing. True, Jesus was a great Teacher, yet some remember Him more for His acts than for His messages. It is no mistake that the book that follows the life of Jesus is called the Acts of the Apostles, not the sermons. It is a testimony of the kind of training Jesus employed and the impact it made in their lives. Jesus' style of training is an example for us all.

As a CEO, supervisor, manager, or leader in an organization, it is your responsibility to see that your staff is trained to do the tasks you assign them. You are only as good as the people you train. If they are unfit for the job, it is likely they were unprepared for it. You may have inherited an untrained staff member, but it is your responsibility to see that he does not remain that way. Just remember that training is not a quick fix, nor is it a cure-all to your problems.

Look at it this way. When we were born, God gave us a key ring. For every situation we go through, we get another key to put on it. As the ring fills up from training and experiences, we learn which keys to use for certain situations. Most people are fumbling around in the dark trying to find a key they might not even have—or do have but they haven't used it in so long they can't find it.

So it is with training. People grow based on what they learn, but most people don't know they are learning something so they feel they are not growing. Training should be a process, not an event. Training, it seems, is more formal than in the days of Jesus. They learned on a raging sea. We learn in a classroom setting. They learned by listening on a hillside. We learn by watching a video series. They learned holding fish and bread. We learn holding pencils and spreadsheets. They learned informally. We learn formally. Their training was free. Our training costs a bundle.

Because of all the factors involved in a training program, many supervisors avoid it. It takes time. It takes talent. It takes money. Essentially, by not training employees to do the job right, we train them to work carelessly, to waste time, and to cover their mistakes. If you don't train, you train regardless. So it is not a question of whether you will train, but a question of why and how.

WHY TRAINING?

Perhaps the first question to ask is this: How do I know when an employee needs training? Drastic as this illustration seems, evaluate it in these terms: if someone held a gun to the employee's head and told him that his life depends on whether or not he can do this task, could he do it? If he can, then he doesn't need training, only sincere motivation. If on the other hand he would die before completing a task correctly, then the time is ripe for training.

The second question to ask: Does this person's work overlap with someone else's? One of the most difficult perspectives in training lies in the blending between two job descriptions. Often one person will hand a nearly completed job to another staff member who works on it and returns it. Employees often interface daily, and their jobs follow suit. It is possible in these blurred areas to consider peer training.

The final question to consider before training: Are you about to train for something that is nearly obsolete? The first formal training I received outside the classroom took place in a computer lab where I promptly learned (and forgot) the necessity and usage of computer cards. Remember those cards with the little rectangular holes punched out? By the time I finished the class, about the only thing those cards were good for was to make Christmas wreaths. So evaluate whether you are training employees to do something that the industry may be phasing out or that your company may need to redesign. Never train before asking whether the item to be trained for can be altered, improved, or eliminated.

Even after your staff is trained, never send them out prematurely. By that I mean, Jesus trained His staff to oversaturation. He trained them until they could do His work in their sleep, and then He sent them out. He cut them loose only when He felt assured they could succeed.

That is the sole purpose of training, whether formal or informal—to make the one being trained successful. It is not to increase your bottom line, nor is it to make the trainer look good. There is little value in training for the wrong reason, or in doing it poorly. When you do a poor job of training, time is wasted. Then there is the question of whether to retrain, possibly making you look silly, or of letting the poorly trained employee stumble on his own. Most of the time we do not repeat training, and we excuse it off to time or money. The truth is, inevitably it will cost you in both time and money to repair the damage done by not training correctly in the first place. Most managers, I'm afraid, would rather blame the employee for "not getting it" than to admit they really blew the job of training.

Are there any valid reasons not to train an employee? After jogging my brain for weeks and reading dozens of books, I came up with a whopping two reasons. First, never train someone to promote them up or out. Is that cantankerous employee giving you indigestion? Have you said to yourself, "If I train him, he might qualify for the position in Ted's department, then he'll be out of my hair for good and in Ted's"? Wrong reason. Training, remember, is for success, not promotion. The second wrong reason is to prove a point. Finance tells you that you must reduce costs (what else?), and to do that you need to improve work habits. They suggest one area in your department ought to be eliminated, so you train more intensively to keep it. Not only have you trained for obsolescence; you did it for the wrong motive.

With the philosophy that you should only train for success, there are three basic reasons for training. They are so obvious that I won't expound on them: (1) The employee can't do the job properly without it, (2) the employee can do the job but not well, and (3) the employee does the job incorrectly.

GET ON THE TRAINING TRAIN

Joe's been pretty irate at Ira the last few weeks. He told Ira twice how to line up the gingleys for the packaging department, and now Sam, the chief packager, says the gingleys are still coming in crooked. Embarrassed and angered, Joe finally blows his top. He marches into Ira's office and says, "For the last time, Ira, all you need to do is put the north end south and the south end north, flip the red button twice, the green button once, call Mabel and tell her the gingleys are on their way, and then fill out a purchase order for the residuals. Got that?"

Chances are Ira only got something about buttons and Mabel and north. Joe never learned the difference between telling and training. *Telling* is best reserved for lectures, sermons, occasional speeches, and eulogies. *Training* requires a mental trip back to kindergarten and a usage of the oldest teaching method known to managers—show and tell. Training must be carried out with as much excitement and wonder as you experienced as a kindergartner showing others how to use your new toy. You showed everyone how the red button did this and how the switch in the back did something else. It is likely you passed it around for all to see, touch, hear, smell, and unfortunately taste. But they learned! When you were all done, they wanted one. Training without the proper attitude by both the trainer and trainee results in lower retention and effectiveness. Jesus knew this. He not only told His men how to calm a storm; He showed them. I imagine after that episode they watched the sky for weeks to try it out themselves. They knew exactly how to do it.

The trainer must explain clearly and in detail. This is difficult at times. Remember, the better they understand the lagoon, the less they will need to surface for air. When training, you must anticipate every question, every glitch, and every objection that might arise. Your ultimate goal is to teach them something they will use more than once. They may learn to hand you a spreadsheet, but you want them to understand why column three is four percentage points below column four and what can be done about the disparity. Training does not teach intuitiveness, wisdom, or inner sense. These things only come after mastery of the skill. For example, I tell my staff that they can come to me with any problem they might have, so long as they have at least one plausible solution in mind to contribute. Not surprisingly, they like that. They are in training for life.

I have worked for several different companies with views on training galaxies apart. One would install a computer and flop a manual on your desk. The other would stand over you, talk you through the difficulties, and encourage the successes. One would demand performance now. The other graduated you in little steps to greater tasks. One said they had neither the time nor the money for training. Yet training was clearly important for the other. Training is absolutely critical to the strength of an organization. It determines the organization's success. It cannot wait until management gets around to it. It must be done with fervency and urgency. If management doesn't take training seriously, neither will anyone else. Management sets the standard.

Training as Jesus did it is quite simple. He followed the three major steps of teaching known for thousands of years:

1. We tell him what to do and then we do it correctly for him.
2. He tells us what to do and then we do it correctly with him.
3. He tells us what to do and then he does it correctly by himself.

A classic example for this in the life of Jesus and Peter took place in the water. I will quote it exactly here from the NIV version. See if you can identify these three steps Jesus uses to teach Peter to walk on water (Matt. 14:25–32).

> During the fourth watch of the night Jesus went out to them, walking on the lake. When the disciples saw him walking on the lake, they were terrified. "It's a ghost," they said, and cried out in fear.
>
> But Jesus immediately said to them: "Take courage! It is I. Don't be afraid."
>
> "Lord, if it's you," Peter replied, "tell me to come to you on the water."
>
> "Come," he said.

Then Peter got down out of the boat, walked on the water and came toward Jesus. But when he saw the wind, he was afraid and, beginning to sink, cried out, "Lord, save me!"

Immediately Jesus reached out his hand and caught him. "You of little faith," he said, "why did you doubt?"

And when they climbed into the boat, the wind died down.

The final point to remember when training is to be a part of the training. Never train facing the persons, but stand alongside them and walk them through it. Be prepared to take their hands. I am currently training my four-year-old son how to use the computer mouse, and I literally place my hand on his as together we move the mouse around. Jesus got onto the water to train Peter. Side-by-side training is the best. It worked two thousand years ago, and it is still valid today.

PRACTICAL TIPS

1. Double your training budget for the next fiscal year.

2. Show and tell in every training session.

3. Determine whether training is necessary or the system needs to be changed.

4. Remember that training's ultimate goal is success. Guard against other motives.

5. Accept responsibility for poor performers and do something about it now.

CONCLUSION

We followers of Jesus Christ are convinced we should follow the teachings of Jesus concerning love, patience, and service. But the idea that Jesus' actions and words extend even to the way we operate our businesses may seem like a real stretch of faith. The early American statesman Patrick Henry said in a speech to the Virginia Convention in 1775, "I have but one lamp by which my feet are guided; and that is the lamp of experience. I know of no way of judging the future but by the past." During Jesus' brief stay here two thousand years ago, He left a legacy for us, and part of that legacy included how we should run our businesses as well as our personal lives. His lamp of experience, shining now for two thousand years, can lead the way.

Since I began writing this book, more than a dozen business books have hit the market, all with differing points of view. If the point of view is from a purely humanistic and selfish one, then the advice will last only as long as the writer does. What separates this book is that the point of view comes from Jesus' words and practices. They are eternal; they transcend the day-to-day. Jesus Christ teaches us more than how to operate our businesses and churches. He teaches us how to operate our lives, if we'll let Him.

Some people will take the words found in the Bible and will try to live by them. It is possible; people have been doing it for centuries. But if you want to truly know what the words of Jesus mean, you will need to have an intimate, personal relationship with Him. That's why I take the words of Jesus so seriously because I know Him personally. I am growing to love and understand Him more every day. Imagine if you could do more than simply take this book with you to work every day; imagine Jesus actually meeting with you before work, standing with you during it, and counseling with you afterward. Well, you don't need to merely imagine it. Millions of businesspeople experience it every day. You can too.

Jesus said of Himself in the Book of John, "Whoever believes in him is not condemned, but whoever does not believe stands condemned already because he has not believed in the name of God's one and only Son" (3:18). Later in John, Jesus said, "Moreover, the Father judges no one, but has entrusted all judgment to the Son, that all may honor the Son just as they honor the Father. He who does not honor the Son does not honor the Father, who sent him" (5:22–23). And John the Baptist, recognizing that Jesus was God, also testified of Jesus saying, "Whoever believes in the Son has eternal life, but whoever rejects the Son will not see life" (3:36). Even though John gave testimony to Jesus' deity, Jesus said, "I have testimony weightier than that of John. For the very work that the Father has given me to finish, and which I am doing, testifies that the Father has sent me" (5:36).

What was the "very work" Jesus spoke of? It was more than miracles and great teachings. His work was to come to earth for the salvation of the human race, to die in our place as a once-for-all sacrifice to God, and to rise from the dead. In the Book of Romans, one of the most vehement haters of

Christians turned from his ways and believed on Jesus. He simplified the change in his heart and life into one piece of hope for us. He said that "if you confess with your mouth, 'Jesus is Lord,' and believe in your heart that God raised him from the dead, you will be saved" (10:9).

My book is not a book of sermons or a religious treatise. It is a business book. I describe twenty-five common business problems and tell how Jesus Christ would solve them. My hope is that you will do more than operate your business on principles Jesus taught. My hope is that you will come to truly know, believe, and follow the teachings of Jesus and will come to know Him personally as many other businesspeople have. True, you can operate your business on Jesus' principles, but how much more rewarding to operate it with Jesus there in person! It's as easy as trusting Him and letting Him take control.

Jesus did so much more than is written in the Bible. It is a fascinating and inspirational Book that has been changing lives (and businesses) for centuries. In fact, the last thing John says in his book is, "Jesus did many other things as well. If every one of them were written down, I suppose that even the whole world would not have room for the books that would be written" (21:25). So we take the things that were written, and we try to apply them to our lives, personal and professional.

We try to make sense of some of the craziness of this world. We are bombarded with advice on business, dieting, parenting, and marriage. Some of it will stick, but most of it will be replaced in a few years with more craziness. The Bible is the one constant, secure Book that transcends every situation we find ourselves in. Somewhere in its pages is the hope and help we need. After we've trusted in Jesus, we must learn to look at life's situations and ask: *How would Jesus solve them?* And if you operate your business by the answer, a transformation will occur. I guarantee it.

NOTES

CHAPTER 1

1. Winston Fletcher, *Meetings, Meetings* (New York: William Morrow and Co., 1984), 20.

CHAPTER 2

1. Leonard Safir and William Safire, *Good Advice* (New York: New York Times Books, 1982), 11.

2. Sam Walton with John Huey, *Sam Walton: Made in America* (New York: Doubleday, 1992), 10.

CHAPTER 5

1. Michael Hodgin, *1,001 Humorous Illustrations for Public Speaking* (Grand Rapids: Zondervan, 1994), 68.

CHAPTER 6

1. Robert L. Desatnick and Denis H. Detzel, *Managing to Keep the Customer* (San Francisco: Jossey-Bass, 1993), 7–8.

CHAPTER 7

1. Tom Peters, *Thriving on Chaos* (New York: Alfred A. Knopf, Inc., 1987), 221.

CHAPTER 8

1. Matthew 10:5–14, NIV.

CHAPTER 10

1. David Thomas, *Not Guilty: In Defense of the Modern Man* (London: Weidenfeld & Nicolson, 1993), 88.

2. James S. Hewett, editor, *Illustrations Unlimited* (Wheaton: Tyndale House, 1988), 192.

CHAPTER 12

1. David J. Schwartz, *The Magic of Thinking Big* (New York: Simon and Schuster, 1981), 163.

CHAPTER 13

1. John W. Gardner, *Excellence: Can We Be Equal and Excellent Too?* (New York: Norton Publishers, 1984), 86.

CHAPTER 14

1. Robert Half, *Finding, Hiring, and Keeping the Best Employees* (New York: John Wiley and Sons, 1993), 21.

CHAPTER 16

1. Charlie Jones, *Life Is Tremendous* (Wheaton: Tyndale House, 1968), 55.

CHAPTER 17

1. Sam Walton with John Huey, *Sam Walton: Made in America* (New York: Doubleday, 1992), 325.

2. James S. Hewett, editor, *Illustrations Unlimited* (Wheaton: Tyndale House, 1988), 153.

BIBLIOGRAPHY

"101 Men's Health Secrets." *Men's Health Magazine*, 1992.

The Supervisor's Handbook. Hawthorne, N.J.: National Press Publications, 1993.

Family Circle, 18 July 1995, 50.

Alexander, John W. *Managing Our Work.* Downers Grove, Ill.: InterVarsity Press, 1975.

Ash, Mary Kay. *Mary Kay on People Management.* New York: Warner Communications, 1984.

Aubrey, Charles A. III, and Patricia K. Felkins. *Teamwork: Involving People in Quality and Productivity Improvement.* Milwaukee: Quality Press, 1988.

Bierman, Harold, Jr. *Strategic Financial Planning.* New York: The Free Press, 1980.

Bolles, Richard Nelson. *What Color Is Your Parachute?* California: Ten Speed Press, 1982.

Booher, Dianna. *First Thing Monday Morning.* Old Tappan, N. J.: Fleming H. Revell, 1988.

Broadwell, Martin M. *The New Supervisor.* Reading, Mass.: Addison-Wesley, 1970.

Buskirk, Richard H. *Your Career: How to Plan It, Manage It, Change It.* New York: New American Library, 1976.

Carnegie, Dale. *How to Win Friends and Influence People.* New York: Pocket Books, 1964.

Chapman, Elwood N. *The Fifty-Minute Supervisor.* California: Crisp Publications, Inc., 1988.

Crystal, John C., and Richard N. Bolles. *Where Do I Go from Here with My Life?* California: Ten Speed Press, 1974.

Culp, Stephanie. *Conquering the Paper Pile-Up.* Cincinnati: Writer's Digest Books, 1990.

Davidson, Jeff. *Breathing Space.* New York: Master Media Limited, 1991.

Deems, Richard S. *How to Fire Your Friends.* Lincoln, Neb.: Media Publishing, 1989.

Delaney, William A. *The 30 Most Common Problems in Management and How to Solve Them.* New York: Amacom, 1982.

Desatnick, Robert L., and Denis H. Detzel. *Managing to Keep the Customer.* San Francisco: Jossey-Bass, 1993.

Dobrish, Cecelia, Rick Wolff, and Brian Zevnik. *Hiring the Right Person for the Right Job.* New York: Franklin Watts, 1984.

Drucker, Peter F. *The Effective Executive.* New York: Harper & Row, 1967.

———. *Managing for Results.* New York: Harper & Row, 1964.

Dun & Bradstreet. *Managing Multiple Priorities.* New York: Business Education Services, 1987.

Eigen, Lewis D., and Jonathan P. Siegel. *The Manager's Book of Quotations.* New York: Amacom, 1989.

Engstrom, Ted, and Edward R. Dayton. *The Art of Management for Christian Leaders.* Waco, Tex.: Word, 1977.

———. *The Christian Executive.* Waco, Tex.: Word, 1979.

———. *60-Second Management Guide.* Waco, Tex.: Word, 1984.

Evered, James F. J., and Erich Evered. *Shirt-Sleeves Management.* New York: Amacom, 1989.

Fletcher, Winston. *Meetings, Meetings.* New York: William Morrow and Co., 1984.

Frank, Milo O. *How to Run a Successful Meeting in Half the Time.* New York: Simon & Schuster, 1989.

Frank, Robert. "For Sale: Mansion on 60-Acre Estate, Amenities, Very Pink." *Wall Street Journal,* 24 August 1994.

Freier, Edmond P. *Revitalizing Your Business.* Chicago: Probus, 1985.

Half, Robert. *On Hiring*. New York: Crown, 1985.

———. *Finding, Hiring, and Keeping the Best Employees*. New York: John Wiley & Sons, 1993.

Hart, Archibald. *The Success Factor*. Old Tappan, N. J.: Fleming H. Revell Co., 1984.

Hersey, Paul, and Kenneth H. Blanchard. *Management of Organizational Behavior: Utilizing Human Resources*. Englewood Cliffs, N. J.: Prentice-Hall, 1977.

Hewett, James S., ed. *Illustrations Unlimited*. Wheaton, Ill.: Tyndale House, 1988.

Hill, Napoleon. *Think and Grow Rich*. Greenwich, Conn.: Fawcett Publications, 1960.

Hill, Napoleon, and W. Clement Stone. *Success through a Positive Mental Attitude*. New York: Pocket Books, 1977.

Hodgin, Michael. *1,001 Humorous Illustrations for Public Speaking*. Grand Rapids, Mich.: Zondervan, 1994.

Januz, Lauren R., and Susan K. Jones. *Time-Management for Executives*. New York: Charles Scribner's Sons, 1981.

Jones, Charlie. *Life Is Tremendous*. Wheaton, Ill.: Tyndale House, 1968.

Keye Productivity Center, *Managing Hourly Employees*. Kansas City, Mo.: Keye, 1988.

Kibel, H. Ronald. *How to Turn Around a Financially Troubled Company*. New York: McGraw-Hill, 1982.

Kingsley, Daniel T. *How to Fire an Employee*. New York: Facts On File Publications, 1984.

Knight, Walter B. *Knight's Illustrations for Today*. Chicago: Moody Press, 1970.

Krackov, Lawrence M., and Surendra K. Kaushik. *The Practical Financial Manager*. New York: New York Institute of Finance, 1988.

Landers, Ann. *Fort Lauderdale Sun Sentinel*, 4 September 1995.

LeTourneau, Richard. *Management Plus*. Grand Rapids, Mich.: Zondervan, 1973.

Maddux, Robert B. *Effective Performance Appraisals*. Los Altos, California: Crisp Publications, Inc., 1987.

———. *Team Building*. Los Altos, California: Crisp Publications, Inc., 1988.

McCartney, Bill. *What Makes a Man*. Colorado Springs: NavPress, 1992.

Noble, Sara. *301 Great Management Ideas*. Boston: Inc. Publishers, 1991.

Olson, Harry A. *Power Strategies of Jesus Christ*. Tarrytown, N. Y.: Triumph Books, 1991.

Peters, Tom. *Thriving on Chaos*. New York: Alfred A. Knopf, 1987.

Peters, Tom, and Nancy Austin. *A Passion for Excellence*. New York: Warner Books, 1985.

Pryor, Fred. *How to Supervise People*. Shawnee Mission, Kans.: Pryor Resources.

Purcell, W. R. Jr. *Understanding a Company's Finances*. Boston: Houghton Mifflin Co., 1981.

Reader's Digest Association. *Write Better, Speak Better*. New York: Reader's Digest Association, 1977.

Rice, Craig S. *Your Team of Tigers*. New York: Amacom, 1982.

Safire, William, and Leonard Safir. *Good Advice*. New York: New York Times Books, 1982.

Sanders, J. Oswald. *Spiritual Leadership*. Chicago: Moody Press, 1967.

Schwartz, David J. *The Magic of Thinking Big*. New York: Simon & Schuster, 1981.

Sloma, Richard S. *No-Nonsense Management*. New York: Bantam Books, 1977.

Sweet, Donald H. *A Manager's Guide to Conducting Terminations*. Lexington, Mass.: Lexington Books, 1989.

Thomas, David. *Not Guilty: In Defense of the Modern Man*. London: Weidenfeld & Nicolson, 1993.

Timpe, A. Dale. *Managing People*. New York: KEND Publications, 1988.

Townsend, Robert. *Up the Organization*. Greenwich, Conn.: Fawcett Publications, 1970.

Trimble, Vance H. *Sam Walton: The Inside Story of America's Richest Man*. New York: Penguin Books, 1990.

Walton, Sam, and John Huey. *Sam Walton: Made in America*. New York: Doubleday, 1992.

Welch, Bob. *More to Life Than Having It All*. Eugene, Ore.: Harvest House, 1992.

Wolff, Richard. *Man at the Top*. Wheaton, Ill.: Tyndale House Publishers, 1969.

Zaccarelli, Brother Herman E. *Training Managers to Train*. California: Crisp Publications, Inc., 1988.